Oxford School Shakespeare

D0246017

Henry V

Edited by

Roma Gill, OBE
M.A. *Cantab.*, B. Litt. *Oxon*

Oxford University Press

Oxford University Press, Great Clarendon Street, Oxford OX2 6DP

Oxford New York Athens Auckland Bangkok Bogota
Bombay Buenos Aires Calcutta Cape Town Dar es Salaam
Delhi Florence Hong Kong Istanbul Karachi Kuala Lumpur
Madras Madrid Melbourne Mexico City Nairobi Paris
Singapore Taipei Tokyo Toronto Warsaw

and associated companies in
Berlin Ibadan

Oxford is a trade mark of Oxford University Press

© Oxford University Press 1995

First published 1995
Reprinted 1997
Trade edition first published 1998

ISBN 0 19 831980 0 (School edition)
ISBN 0 19 831997 5 (trade edition)

Illustrations by Victor G. Ambrus

Cover photograph by Donald Cooper shows Kenneth Branagh as Henry V in the Royal
Shakespeare Company's 1984 production of *Henry V.*

For Cyril

Oxford School Shakespeare
edited by Roma Gill

A Midsummer Night's Dream
Romeo and Juliet
As You Like It
Macbeth
Julius Caesar
The Merchant of Venice
Henry IV Part I
Twelfth Night
The Taming of the Shrew
Othello
Hamlet
King Lear
Henry V
The Winter's Tale
Antony and Cleopatra
The Tempest

Typeset by Herb Bowes Graphics
Printed in Great Britain at the University Press, Cambridge

Contents

A Play for all Seasons v

People in the Play vii

Family Tree x

Henry V: commentary xii

Hal to Henry: From Prince of Wales to King of England xxxi

Shakespeare's Verse xxxv

Date and Text xxxvi

Characters in the Play xxxviii

Henry V I

The Sources of *Henry V* 127

What the Critics have said 130

Classwork and Examinations 133
    Discussion 133
    Character Study 134
    Activities 137
    Context Questions 138
    Comprehension Questions 139
    Essays 140
    Projects 141

Background 143
    Government 143
    Religion 143
    Education 144
    Language 144
    Drama 145
    Theatre 145

Suggested Further Reading 147

William Shakespeare 1564–1616 148

List of Shakespeare's Plays 150

A Play for all Seasons

Mention *Henry V* nowadays and most people will think of a *film*—either Laurence Olivier's gallant attempt in 1944 to rally a nation exhausted by war but still intensely patriotic; or the more recent (1989) version made for a very different audience by Kenneth Branagh. In both films a distinguished actor-director with great personal charisma (and very sharp cutting-scissors) drove the action at full speed from the city of London to the walls of Harfleur and the plains of Agincourt, thence to the council-chamber of Troyes. But neither of these is Shakespeare's *play*!

Henry V was the last in a group of four related plays (a 'tetralogy') showing the fortunes of the English monarchy between 1398 and 1420. The first of these, *Richard II*, dealt with the downfall of one king and the rise of his successor. Richard II banished Henry Bullingbrook and confiscated his lands. Bullingbrook returned to England, led a rebellion against Richard (who was forced to abdicate), and was himself crowned Henry IV. His reign was restless: he was threatened constantly by insurrection, and greatly distressed by the conduct of the Prince of Wales, his only son and heir. The second part of the tetralogy, *Henry IV Part 1*, is most memorable for the royal tearaway, Prince Hal, who begins to redeem his riotous youth at the end of the play when he fights valiantly in his father's cause against the rebels. The relationship of father and son is further explored (still with the background of civil strife) in *Henry IV Part 2*. Prince Hal distances himself from his old mates, discarding the ringleader of their riots, Sir John Falstaff, and assuming the royal personality. At last he is crowned as King Henry V.

This is the second of Shakespeare's historical tetralogies; the first, mentioned by the Chorus in the closing speech of *Henry V*, consisted of *Henry VI*—in three parts—and *Richard III*. Such plays were very popular in Elizabethan England. As well as themes of perennial interest—greed, envy, lust, the struggle for power and the clash of ideologies—they were able to reveal some aspect of its past to a nation which was searching for its own identity. Henry VIII had severed all links with the Church of Rome when he declared himself head of the Church in England, and now his country was trying to find its own individuality, distinct from Europe, by learning about its history. 'What is my nation?' (*3*, 3, 68). Official historians, such as Raphael Holinshed, had been appointed to research the archives and to chronicle events of the past in vast tomes—but these were largely inaccessible to the multitudes (most of whom were illiterate anyway). The popular writers—ballad-makers, pamphleteers and, above all, dramatists—found themselves with avid audiences and a plentiful supply of source material. A character in one of Ben Jonson's plays, commended for his knowledge of history, disclaimed any academic study and confessed 'I ha't from the *play-books*, And think they are more authentic' (*The Devil is an Ass*, II, iv, 13–14).

Once again, at the end of the twentieth century, we are at a cultural crossroads. England, together with Wales, Scotland, and Northern Ireland, is now a full member of the European Community. Sharing a common future, but possessed of an individual past, we should be one in spirit but distinct in character. And however this ideal may be realized, it is certain that the theatre, with dramatists past and present, will have a very large part to play.

People in the Play

Henry V is a play with, unusually for Shakespeare, very few 'in-depth' characters. Mostly they are 'cameo' parts, where one or two pointers are given to direct the actor in his performance, but the actor himself must supply the internal motivation for what he does.

The Chorus however, seems to be more fully characterized than one might expect! The part is traditionally played by a male actor wearing a black cloak—although productions in recent years have 'modernized' him with jeans and sweater, overalls, and rehearsal clothes. His speeches show him to be excited and excitable, very enthusiastic about the events he is describing, and intensely patriotic. He would seem to be a 'gentleman' rather than a 'player': his words are addressed to the 'gentles' and to those who '*sit and see*' (Chorus 4, line 52) rather than to the groundlings who stood around the stage.

King Henry V is the character about whom we know the most. There are no secrets about his past life (as Shakespeare's Prince Hal), and we are given full details of the outward manifestation of his conversion. He is a man with a great mission—called by God (he feels) to confirm the Plantagenet dynasty on the throne of England, and to unite the kingdoms of France and England. He prays for God's guidance in all his actions; and his triumphs are always ascribed to the wonderful power of God's strength. Until the night before Agincourt (*Act 4*, Scene 1) we do not see Henry alone, and his motives might be open to misconstruction, but his soliloquy at the end of this scene leaves no room for doubt as to his personal sincerity. For the Elizabethans, Henry V was the ideal monarch, deserving of comparison only with Alexander the Great, and he featured in many other writings before Shakespeare's play. But by the turn of the century (when this play was written) the mood of the times was changing—and Shakespeare himself was becoming increasingly sceptical. As a result, the character of his Henry is capable of many interpretations.

The two churchmen are also somewhat ambiguous figures. Their respect and admiration for their new king in his conversion *seems* to be from the heart—but how much is their concern for their own Church property? Should the men of God advocate warfare? Is the Bishop of Ely any more than a 'yes-man' to the machiavellian Archbishop of Canterbury?

The English nobility are barely differentiated. Exeter, the older man, is given most responsibility in Henry's campaigns—and consequently the most lines to his part. The men closest to the king, his counsellors, are also related to him in blood: it is indeed a 'band of brothers'. They are all—except the three conspirators—honourable, trustworthy, and loyal.

The army. Shakespeare's introduction of the four captains is unhistorical—but it may have been politically diplomatic and prophetic, anticipating the formation of the United Kingdom. He uses the captains to provide light comic relief with their squabbling, but the issues they raise are quickly abandoned. The English captain is characterized by his quiet reserve; the Scot is taciturn; and the Irish captain is impetuous. Only Llewellyn is developed into a full personality, staunchly defending his nation and his king—whom he greets as a fellow Welshman. He is old-fashioned, strict on the subject of military etiquette—and romantically sentimental. Early editions of the play spell his name phonetically as 'Fluellen'.

The private soldiers, weary of fighting with danger and trudging through the mud of France, are critical of their leader but mindful of their duty. By giving them personal names (rather than referring simply to '1 Soldier' etc.), Shakespeare insists that they are all individuals.

The Eastcheap mob are fairly static characters who have changed little since their first appearance as the companions of Prince Hal. Bardolph's red nose is as spectacular as it ever was, and his end—he is hanged for pilfering—was predicted in *Henry IV Part 1*. Pistol 'swaggers' as much as he did in *Henry IV Part 2*, strong in words and threats but empty of deeds. He sees himself as an epic warrior, but comes at last to a bleak reality of destitution, losing even the ransom money promised by his French captive when the prisoners' throats are cut. Mistress Quickly makes a brief appearance with her elegiac account of the death of Falstaff—but she is needed in this play only as a reporter and not for her character. Falstaff's Boy—the page given to him by Prince Hal in *Henry IV Part 2*—is streetwise, and sees his companions for what they really are.

The French monarchy   Contrary to his sources (which suggest that Charles VI was incompetent and even insane) Shakespeare presents the French king as a judicious monarch who takes the English threat very seriously, controlling his son, the scornful Dauphin, with a firm hand. The part of Katherine, his daughter, is a tricky one for the actress—just as it was indeed for the real princess! Knowing that it is her destiny to marry the English king, Katherine must act out the wooing scene as though she were free to choose or reject her lover, and make a personal relationship out of a political alliance.

The French nobility   are shown collectively as being frivolous and boastful—although they are perhaps a little more distinguishable than their English counterparts. Bourbon is the one who excels in silliness on the night before Agincourt (*Act 3*, Scene 8). In the Folio text the lines here assigned to Bourbon are spoken by the Dauphin, and they certainly seem more appropriate for the sender of the tennis balls; but in historical fact the Dauphin was not present at the battle of Agincourt, and in *Act 3*, Scene 6 of the play Shakespeare's character is expressly ordered to remain in Rouen. Burgundy stands out from the rest in honour and dignity, partly because he was historically not of the French king's party but the ruler of an independent power—and therefore best able to act as a go-between at the Council of Troyes.

Montjoy   the French herald, is given unusual opportunities to develop a relationship with King Henry. His manner changes from armed neutrality to an almost affectionate respect.

Family tree : *French and English Royal Families*

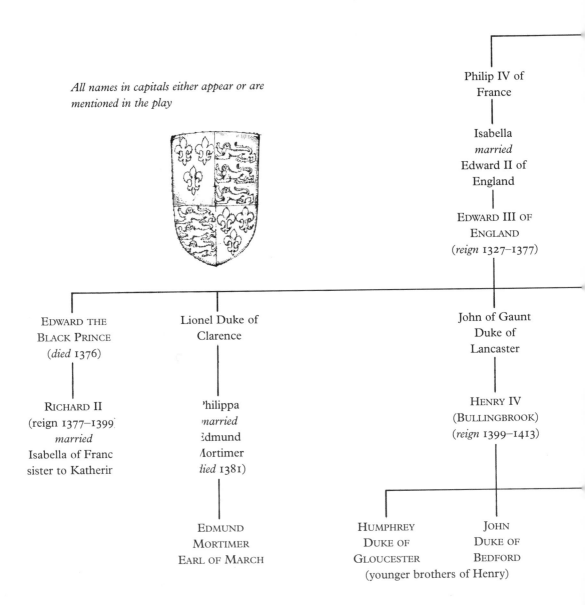

All names in capitals either appear or are mentioned in the play

Philip IV of France

Isabella
married
Edward II of England

EDWARD III OF ENGLAND
(*reign* 1327–1377)

EDWARD THE BLACK PRINCE
(*died* 1376)

Lionel Duke of Clarence

John of Gaunt Duke of Lancaster

RICHARD II
(reign 1377–1399)
married
Isabella of Franc
sister to Katherir

ʼhilippa
ʼnarried
ʒdmund
ʌortimer
ʽied 1381)

HENRY IV
(BULLINGBROOK)
(*reign* 1399–1413)

EDMUND MORTIMER EARL OF MARCH

HUMPHREY DUKE OF GLOUCESTER

JOHN DUKE OF BEDFORD

(younger brothers of Henry)

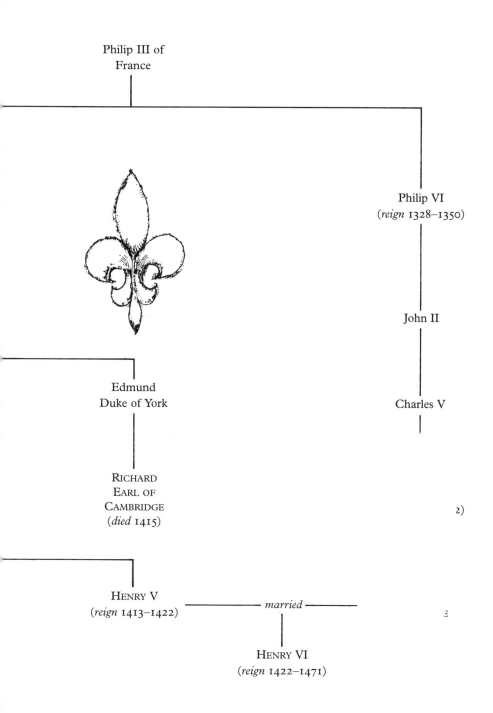

Philip III of
France

Philip VI
(*reign* 1328–1350)

John II

Edmund
Duke of York

Charles V

RICHARD
EARL OF
CAMBRIDGE
(*died* 1415)

2)

HENRY V ———— *married* ————
(*reign* 1413–1422)

3

HENRY VI
(*reign* 1422–1471)

Henry V: commentary

Act I

Prologue   The 'Chorus' (a part traditionally played by a single male actor, wearing a black cloak) begins a tale of epic dimensions, using language in the 'grand style' appropriate for such an exalted theme. But his tone soon changes as he reminds the audience where they really are, in the little 'wooden O' made by the circular walls of the playhouse. Yet these can be transcended if the audience will only put their imaginations to work!

The Chorus manipulates audience response through the words and rhythms of his speech, contrasting the simple 'cockpit' with the 'vasty fields of France' and the poor 'crooked figure' with 'a million'. In the first eight lines the verse builds up to the horrific vision of a conqueror who can bring total devastation with 'famine, sword and fire'; and then, with a strongly marked pause (a 'caesura') in the middle of one line, drops down to a humble confession of the actors' unworthiness: 'pardon, gentles all'.

And now, like the 'warm-up man' in a modern television studio, he begins to stir up his hearers to participate in the action, with himself as their guide.

Scene I   Having prepared ourselves mentally for the excitement of a battle, it is rather disconcerting to find that we are now eavesdropping on a private and highly confidential conversation between two eminent churchmen. They are discussing the perennial problem of money! Church property before the Reformation was enormous, and much of it (having been bequeathed by legacy) was exempt from tax. Successive governments tried to wrest some of this wealth for themselves, to pay for national debts—and now these efforts are being renewed. The Archbishop of Canterbury, head of the Church in England, is acutely aware of the situation, but he has also got hopes of the new king. With awe and wonder he describes the change that has come over the wild Prince Hal since he ascended the throne of England after his father's death. Canterbury's language comes from the Bible and the Prayer Book, presenting the king's reformation as a religious conversion. Henry has become a model of learning, wisdom, temperance, and prudence—the ideal monarch.

Although it is undramatic, the speech, which has the approval of the Bishop of Ely, serves to prepare the audience to receive his gracious majesty, King Henry V. Regular theatre-goers would remember, and Shakespeare intends that they *should* remember, the impact made by Prince Hal and his unruly comrades in the two *Henry IV* plays; but they must now believe in the transformation that has been accomplished.

As well as accepting, reverencing, and applauding the change that has come over the new king, the Archbishop of Canterbury has also found a means of solving the royal economic difficulties— without damaging the Church's own finances!

Scene 2   In the previous scene the archbishop spoke of some property in France—perhaps even extending as far as the French throne— which the English king might rightfully claim as his own. Now Canterbury comes into the royal presence to explain himself. King Henry is conscious of the seriousness of the enterprise, and the probable cost in human lives if he were to pursue his claim. Is the warfare justified? The archbishop must examine his conscience before he gives the king an answer, and speak with all religious sincerity.

The king speaks in measured terms, in a regular formal blank verse; and the archbishop replies in the same manner. His researches have been thorough, and the results are presented in meticulous detail as he expounds the Salic law and the fallacy that has deprived the English crown of territory that properly belongs to it. He points out that the Salic land is not in France at all, but is a French possession in Germany (between the rivers Elbe and Sala). He argues, moreover, that three French kings have themselves asserted their rights to the crown by claiming descent through a female line—which is precisely what is now being *denied* to Henry.

It is reassuring to know that Henry's claims can be thus validated—but for the reader the archbishop's speech seems tedious and long-winded, whilst in performance the director must decide how to keep his audience entertained.

In Olivier's film the scene was played as comedy, where a flustered archbishop was encumbered with massive volumes of untidy manuscripts and impeded by scurrying clerics. But this is surely wrong! Shakespeare's character may be verbose, but he is by no means stupid. And although he is being a little devious in turning the king's attention towards France (and consequently away from Church financial affairs), he is a sincere and loyal churchman.

Kenneth Branagh's recent film was, I think, closer to Shakespeare's intentions. This shows a well-briefed archbishop expounding his case, in all its precise legalistic details, to a bewildered audience until eventually the king, no less confused than are his peers, cuts through the verbiage with a curt question:

May I with right and conscience make this claim?

The question is answered in the affirmative. Canterbury brings the authority of Holy Writ (the Book of Numbers) to endorse his thesis, and urges a precedent in the battle of Crécy (1346), when Edward III and his son, the Black Prince, conquered the French and captured Calais. The other nobles, as if brought to life by a magic touch, join the churchmen in urging the king to fight. Henry still demurs, mindful now of the threat posed by the Scots, who, as they have always done, will maraud into England as soon as the country's defences are removed. His counsellors answer all Henry's objections until at last the Archbishop of Canterbury, taking up a remark from the Duke of Exeter, delivers a speech that is almost a sermon on the subject of the well-ordered state.

Exeter compares the state to a piece of music: the high and the low—both notes in music or human beings in their social ranks—combine to form one perfect harmony. The archbishop develops this notion, using the analogy (first proposed by the Roman poet Virgil) of a beehive, where each individual cheerfully performs the allotted task to the benefit of the whole colony. This leads to the conclusion that it is the king's *duty* to go to war, a moral obligation upon him for the good of his country, 'your happy England'.

Whether or not this poetic argument (commonplace in the sixteenth century) has any force on him, Henry at the end of the oration is fully resolved on action, and he declares his mind with bravura; 'France being ours, we'll bend it to our awe, Or break it all to pieces'.

Calling in the French ambassadors, he listens to the Dauphin's contemptuous message which taunts him by recalling his licentious past. Even the messengers are embarrassed, but Henry, unruffled, replies with a dangerously icy calm that returns the 'tennis ball' image back to the server. Henry's anger, like his other passions, is 'fettered' (line 243)—but his spirit is now aroused. Hitherto in this play he has been a man of few words, but here the kingly lion is stretching his limbs and showing what he is made of. He admits the 'barbarous licence' of his 'wilder days', his neglect and under-valuation of 'this poor seat of England', but he promises henceforth to be 'like a king' and show a 'sail of greatness'. The humility of his confession makes us—and the French ambassadors—take his threats very seriously. The man means what he says!

Shakespeare has here made a significant alteration to the history as it was reported by Holinshed, who says that the 'tennis balls' incident occurred *before* the king had determined to fight for his rights and pursue his claim as far as the throne of France. By making this change Shakespeare ensures that there can be no suspicion that Henry's decision was in any way affected by the personal insult, which is only a spur to urge him forward. The incident also prepares us—audience and readers—to greet the French with hostility. The Dauphin is the immediate target.

After the departure, in silence, of the ambassadors, the tense atmosphere is eased by Exeter's wry comment: 'This was a merry message'. Henry is now businesslike, calling for action—'with reasonable swiftness'. But he does not forget the vocational aspect of his expedition:

> God before,
> We'll chide this Dauphin at his father's door.

With God helping them, the mission will be divinely sanctioned and will indeed be a *fair* action. Rhyming couplets bring the episode, the scene, and the whole first movement of the play to a neat conclusion.

Act 2

Chorus   The Chorus returns, eager to tell us of the intense wave of patriotic fervour that is sweeping England. But not all men are loyal. We hear of treachery which must be foiled—or else all will be lost! Carried away by the magnitude of the events he is relating—and by his own importance and cleverness as narrator—the Chorus becomes melodramatic, with a rhetorical question addressed to 'O England'. His word-play ('kind and natural', 'hollow bosoms', 'gilt'/'guilt') gets increasingly self-conscious, and he almost giggles as he assures the audience that in the imaginary sea-crossings between England and France the play will not 'offend one stomach'.

Scene 1   Although, as we learned from the Chorus, 'The king is set from London', the setting of this scene is still within the city—in one of London's most seedy areas, a 'red light' district, where street-violence was common. *Henry IV Part 1* showed this as one of the favourite haunts of Prince Hal, before he became Henry V, and the characters who now assemble belong to the past he has so decisively rejected. By turns squabbling, threatening, joking, and grumbling, they speak a language which is all their own, made up of thieves' cant, bawdy innuendo, vulgarisms, and clichés, and enlightened with snatches of popular songs. Their words—those of Nym especially—often have no precise meanings. Intonation says it all.

Absent from the company is the man who was once the ringleader in mischief, Sir John Falstaff, but his presence is strongly felt. He was the personification of lawlessness, disorder, and misrule—but in another aspect he also represented carefree pleasure, comradeship and, in a word, fun. All that is past. Now Falstaff is dying, and a few shabby ruffians are all that remain of the life he embodied.

When Henry was newly crowned, he refused to acknowledge Falstaff and publicly rejected his claim for friendship—and also the association with his former mates. We must agree that these are most undesirable companions for a king of England; a knowing audience—those familiar with Prince Hal from *Henry IV Parts 1* and *2*—should feel glad that he is no longer part of such a low-life fraternity. They should rejoice, like the bishops and the nobles, in the reformation (which he had always promised), and look forward to seeing 'what use' he has made of his 'wilder days' (1, 2, 267–8) and yet . . . These characters seem to have a warmth that has so far been lacking in the play. They care about each other, and their quick, unruly passions are a welcome contrast to the deliberate calculations of the politicians.

The news of Falstaff's sickness is sobering, and the Hostess's accusation, coming so suddenly, casts a different light on King Henry's much praised reformation. Falstaff is very ill: 'The king has killed his heart'. At the end of the scene Nym's criticism, though imperfectly articulated, cannot pass unnoticed: 'The king is a good king, but it must be as it may. He passes some humours and careers'.

Scene 2   Time has passed whilst we lingered in Eastcheap—long enough for
the king to have journeyed as far as Southampton. Before he
himself appears, we are given some preparation for the scene that
will take place. Although Bedford and Westmorland seem
apprehensive, Exeter is confident that the king is fully in control of
the situation.

Trumpets sound, and Henry enters with three men who seem
to be his very close friends. Apparently he sets great store by their
judgements and their loyalty, and each of them, in turn, affirms his
devotion to the king and his cause. Reassured, Henry turns his
attention to a minor misdemeanour—verbal abuse from a drunken
man. The king is ready to pardon the man, but Scroop,
Cambridge, and Gray counsel against such clemency and
recommend 'much correction' for the offender, 'lest example
Breed by his sufferance more of such a kind'. Henry thanks them
for their advice, but for the moment he ignores it and the drunkard
is set free. The king turns to more weighty business.

Cambridge, Scroop, and Gray are to rule the kingdom during
the king's absence in France, and they are now given the official
documents which should—or so they expect—detail the extent of
their powers and responsibilities. But when they read the papers
they find themselves indicted of the most heinous treachery. They
have taken bribes from the French to murder King Henry, and
(although little is made of this in the play) they are hoping by
Henry's death to secure the throne for the Earl of March and then,
since March has no children, for the descendants of the Earl of
Cambridge (see 'Family Tree', p. x). In fact the Earl of March
himself was loyal to the king—and it was he who revealed the plot
to Henry.

The guilty traitors confess their crimes and beg for mercy—
but they stand condemned out of their own mouths: the king metes
out their punishment with the same strict justice that they
themselves recommended for the abusive drunkard. The treachery
of Cambridge and Gray angered the king, but he is most cruelly
hurt by Lord Scroop's betrayal of his friendship. He denounces
Scroop with a passion such as we have never heard from this
otherwise self-controlled king: repeated rhetorical questions build
to a climax of emotion which dissolves into tears.

With a few words of cold prose, Exeter makes a formal arrest
to which all the traitors react with signs of relief, appearing glad
that they have been prevented from acting out their own evil
schemes. Henry, once more in full possession of himself, briefly

points out what would have been the consequences of their crime, not for himself alone, but for his entire kingdom. Sentences of death are pronounced, and the king moves off to war. Surely, he argues, this timely discovery of the conspiracy must be a sign that God is in favour of the expedition.

The director of a production, the actor playing the part of Henry V, or the solitary reader, must determine the extent to which the king is in control of this scene. He instructed the three traitors to expect that their 'commissions' would be given to them now (see line 61), and clearly he introduced the subject of the drunkard to allow them to sentence themselves. But in the denunciation of Lord Scroop—how much of his passion is performance?

Scene 3   Whilst the king's party sets sail boldly from Southampton, a less heroic bunch of warriors in Eastcheap is preparing to follow him. They are leaving behind them a past life that has died with Sir John Falstaff, and they listen in silence to the Hostess's account of the knight's death. They must have heard her words many times already. She speaks a poetic elegy in which her simple grief is emphasized by those idiosyncrasies of her language which, at other times, are so amusing—the homely wisdom ('at turning of the tide'), the mistaken allusions ('Arthur' for 'Abraham') and the 'malapropisms' (verbal misapprehensions—such as 'in carnation' for 'incarnate', 'rheumatic' when she intends 'lunatic'). At last, after brief words of parting, the men begin their trudge to Southampton.

Scene 4   Across the channel the French are preparing to resist the threatened invasion. The French king is taking all precautions, being mindful of previous Anglo-French engagements, but the Dauphin makes light of his fears. He scoffs at the English king, seeing only the wild Prince Hal (whom he insulted with his gift of tennis balls in *Act 1, Scene 2*) and refusing to recognize the reformed King Henry.

In the Dauphin's mind is a picture of the parody king of English folk-festivals, but the French king and the Constable, older and wiser men, are thinking of distinguished precedents—the early Roman Brutus, and the almost legendary Black Prince of England who was Henry's ancestor. To the French king the English seem a fighting-dogs, bred from a 'bloody (= bloodthirsty) strain' and trained ('flesh'd') on the meat they are to kill. To the Dauphin they are merely 'coward dogs' who make a lot of noise but who will turn tail and run as soon as they meet any resistance.

Exeter comes as the English ambassador—the situation is grave enough to warrant a member of the royal family to perform this function. He makes his demands in formal language, invoking all laws, divine as well as human and international, to sanction Henry's claim to the French throne. And if the king of France will not yield? In calm, measured tones Exeter declares the full horrors of war, and his almost matter-of-fact description makes the threat sound very, very real.

Act 3

Chorus   The Chorus now has the immediacy of a 'live' outside-broadcast on television news: we see through his eyes as through a video-camera. First we focus on the royal party as the king embarks at Southampton Pier, all flags flying. Henry is showing himself in all his glorious majesty—and the rising sun is a most fitting comparison. We watch the ship-boys who swarm up the rigging to unfurl the great sails, and we can even hear the bo'sun's pipe which gives the orders. The sails billow out and the huge galleons move off. This is (as the Chorus presents it) truly heroic action, and it is impossible to resist the exhortation to become part of it and join the expedition—especially when we look back at sleepy old England!

Before we know it, we are in France and laying siege to Harfleur. The graphic details of cannon pointing at the city speak their threats as eloquently to a twentieth-century mind as ever they could to Shakespeare's audience.

A 'news-flash' of information comes to let us know the official response to the demands made by Exeter in the previous scene. Understandably, the French king is refusing to surrender his crown—but he is willing to compromise with Henry, offering his daughter's hand in marriage (which would secure the throne of France for Henry's descendants) and, as a dowry for her, certain 'dukedoms' (which were described as 'almost kingly' in 1, 2, 227 but which are now despised as 'petty and unprofitable'). The offer has been rejected, and war is declared. As the Chorus is speaking, we hear the sound of cannonfire.

The speech sounds urgent and impassioned; strong, active verbs and frequent alliterations hurry the lines along at a great pace.

Scene 1   The stage should be alive with frenzied activity (or the impression of this) as soldiers with weapons and ladders charge the breach the artillery has made in the city wall at Harfleur. But their first assault has failed, and they are now in retreat.

Henry rallies his troops, speaking first to the commanders of the campaign (and perhaps meaning particularly the three lords who accompany him). His 'dear friends' now, they must adopt the monstrous appearance of fighting machines. The 'noble English' (the knights and cavalry officers) are reminded of their forefathers, war heroes who must not be betrayed by their descendants: don't let the side down—and set a good example to the men who are (both socially and in military terms) beneath you! The common soldiers, 'men of grosser blood', are not forgotten. Henry speaks to the 'yeomen of England' in the language of farmstock—the language that they, as countrymen, ought to appreciate. The exhortations are effective, and the king leads a fresh assault on Harfleur.

The scene—merely an oration spoken against a background of activity—shows us yet another aspect of this new Henry. Here he is the military leader, the inspiration of his soldiers, who must be able at once to persuade, flatter, and stir up to action. With one of the most famous of opening lines, the speech is by no means easy to deliver!

Scene 2   Once again, the earlier heroics of the flag-waving Chorus and the militaristic king seem to be deflated by the baser realities. Although Bardolph has caught something of the spirit of Henry's fervour, Nym and Pistol are resistant. Nym is frightened and Pistol is too much of a coward to go anywhere near the fighting. The Welsh captain Llewellyn, making his first appearance in the play, rounds them up and drives them to where the action is. The Boy remains behind, alone on the stage. He knows and despises all three— braggarts, cowards, and petty thieves. Any sympathy the audience might remember for these former companions of Sir John Falstaff (and associates of Prince Hal) is quickly being dispersed.

Scene 3   There is still another aspect of war that has not yet been touched upon—the point of view of the professionals. The trio that comes before us now—the Welshman, the Irishman, and the Scotsman— are all of them experienced soldiers.

These three nations were all represented in Henry's French campaigns, and in the Folio text the characters are identified simply as 'Welch', 'Irish', and 'Scot'. Shakespeare has used the national

speech-habits to give each man a separate voice—and they all have
different ideas about the proper way to do things. Shakespeare does
not find the Welsh accent difficult to imitate: a single phrase ('look
you'), a few unusual grammatical forms ('is' for 'are', 'is digged' for
'has dug'), and the fairly regular *p/b* substitution are all that is
necessary. Llewellyn is formal and old-fashioned, as his language
('beseech', 'vouchsafe') shows; and he works strictly by the book—
perhaps even using Thomas Digges's *Stratioticos*, a volume which
describes the classical battles of the ancient Romans and their
'disciplines of war'.[1] Llewellyn has no regard for the Irish captain
who, he suspects, 'will plow up all, if there is not better directions'.

Macmorris himself is near to panic and throws up his hands in
despair: 'there ish nothing done, so Christ sa' me law'. For 'the
Scots captain', however, Llewellyn has nothing but praise: 'Captain
Jamy is a marvellous falorous gentleman . . . and of great expedition
and knowledge in th'anchient wars'. Jamy is a man of few words,
but his resolution is certain: 'I'll dee guid service, or I'll lig i'the
grund for it'. A quarrel is being threatened, but the trumpet-call
sounds a truce: for the present, all hostilities will be postponed.

The little episode has served to introduce to the audience three
new characters—who will take the places of Bardolph, Nym, and
Pistol in providing some prose entertainment and light relief from
the epic seriousness.

Scene 4   Henry seems now to have become the bloody-minded fighting
monster that he himself described. His threat of the horrors of war
is terrible, depicting brutal soldiers who rape and massacre,
uncontrolled in their destructive rage which spares no one: old men
and infants alike, both mothers and daughters. Thanks to Henry's
gracious restraint, the air is clear now; but in a moment, unless the
French will yield, it will be dark and thick with gunsmoke and the
screams of the victims. Once again, the twentieth-century
audience/reader—educated by television—knows even better than
Shakespeare's first audiences that what Henry describes is all too
possible. It is frightening to think that one man can unleash such
forces!

From the walls of Harfleur (or, in theatre terms, the balcony at
the back of the stage), the Governor concedes defeat: the Dauphin
has disappointed them, and now the city is at the mercy of the

---

[1] This book was re-issued in 1590 by a Stratford man, Richard Field, who subsequently
published Shakespeare's poems.

English king. Shakespeare's King Henry is more generous than his historical counterpart. Setting Exeter in command, he orders 'Use mercy to them all': Holinshed reports that in reality the town was ransacked. No victory was more easily won!

The English, when they are rested, will retire to Calais—which at this time was an English possession.

Scene 5   A complete and most welcome change. From the outdoor, very 'masculine', atmosphere of the previous scenes we go inside to the enclosed and 'feminine' world of the French court where the princess (already conscious of her destiny) is learning about the English language from her lady-in-waiting—whose own knowledge is rather uncertain! The parts of speech for the parts of the body meet with girlish giggles. By learning the new language, the princess is preparing to begin a new life.

Scene 6   At the French king's court, things are beginning to look serious. The king himself speaks little, allowing his nobles to give their opinions. The French lords are proud, despising the English as a 'barbarous people' who live in a 'nook-shotten isle' with a disgusting climate, 'foggy, raw and dull'! Even their national drink, 'sodden [boiled] water' making 'barley-broth', is not fit to be compared with the wine which gives spirit to the blood in France. Honour demands that the French lords must demonstrate their superiority in birth, breeding, and manhood. Occasional phrases such as '*O Dieu vivant*', '*Mort de ma vie*' are enough to sketch in the foreign language.

Having heard the counsel of the lords, who are shamed into unanimity, the king responds with an impressive roll-call of French nobility—and a complicated image that likens his forces to an avalanche that will quite overwhelm the English invaders. Confident of victory, the French prepare to fight—but the Dauphin is forbidden to join in the fun.

Scene 7   There has been a skirmish on the road to Calais where the French were trying to block the English retreat by breaking down a bridge over the river Ternoise. The fighting is now over; the French are defeated; and the Duke of Exeter is in command (although according to Holinshed he did not re-join the king until the action reached Agincourt).

Llewellyn speaks highly of the duke, and singles out for high praise 'an anchient lieutenant' who has done 'gallant service'. But when we hear his name, we recognize the man (who comes on to the stage) as the loud-mouthed braggart from Eastcheap—all word and no deed. But Pistol has a heart, and he pleads now for Bardolph. That incurable thief—no more than a petty pilferer (we remember the Boy's observation in Scene 2)—has stolen again. Military rules are strict and must be obeyed: Bardolph must die. Pistol, with a rude gesture, quits the scene.

The incident is based on Holinshed's *Chronicles*, which describe how

> in this great necessity, the poor people of the country were not spoiled, nor any thing taken of them without payment, nor any outrage or offence done by the Englishmen, except one, which was, that a soldier took a pix out of a church, for which he was apprehended, and the king not once removed [from the place] till the box was restored, and the offender strangled.

Shakespeare, identifying the soldier with his fictional character Bardolph, has changed the 'pix', a box holding communion wafers, to a 'pax', a plate—less valuable and less sacred—kissed by the communicants. With a quick stroke he dismisses another part of the king's youth. When Henry is told of Bardolph's crime and punishment, he is apparently unmoved: 'We would have all such offenders so cut off'.

As though to allow Henry to demonstrate afresh his new personality, the French herald brings another challenge. Its wording is contemptuous, but it is spoken 'fairly', and the king answers with dignity and courage: the English are in no fit state to fight, but they will not refuse the French challenge. Everything is in God's hand.

Scene 8   The French lords are restive, eager to join battle with the English. Time passes slowly for them, enlivened only by Bourbon's rhapsody on his horse, which is almost a formal rhetorical exercise. His companions tease him—and when he has gone out they scoff at Bourbon's empty boasting. But they are confident of victory.

Act 4

Like the previous one, this act is made up of cross-cutting scenes that move the audience into different parts of the field and show contrasting attitudes to warfare in general and to the battle of Agincourt in particular.

Chorus Now the Chorus beckons us conspiratorially to come to the battlefield. We must create darkness in our imaginations (in the Elizabethan theatre all performances took place in the afternoon), and peer through the night, lit by the occasional campfire, to see the army preparing for the next day's fighting. All is still—but we become aware of a hum of activity. Noises sound louder at night— the neighing of war-horses, the clunk of hammers, the rasp of metal against metal. The sound of the words echoes their sense: 'creeping murmur', 'hum . . . stilly sounds', 'high . . . neighs Piercing'. Every word in this speech adds to the picture in sight and sound.

The Chorus seems to speak louder now, contrasting the two armies who wait, with such different expectations, for morning. Although the night, personified as 'a foul and ugly witch', fills all his men with foreboding, the English king appears unaffected. His presence amongst them gives comfort, light and life: the royal sun shines on all alike.

Scene 1 Henry is fully aware of the danger of the situation, but although he can admit this to his nobles he must show no signs of panic. He moralizes on the subject, 'gather[ing] honey from the weed' to 'make a moral of the devil himself'. Gloucester and Erpingham listen dutifully and then Henry, disguised under Erpingham's cloak, embarks on a 'walkabout'. His first encounter is with Pistol, who attempts to 'pull rank' as an 'ancient' or standard-bearer (= second lieutenant). Pistol's hostility to Llewellyn is re-introduced, but there is no doubt where our sympathies should lie—especially after Henry's comment:

> Though it appear a little out of fashion,
> There is much care and valour in this Welshman.

So far there has been nothing to worry the king. But three common soldiers (who, unusually for Shakespeare, are given individual names) raise serious problems. How far is a king responsible to and for his subjects? What are the subject's duties to the king, to his own family, to his own soul, and to God? Disobedience to the king is disobedience to God—because the king is God's deputy on earth. But if the king's cause is not just . . . ?

Henry tries to make the soldiers understand that the king is a man just the same as they are, but they are unconvinced. Accepting a challenge from Williams, Henry watches the soldiers depart and, alone on the stage, meditates on the lonely burden that a king must bear and the inadequacy of empty ceremonious formalities to compensate.

This is the central scene of the play: all the issues seem to come to a head here, and for the moment they are resolved—insofar as they are capable of resolution—in Henry's final prayer. We can now appreciate what has been always at the back of his mind—and which is perhaps the real reason for this entire campaign: Henry's insecurity on the throne! Again we are reminded that Henry, guiltless himself, owes his crown to the murder by Henry Bullingbrook (Henry IV) of Richard II.

Scene 2   In the opposing camp the French are excitedly waiting for the battle to commence. They are fresh, in tiptop condition, and scornful of the pathetic band of British soldiers. Sickness—dysentery—had taken its toll of Henry's army even before the siege of Harfleur; and the march to Calais had taken twice as long as expected. By the time they reached Agincourt the men were exhausted—cold, wet, hungry, and ill—and their horses were in no better state. The French gloat over their expected victims.

Scene 3   The English nobles reckon up the odds against them. The actual numbers are in dispute, but it is certain that the English were heavily outnumbered (perhaps by as many as 30,000 French against 7,000 English). The king enters just in time to hear Westmorland longing for reinforcements. The great speech that follows is one of the finest dramatic expressions of military patriotism, and celebrates the achievements—as yet unaccomplished—of the 'few': 'We few, we happy few, we band of brothers'. Henry anticipates the festive celebrations that will annually commemorate the glorious victory. Those who fought at Agincourt will be united in a blood brotherhood that will transcend all the social barriers that divide 'high and low and lower' (*1*, *2*, *180*).

Westmorland is convinced. Now the English are ready to fight—but the French herald interrupts with yet another insulting demand for the king's ransom. Henry, enraged, sends back a proud retort which Montjoy, the herald, hears with respect and addresses him for the first time as 'King Harry'. The quickest of prayers, 'how Thou pleasest, God' ('Thy will be done'), and the battle is on.

Scene 4   The first sign of victory is a parody of conquest: Pistol has captured an unfortunate Frenchman—who is an even greater coward than Pistol and will plead and flatter and *pay* to save his life. The Boy scornfully translates Pistol's empty threats and, before he leaves the stage, makes the apparently irrelevant observation that the English camp is unprotected: 'there is none to guard it but boys'.

Scene 5   With disgust and shame the French nobles contemplate their overthrow, determining to re-join the battle and die with some honour rather than live with such disgrace. Their resolution, because it is expressed with such exaggerated language, is laughable rather than heroic.

Scene 6   The English take time for a moment's grief. Hearing a trumpet, Henry assumes that the French must be about to make a renewed onslaught and, contrary to all conventions of warfare, orders his soldiers to kill their prisoners.

Scene 7   Llewellyn has just heard of an outrage 'against the law of arms' committed by the French, who have murdered innocent civilians and looted the English tents (now we understand the Boy's comment in Scene 4). Lines of communication seem to have crossed—Gower believes that the king had ordered the killing of all prisoners as a form of retaliation, and he applauds the deed as 'most worthily' done by 'a gallant king'. Llewellyn joins in his praise of Henry, reiterating the comparison (see *1, 1, 46*) with the classical model of conquering kings, Alexander the Great. Even the rejection of Falstaff by the newly-crowned King Henry V (see *2, 1, 80 note*) is seen by Llewellyn to have its counterpart in the life of Alexander. But Henry was, as the Welshman himself recalls, 'in his right wits and his good judgements' when he 'turned away the fat knight with the great belly doublet'.

It is interesting that Shakespeare chooses this moment of Henry's greatest triumph to remind us of the price that had to be paid in personal relationships. Prince Hal could only become Henry V by sacrificing his friend—and renouncing all that Falstaff represented.

Another crossed line! The king has only just learned of the massacre of the boys in the camp. His claim to have his emotions well under control (see *1*, 2, 242–3) is momentarily forgotten, and he is now very angry and threatens the French. His language is strong and confident: the alliteration—'skirr away as swift as stones'—makes the task sound easy. Again he orders (apparently for the first time) that the prisoners' throats are to be cut.

The English herald departs—but meets the returning French herald, who presents a very different appearance, 'His eyes are humbler than they used to be'. Henry, still angry, assumes that this is another ransom demand, but Montjoy is submissive now, asking permission for the French to rescue the bodies of their dead—who even in death must observe social distinctions. As though taken by surprise, Henry can only ask who has won the battle!

A kind of light relief is needed here to relax after the tensions of fighting. The king turns to Llewellyn, and they rejoice in their Welsh kinship. Henry, when he was Prince Hal, was fond of practical jokes, and he now sets up a duel (which was in fact prepared for earlier—in Scene 1—when he walked through the camp the previous night).

Scene 8   The joke continues, involving more people. The soldiers' loyalty is praiseworthy, and it seems hard that Henry should take such pleasure in the discomfiture of Williams and the embarrassment of the officers. Williams is dignified in his reproach to the king and in his refusal of the shilling offered by Llewellyn in imitation of the royal gesture. All's well that ends well—but class distinctions, abandoned before Agincourt, seem to be returning: Williams is now 'this fellow'.

The French and English casualty lists are compared. The French seem to have lost more noblemen than common soldiers—truly 'a royal fellowship of death'. The English, however, are almost unscathed: only five men 'of name', and no more than twenty-five 'other men' (the total is taken from Holinshed's reckoning—although the historian remarks that other estimates of the dead range between one hundred and six hundred). God's is the glory, and His must be the praise. Insisting on this, and claiming a victory won 'without stratagem', Shakespeare's king ignores the role of military tactics and the 'politic invention' described by Holinshed whereby Henry

> sent privily two hundred archers into a low meadow which was near to the vanguard of his enemies, but separated with a great ditch, commanding them there to keep themselves close till they had a token to them given, to let drive at their adversaries . . . [and] he caused stakes bound with iron sharp at both ends,

of the length of five or six foot to be pitched before the archers, and of each side the footmen like an hedge, to the intent that if the barded horses ran rashly upon them, they might shortly be gored and destroyed . . . This device of fortifying an army was at this time first invented.

Singing hymns of thankfulness, the army retires to Calais—and then home to England.

Act 5

Chorus   The Chorus is now brisk and businesslike: his speech must cover a lot of ground, and account for several years of historical time, for the benefit of those in the audience who are not already familiar with the story of Henry V (from history books, ballads, and from earlier plays). Making the usual apologies for the theatre's inadequacies, he takes the king to Calais—and immediately across the Channel to a vociferous welcoming crowd, then quickly into London. A victorious conqueror should be honoured (as Julius Caesar was) with a triumphal procession, but Henry's religious modesty forbids this.

A sudden change of rhythm and line-length introduces a contemporary allusion—which also ties the date when the play was written to the period between April and September 1599, when the Earl of Essex was commanding the English forces in Ireland (see 'Date and Text', p. xxxvi). After a short time at home—about five years, in fact—the king returns to France.

Scene 1   As so often in this play, the Chorus's formality is broken by a comedy scene. Fighting in France continued for some time after the Battle of Agincourt (25 October 1415). This scene would appear to take place on 2 March, the day after St David's day. The quarrel between Llewellyn and Pistol still goes on, but now there is leisure to settle it. Pistol is most ignominiously defeated, and the news from England—'my Doll is dead i'th'Spital of a malady of France'—demoralizes him further; he is also penniless (having lost even the promised ransom money when all prisoners were killed). But Pistol, the last of the Eastcheap mob, is irrepressible: punning on 'steal' and 'steal' he exits with characteristic bravado in a rhymed couplet and an allusion to Caesar's *Gallic Wars*.

Scene 2   This time we are really, as the Chorus promised us, with the king at a summit conference in Troyes. The two parties assemble on opposite sides of the stage, 'eyeballing' each other and speaking formal words of greeting.

In the centre of the stage stands Burgundy, lord of an independent French dukedom and, therefore, an ideal mediator between the two kings. He delivers a lecture to the warring factions on the beauties of peace, developing an analogy of the wasteland of a neglected countryside and the uncivilized savagery of a nation at war. The regular rhythms and rich language emphasize the content of his speech.

Delegates are appointed to negotiate terms of conciliation. King Henry ensures that he is represented by all his kinsmen—including the Earl of Huntington, who has not before appeared in the play (although in fact he fought at Harfleur). The French queen accompanies the negotiators to make sure that a woman's voice is heard.

Alone on the stage (apart from the interpreting Alice) are Henry and his 'capital demand', the Princess Katherine. Henry's demands have been considerably modified since he insisted (2, 2, 189) 'No king of England if not king of France'. Now he is asking only that his heirs should inherit the French crown through his marriage to the French princess.

The scene is a tricky one to play. Both characters must know their political roles, yet by teasing and joking they must act out a romantic comedy of love (whose outcome is preordained). Henry is content to make a fool of himself in pretending to be no lover, secure in the knowledge that he is 'the best king of good fellows' and Katherine—by extension of the proverb—'the queen of beggars'. Katherine's French nicety yields to English customs, and their contract is sealed with a kiss: 'nice customs curtsy to great kings'. The counsellors return, having made equally good progress in their negotiations. Burgundy tries to make a joke of the situation with some rather crude humour, and Henry joins in—showing more restraint and wit than the French lord. Finally, when all parties are in full agreement, the French queen speaks a blessing. The stage is left to the Chorus to wind up the history.

Chorus
Still apologizing for the theatre's inadequacies, the Chorus has a
last word of praise for Henry V, 'This star of England', before
pointing the audience towards Henry's son, Henry VI. In looking
forward he also looks back—to the three *Henry VI* plays of
Shakespeare's first tetralogy.

Hal to Henry:
From Prince of Wales to King of England

No one can forget Prince Hal! All the characters in *Henry V* remember the prince who was created by Shakespeare (with only a little help from historical sources) in the early scenes of *Henry IV Part 1*, and they make sure that we—the twentieth-century audiences and readers—are not allowed to forget either. A royal prince, apparently an adolescent (his age is never ascertained), is led astray by a much older man (Sir John Falstaff), and joins with a bunch of hooligans and petty criminals ('unlettered, rude and shallow') in sessions of heavy drinking and practical joking ('riots, banquets, sports'—*I*, 1, 55–6). To the bystanders, it all seems fairly harmless, and even quite amusing—but to the prince's father, and to all representatives of law and order in the state, such misconduct appears dangerously subversive. The future of the English monarchy is threatened by it!

Those who *understand* Prince Hal, however, and who become intimate with his thoughts by listening to his soliloquies, know better what to expect. From his earliest appearance in the play, Hal shows a streak of determined calculation. As he parts from his drinking pals, he excuses and justifies his actions:

> I know you all, and will awhile uphold
> The unyok'd humour of your idleness.
> Yet herein will I imitate the sun,
> Who doth permit the base contagious clouds
> To smother up his beauty from the world,
> That, when he please again to be himself,
> Being wanted he may be more wonder'd at
> By breaking through the foul and ugly mists
> Of vapours that did seem to strangle him . . .

The effect, he promises, will be spectacular:

> . . . like bright metal on a sullen ground,
> My reformation, glitt'ring o'er my fault,
> Shall show more goodly, and attract more eyes
> Than that which hath no foil to set it off.
>
> *Henry IV Part 1, I, 2, 197–205; 214–7.*

Throughout *Henry IV Part 1* Prince Hal is contrasted with Henry Hotspur, son of the Earl of Northumberland. Hotspur, 'the theme of honour's tongue' (*1*, 1, 80), has earned the admiration of Henry IV, Hal's own father, even whilst he is fighting in rebellion against the king. At the battle of Shrewsbury, which ends the play, Hal overcomes Hotspur in physical combat. Their duel also, metaphorically, strikes a blow against Falstaff, who, like the allegorical Riot, misleader of Youth in the Morality Plays, seems to tempt Prince Hal away from the straight and narrow path of his royal calling. Much of *Henry IV Part 2* is taken up by the gradual undermining of Falstaff's influence. Shakespeare shows the fat knight in an increasingly unfavourable light—cowardly, unscrupulous, and diseased. At the end of the play Prince Hal, newly crowned Henry V, disclaims his former friend: 'I know thee not, old man' (5, 5, 47). Falstaff, and all that he represents, has to be sacrificed for the sake of the kingdom.

By the grace of God—or so it appears to the clerics in the opening scene of *Henry V*—a religious conversion has taken place. 'The king is full of grace and fair regard' (*1*, 1, 22). The Christian concept of 'grace' is important in this play. The word has many connotations, but it generally refers to the assistance given freely by God to any human being who will freely accept it, and particularly to those whose efforts (whether or not they understand what they are doing) ensure that the will of God is being carried out. Prince Hal was given the grace to recognize the error of his adolescent past, to repent and reform; he will now hope and pray for still further grace to accomplish the task for which—he believes—God has called him.

But in shaking off the burden of his own past, Henry has been compelled to recognize and shoulder the burdens which were his father's.

Henry IV attained the crown by rebellion against the rightful king, Richard II, and his reign was an uneasy one. He confesses this, shortly before he dies, to Prince Hal:

> God knows, my son,
> By what by-paths and indirect crook'd ways
> I met this crown, and I myself know well
> How troublesome it sat upon my head.
> To thee it shall descend with better quiet,
> Better opinion, better confirmation . . .

He gives his son a warning:

> . . . though thou stand'st more sure than I could do,
> Thou art not firm enough, since griefs are green . . . ;

and the advice:

> Therefore, my Harry,
> Be it thy course to busy giddy minds
> With foreign quarrels, that action hence borne out
> May waste the memory of the former days.
> *Henry IV Part 2, 4, 5, 182–215*

All this Henry V must bear in mind at the important crises of the play—when the Archbishop of Canterbury urges him to war with France; when he discovers the treachery of Cambridge, Scroop, and Gray; and when he prepares himself mentally and spiritually for the battle of Agincourt.

Shakespeare's Verse

Shakespeare's plays are mainly written in 'blank verse', the form preferred by most dramatists in the sixteenth and early seventeenth centuries. Blank verse is a very flexible medium, which is capable—like the human speaking voice—of a wide range of tones. The lines, which are unrhymed, are ten syllables long and divide into five 'feet' with alternating stresses, just like normal English speech. The technical name for this is 'iambic pentameter'.

> **Canterbury**
> It múst be só, for míraclés are céas'd,
> And thérefore wé must néeds admít the meáns,
> How thíngs are pérfectéd.
> > **Ely**
> > But mý good lórd,
> How nów for mítigátion óf this bíll
> Urg'd bý the Cómmons? Dóth his májestý
> Inclíne to ít or nó?
> > **Canterbury**
> > > He séems indífferént . . . (*1*, 1, 67–72)

Here the two prelates, men of great seriousness and in complete agreement with each other, are speaking a verse which is fairly regular (there is an extra foot in the last line), and where the lines are divided between the speakers without losing the rhythm.

Sometimes the verse line contains the grammatical unit of meaning, thus allowing for a pause at the end of the line before a new idea is started—'It must be so, for miracles are ceased'. At other times the sense runs on from one line to the next—'we must needs admit the means / How things are perfected'. This makes for the natural fluidity of speech, avoiding monotony but still maintaining the basic iambic rhythm. On occasion Shakespeare deviates from the norm, writing lines that are longer or shorter than ten syllables, and varying the stress patterns for unusual emphasis. In the king's meditation the night before Agincourt there are two short lines whose 'missing' syllables speak more than words:

> What ínfiníte heart's eáse must kíngs negléct
> That prívate mén enjóy?   (*4*, 1, 233–4)

and

> Wherein thou árt less háppy béing féar'd
> Than théy in feáring?   (lines 245–6)

Again, in the Chorus's speech introducing *Act 5* (lines 28–31) there is a sudden change of rhythm and line-length when Shakespeare inserts a contemporary allusion: the citizens

> Go fórth and fétch their cónquering Cáesar ín —
> As, bý a lówer bút by lóving líkelihoód
> Were nów the géneral óf our grácious émpress,
> (As ín good tíme he máy) from Íreland cóming . . .

Much of *Henry V* is written in prose, which is the proper medium for comic scenes and those involving 'low-life' characters. King Henry sometimes speaks in prose—but only when he is adopting a persona different from his usual character—the 'man amongst men' on the night before Agincourt (*Act 4*, Scene 1), for instance, or the unskilled wooer of the French princess.

Date and Text

The date of Shakespeare's play is fairly certainly established by a topical allusion in the Chorus's *Act 5* speech (lines 30–2). He compares Henry's reception in London to that which would be given

> Were now the general of our gracious empress,
> As in good time he may, from Ireland coming,
> Bringing rebellion broached on his sword . . .

The reference is to the Earl of Essex, whose campaign left England for Ireland on 27 March 1599, returning—unsuccessful—in September of that year.

There are two early editions of the play—the Quarto (Q) published in 1600 and reprinted, with some few corrections, in 1602 and 1619; and the Folio (F) of 1623. F seems to have been based on Shakespeare's own manuscript and, although much later, is more authoritative than Q, which could have originated from a reconstruction of the play by one or more actors working from memory. The present edition uses the text established by Professor Andrew Gurr (*The New Cambridge Shakespeare*, 1992). Significant variations are remarked in the Notes, as are some omissions.

Characters in the Play

ON THE ENGLISH SIDE

The Chorus

The Monarch	King Henry V	
The Church	The Archbishop of Canterbury The Bishop of Ely	
The Nobility	Duke of Exeter	King Henry's *uncle*
	Duke of Gloucester	King Henry's *brothers*
	Duke of Bedford	
	Duke of Westmorland	King Henry's *cousins*
	Duke of York	
	The Earl of Warwick The Earl of Salisbury Sir Thomas Erpingham	
	Lord Scroop The Earl of Cambridge Lord Gray	*conspirators against* King Henry
The Army	Gower Llewellyn Macmorris Jamy	*an English captain* *a Welsh captain* *an Irish captain* *a Scots captain*
	John Bates Alexander Court Michael Williams	*private soldiers*
	The English Herald	
The Eastcheap Mob	Bardolph Nym Pistol	*former friends of* Prince Hal
	Hostess (Mistress Quickly) Boy	*wife of* Pistol *page to* Falstaff

ON THE FRENCH SIDE

Royalty	King Charles VI	
	Queen Isabel	*his wife*
	The Dauphin	*their eldest son*
	Princess Katherine	*their daughter*
The Nobility	Duke of Berri	
	Duke of Bourbon	
	Duke of Orléans	
	Duke of Burgundy	
	The Constable of France	
	Rambures	
	Grandpré	*Lords of France*
	Beaumont	
Citizens	Governor of the city of Harfleur	
	Montjoy	*the French Herald*
	Alice	*lady-in-waiting to* Princess Katherine
	Ambassadors	*to the English court*
	Monsieur Le Fer	*a French gentleman captured by* Pistol

Attendants at both courts, and soldiers in both armies
The action of the play takes place in England and in France

Prologue

Prologue

The Prologue to the play, which is spoken by a single actor known as the 'Chorus' (see p. vii), laments the inadequacies of the theatre, and urges the audience to use their own imaginations to supply the actors' deficiencies.

1 *muse*: In Greek mythology, the nine Muses were goddesses of inspiration; creative artists invoked the one they thought most appropriate for their purposes.
fire: the lightest of the four elements—earth, water, air, and fire—of which the world (according to Elizabethan cosmology) was composed. The astronomer Ptolemy taught that fire would always rise to the highest heaven, the empyrean.

2 *invention*: poetic creation.

3–4 *princes . . . behold*: See the description of the Battle of Crécy (*1*, *2*, 105–10) in which the Black Prince 'played a tragedy', watched by his father, Edward III.

4 *swelling*: increasingly splendid.

5 *warlike*: skilled in military matters.
Harry: the familiar form of 'Henry'.
like himself: presented in an appropriate manner.

6 *port*: bearing (with a possible pun on 'part' = actor's role).
Mars: the Roman god of war.

7 *famine, sword, and fire*: the instruments of war, personified as hounds which, for hunting, were fastened in a 'leash' of three.

8 *gentles all*: ladies and gentlemen.

9 *flat unraised spirits*: dull and uninspired creatures—i.e. the author of this play, and the actors.
hath: Shakespeare often mixes singular and plural verbs and subjects.

Prologue

Enter Chorus

Chorus
O for a muse of fire, that would ascend
The brightest heaven of invention,
A kingdom for a stage, princes to act,
And monarchs to behold the swelling scene.
5 Then should the warlike Harry, like himself,
Assume the port of Mars, and at his heels
(Leash'd in, like hounds) should famine, sword, and fire
Crouch for employment. But pardon, gentles all,
The flat unraised spirits, that hath dar'd,

10 *scaffold*: platform, stage.
11 *cockpit*: pit for cock-fighting.
12 *vasty fields*: huge battlefields.
13 *wooden O*: small circular building made
    of wood—i.e. the theatre.
    the very casques: the actual helmets (*and
    the men who wore them*).
14 *affright*: frighten.
15 *a crooked figure*: i.e. the *o* of arithmetic:
    o added to 100,000 makes a million—
    1,000,000.
16 *Attest*: signify.
17 *us*: i.e. the actors.
    ciphers: nothings, nonentities.
    to: compared to.
18 *imaginary forces*: powers of imagination.
19 *Suppose*: imagine.
    girdle: surroundings.
21 *high upreared*: The image is of warhorses
    rearing to challenge each other: the ref-
    erence is to the cliffs of Dover, standing
    opposite to the shores of France.
    abutting: adjacent.
    fronts: foreheads, frontiers.
22 *the . . . ocean*: the English Channel,
    which is particularly treacherous for
    shipping.
23 *Piece out*: augment.
25 *puissance*: power, forces (the word is
    pronounced with three syllables).

10 On this unworthy scaffold, to bring forth
    So great an object. Can this cockpit hold
    The vasty fields of France? Or may we cram
    Within this wooden O the very casques
    That did affright the air at Agincourt?
15 Oh, pardon: since a crooked figure may
    Attest in little place a million,
    And let us, ciphers to this great account,
    On your imaginary forces work.
    Suppose within the girdle of these walls
20 Are now confin'd two mighty monarchies,
    Whose high upreared and abutting fronts
    The perilous narrow ocean parts asunder.
    Piece out our imperfections with your thoughts.
    Into a thousand parts divide one man,
25 And make imaginary puissance.
    Think when we talk of horses that you see them

27 *proud*: spirited.

28 *deck*: equip.

30 *th'accomplishment . . . years*: that which took many years to achieve: the events of the play took place between 1414 and 1420.

31 *for the which supply*: to help you with this.

32 *Admit*: accept.

32–3 *Chorus . . . Prologue-like*: Although he appears as a 'Prologue' now, he will return from time to time to comment on the action as a 'Chorus' would do.

Printing their proud hooves i'th'receiving earth,
For 'tis your thoughts that now must deck our
    kings,
Carry them here and there, jumping o'er times,
30 Turning th'accomplishment of many years
Into an hour-glass. For the which supply
Admit me Chorus to this history,
Who, Prologue-like, your humble patience pray,
Gently to hear, kindly to judge our play.

[*Exit*

Act 1

Act 1   Scene 1

The Archbishop of Canterbury and the
Bishop of Ely have a problem; a bill has been
presented in Parliament which, if it is passed,
will deprive the Church of much of its great
wealth. But there is a new king on the
throne, and the two churchmen are encour-
aged by his amazing abilities. The
Archbishop of Canterbury has a scheme
which may solve their dilemma. This scene is
not present in Q.

1–19 These lines are particularly close to
    the wording of Shakespeare's source;
    see 'The sources of *Henry V*' p. 127.
  1 *that . . . urg'd*: the very same bill is
    being presented. In 1410—'th'eleventh
    year of the last king's reign'—the House
    of Commons had tried to wrest from
    the Church some of its enormous,
    untaxable, property holdings. This
    problem was not a new one in 1410—
    and was still unsolved in 1599.
  3 *Was . . . pass'd*: was likely to be, and
    would indeed have been passed.
  4 *scambling*: violent, unruly.
  5 *question*: debate.
  8 *the better . . . possession*: more than half
    of what we own.
  9 *temporal*: secular—i.e. land which had
    been bequeathed to the Church and
    was consequently exempt from taxation.
 10 *By testament*: as a legacy.
 15 *lazars*: lepers; the term came from the
    story of Lazarus (St Luke's Gospel,
    16:20), and was generally applied to all
    chronically sick persons.
 16 *indigent*: needy, destitute.
    corporal: physical.
 19 *by th'year*: annually.
    the bill: the bill before Parliament; *and*
    the cost.
 20 *drink deep*: take a lot away from us.
 22 *grace*: Christian goodness; see p. xxxii.
    fair regard: highly respected and with

Scene 1

Enter the two Bishops *of* Canterbury *and*
Ely

Canterbury
My lord, I'll tell you, that self bill is urg'd
Which in th'eleventh year of the last king's reign
Was like, and had indeed against us pass'd
But that the scambling and unquiet time
5 Did push it out of farther question.
    Ely
But how, my lord, shall we resist it now?
    Canterbury
It must be thought on. If it pass against us
We lose the better half of our possession,
For all the temporal lands, which men devout
10 By testament have given to the Church
Would they strip from us, being valu'd thus:
As much as would maintain to the king's honour
Full fifteen earls and fifteen hundred knights,
Six thousand and two hundred good esquires,
15 And to relief of lazars and weak age
Of indigent faint souls, past corporal toil,
A hundred alms-houses, right well supplied;
And to the coffers of the king beside
A thousand pounds by th'year. Thus runs the bill.
    Ely
20 This would drink deep.
    Canterbury
                                'Twould drink the cup and all
    Ely
But what prevention?
    Canterbury
The king is full of grace, and fair regard.

24 *courses of his youth*: undisciplined behaviour when he was a boy; see 'Hal to Henry', p. xxxi.

great respect for [the Church].

26 *mortified*: put to death.

27 *Yea*: yes indeed.

28 *Consideration*: self-awareness.

29 *Adam*: the first man (according to the Book of Genesis), who was expelled from the Garden of Eden because he broke God's law.

30 *paradise*: the Garden of Eden, and *also* Heaven, the home of all divine spirits.

32 *was . . . made*: did anyone become a theologian so quickly.

33 *in a flood*: Here, and also in line 35, Shakespeare alludes to the twelve labours imposed on Hercules, the superman of classical mythology. The fifth of these was the cleansing of the Augean stables, which Hercules achieved by diverting a river through them.

34 *heady currance*: rush of flowing water.
scouring: scrubbing out.

35 *Hydra-headed*: manifold and persistent—i.e. with as many heads as the Hydra. The monster (which was killed by Hercules as his second labour) had nine heads; when one was cut off, two more grew in its place.

36 *seat*: power.

38 *reason in*: discuss.

42 *all . . . study*: his special subject.

43 *List*: listen to.
discourse: talking about.

44 *render'd you in music*: narrated with eloquence.

45 *cause of policy*: argument about politics.

46 *gordian knot*: The intricate knot tying the chariot of Gordius would only—according to ancient prophecy—be unloosed by the man who was to conquer Asia. Alexander the Great cut through the knot with his sword.

Ely
And a true lover of the holy Church.
　　Canterbury
The courses of his youth promis'd it not.
25 The breath no sooner left his father's body
But that his wildness, mortified in him,
Seem'd to die too. Yea, at that very moment
Consideration like an angel came,
And whipp'd th'offending Adam out of him,
30 Leaving his body as a paradise
T'envelop and contain celestial spirits.
Never was such a sudden scholar made,
Never came reformation in a flood
With such a heady currance scouring faults,
35 Nor never Hydra-headed wilfulness
So soon did lose his seat, and all at once,
As in this king.
　　Ely
　　　　　　We are blessed in the change.
　　Canterbury
Hear him but reason in divinity,
And all-admiring, with an inward wish,
40 You would desire the king were made a prelate.
Hear him debate of commonwealth affairs,
You would say it hath been all in all his study.
List his discourse of war, and you shall hear
A fearful battle render'd you in music.
45 Turn him to any cause of policy,
The gordian knot of it he will unloose,
Familiar as his garter, that when he speaks

47 *Familiar*: i.e. as easily.
48 *charter'd libertine*: licensed free-ranger.
49 *the mute wonder*: silent amazement.
50 *honey'd*: well-spoken.
    sentences: maxims.
51 *art and practic*: practical experience.
52 *mistress to*: controller: practice is more important than theory ('*theoric*').
53 *his grace*: his majesty; but see also line 22 and *note*.
    glean: pick up, learn.
54 *courses vain*: useless activities.
55 *companies*: companions.
    unletter'd: uneducated.
    rude: ignorant.
    shallow: frivolous.
58 *sequestration*: withdrawal into some privacy.
59 *open haunts*: public places.
    popularity: throngs of common people.
60 *strawberry*: The strawberry was used as an emblem of righteousness because it was untainted by neighbouring plants 'of baser quality' (such as onions or garlic). The strawberries of Ely House, the London home of the Bishop of Ely, were famous.

63 *obscur'd his contemplation*: hid the seriousness of his thinking.
66 *crescive in his faculty*: increasing because it was in its nature to increase.
67 *miracles are ceas'd*: The Protestant Church taught that the only miracles were those recorded in Holy Scripture. In the time of Henry V, England was still a Catholic country, but Shakespeare's audience would be unlikely to notice the anachronism.
68 *admit the means*: find a natural cause.
69 *perfected*: brought to spiritual perfection; the stress is on the first syllable.
72 *indifferent*: impartial.

The air, a charter'd libertine, is still,
And the mute wonder lurketh in men's ears
50 To steal his sweet and honey'd sentences,
So that the art and practic part of life
Must be the mistress to this theoric.
Which is a wonder how his grace should glean it,
Since his addiction was to courses vain,
55 His companies unletter'd, rude and shallow,
His hours fill'd up with riots, banquets, sports,
And never noted in him any study,
Any retirement, any sequestration
From open haunts and popularity.
    Ely
60 The strawberry grows underneath the nettle,
And wholesome berries thrive and ripen best
Neighbour'd by fruit of baser quality.
And so the prince obscur'd his contemplation
Under the veil of wildness, which, no doubt,
65 Grew like the summer grass fastest by night,
Unseen, yet crescive in his faculty.
    Canterbury
It must be so, for miracles are ceas'd,
And therefore we must needs admit the means
How things are perfected.
    Ely
                        But my good lord,
70 How now for mitigation of this bill
Urg'd by the Commons? Doth his majesty
Incline to it or no?
    Canterbury
                        He seems indifferent,
Or rather swaying more upon our part
Than cherishing th'exhibiters against us,
75 For I have made an offer to his majesty
Upon our spiritual convocation
And in regard of causes now in hand
Which I have open'd to his grace at large,
As touching France, to give a greater sum
80 Than ever at one time the clergy yet
Did to his predecessors part withal.
    Ely
How did this offer seem receiv'd, my lord?

74 *exhibiters*: sponsors, those who are presenting the bill.
76 *Upon*: on behalf of.
   spiritual convocation: assembly of the
   higher clergy.
77 *causes*: legal matters.
78 *open'd*: explained.
79 *touching*: concerning.
81 *withal*: with.
83 *of*: by.
85 *fain*: like to.
86 *severals*: separate details.
   unhidden passages: clear and undisputed
   lines of descent.
88 *seat*: throne.
89 *Deriv'd*: descended from; see 'The
   Family Tree', p. x.

95 *embassy*: ambassador's message.

Canterbury
With good acceptance of his majesty,
Save that there was not time enough to hear,
85 As I perceiv'd his grace would fain have done,
The severals and unhidden passages
Of his true titles to some certain dukedoms,
And generally to the crown and seat of France
Deriv'd from Edward, his great-grandfather.
        Ely
90 What was th'impediment that broke this off?
        Canterbury
The French ambassador upon that instant
Crav'd audience, and the hour I think is come
To give him hearing. Is it four o'clock?
        Ely
It is.
        Canterbury
95 Then go we in, to know his embassy,
Which I could with a ready guess declare
Before the Frenchman speak a word of it.
        Ely
I'll wait upon you, and I long to hear it.

                              [*Exeunt*

Act I   Scene 2

King Henry asks the archbishop if it is right
that England should declare war on France.
Henry knows that many lives will be lost in
the fighting, and he wants to make sure that
his cause is just. The archbishop explains, at
great length, why Henry can lay claim to the
throne of France, and he urges the king to
fight for his right. King Henry is convinced,
but he is reluctant to leave England in case
the Scots attack the country whilst the best
of its armed forces are abroad. The archbishop sets the king's mind at rest, and then
delivers a short sermon on the proper ordering of a state. King Henry is determined to
fight, and he calls in the ambassadors from
the French court, who deliver a very insulting message from the Dauphin. The king
declares war.

Scene 2

        Enter the King, Gloucester, Bedford,
        Clarence, Westmorland, *and* Exeter *and*
        Attendants

        King
Where is my gracious lord of Canterbury?
        Exeter
Not here in presence.
        King
                          Send for him, good uncle.
        Westmorland
Shall we call in th'ambassador, my liege?
        King
Not yet, my cousin. We would be resolv'd,
5 Before we hear him, of some things of weight
That task our thoughts, concerning us and France.

os.d. *Clarence*: the Duke of Clarence has no speaking part in this scene, and he does not appear anywhere else in the play. But his entrance is marked in both Q and F texts. See 'Date and Text', p. xxxvi.

2 *presence*: the royal presence.

3 *liege*: royal lord.

4 *cousin*: Westmorland was related to Henry by marriage.
we: King Henry speaks in 'the royal plural'.
resolv'd: satisfied.

5 *of . . . weight*: about matters of importance.

6 *task*: burden.

8 *become*: grace it with your presence.

10 *justly . . . unfold*: honestly and in all good faith explain.

11 *the law Salic*: The Archbishop of Canterbury expounds the Salic law in lines 37–95.

12 *Or . . . or*: either . . . or.

13 *faithful*: of good Christian faith.

14 *fashion*: give a false shape to.
bow: distort.

15 *nicely charge*: lay a burden on [your soul] with subtle arguments.
understanding: comprehending, learned; and obedient to, standing under, God.

16 *opening*: raising the question of.
titles miscreate: illegitimate claims.

17 *Suits . . . colours*: does not match up.

19 *approbation*: support.

20 *your reverence*: This is an appropriate form of address for the Archbishop of Canterbury—but it could be spoken with some sarcasm.

21 *impawn*: risk, hazard.

26 *sore*: serious.

27 *wrongs*: wrong-doings.
gives edge: sharpens; singular verbs might be used with plural nouns.

29 *Under this conjuration*: in response to this solemn invocation.

32 *sin*: the 'original sin' of which—according to the Catholic Church—every human being is guilty: all share Adam's sin (see *1, 1, 29 note*) until this is cleansed by Christian baptism.

Enter Canterbury *and* Ely

Canterbury
God and his angels guard your sacred throne,
And make you long become it.
    King
                                    Sure, we thank you.
My learned lord, we pray you to proceed,
10 And justly and religiously unfold
Why the law Salic that they have in France
Or should or should not bar us in our claim.
And God forbid, my dear and faithful lord,
That you should fashion, wrest, or bow your reading,
15 Or nicely charge your understanding soul
With opening titles miscreate, whose right
Suits not in native colours with the truth.
For God doth know how many now in health
Shall drop their blood in approbation
20 Of what your reverence shall incite us to.
Therefore take heed how you impawn our person,
How you awake our sleeping sword of war.
We charge you in the name of God take heed,
For never two such kingdoms did contend
25 Without much fall of blood, whose guiltless drops
Are every one a woe, a sore complaint
'Gainst him whose wrongs gives edge unto the swords
That makes such waste in brief mortality.
Under this conjuration speak, my lord,
30 For we will hear, note, and believe in heart
That what you speak is in your conscience washed
As pure as sin with baptism.

Canterbury

Then hear me, gracious sovereign, and you peers
That owe your selves, your lives and services
35 To this imperial throne. There is no bar
To make against your highness' claim to France
But this which they produce from Pharamond:
In terram Salicam mulieres ne succedant,
—No woman shall succeed in Salic land—
40 Which Salic land the French unjustly glose
To be the realm of France, and Pharamond
The founder of this law and female bar.
Yet their own authors faithfully affirm
That the land Salic is in Germany,
45 Between the floods of Sala and of Elbe,
Where Charles the Great, having subdu'd the
    Saxons,
There left behind and settled certain French,
Who, holding in disdain the German women
For some dishonest manners of their life,
50 Establish'd then this law: to wit, no female
Should be inheritrix in Salic land,
Which Salic (as I said) 'twixt Elbe and Sala
Is at this day in Germany called Meissen.
Then doth it well appear the Salic law
55 Was not devised for the realm of France.
Nor did the French possess the Salic land
Until four hundred one-and-twenty years

35 *imperial*: having absolute sovereignty.
   bar: objection. The archbishop could
   have explained that Henry's claim to
   the French throne was through his
   descent from Queen Isabella, the
   mother of Edward III and daughter of
   Philip IV of France (see 'Family Tree',
   p. x).
37 *Pharamond*: legendary king of the Salian
   Franks.
39 *succeed*: inherit the throne.
40 *glose*: gloss, interpret.
42 *female bar*: prohibition against women;
   the law was in fact devised by the
   French nobles who had elected Philip
   of Valois to the throne of France.
43 *authors*: scholars.
45 *floods*: rivers.
46 *Charles the Great*: Charlemagne, AD
   742–814.
47 Charlemagne colonized the 'Salic land'
   with Frenchmen.
49 *dishonest manners*: unchastity.

57 *four hundred one-and-twenty*: In actual
   fact, it was 379 years later—four hundred *less* one-and-twenty; the arithmeti-
   cal error came from Holinshed.

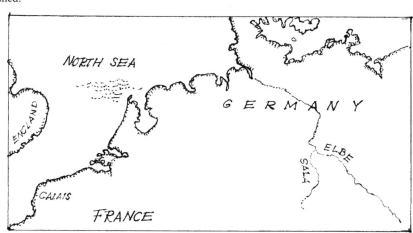

58 *defunction*: decease.
59 *Idly*: falsely.
60 *the year of our redemption*: anno Domini, the year of the Lord—Jesus Christ, whose birth and death redeemed mankind from all their sins.
62 *seat*: settle.
64 *Besides*: in addition.
   writers: scholars.
66 *heir general*: one who inherits regardless of whether the descent is through the male or female line.

72 *fine*: refine, complete.
   shows: appearance.
73 *naught*: rubbish.
74 *Conveyed*: dishonestly presented.
75 *Charlemagne*: This was really Charles the Bald; Shakespeare follows Holinshed's slip.
76 *Louis*: The name was pronounced as 'Lewis' by the Elizabethans.

82 *lineal of*: descended in a straight line from.

88 *Louis his satisfaction*: Louis's satisfaction.
89 *title*: entitlement.

91 *Howbeit*: notwithstanding.

93 *hide them in a net*: take refuge in a tangle of obvious contradictions.
94 *amply*: honestly and openly.
   embar their crooked titles: prevent discovery of the weakness of their own titles (which are not in a direct line of descent).

After defunction of King Pharamond,
Idly suppos'd the founder of this law,
60 Who died within the year of our redemption,
Four hundred twenty-six, and Charles the Great
Subdu'd the Saxons and did seat the French
Beyond the River Sala in the year
Eight hundred five. Besides, their writers say
65 King Pepin, which deposed Childeric,
Did as heir general, being descended
Of Blithild, which was daughter to King Clothair,
Make claim and title to the crown of France.
Hugh Capet also, who usurp'd the crown
70 Of Charles the Duke of Lorraine, sole heir male
Of the true line and stock of Charles the Great,
To fine his title with some shows of truth,
Though in pure truth it was corrupt and naught,
Conveyed himself as th'heir to the Lady Lingard,
75 Daughter to Charlemagne, who was the son
To Louis the emperor, and Louis the son
Of Charles the Great. Also King Louis the Ninth,
Who was sole heir to the usurper Capet,
Could not keep quiet in his conscience,
80 Wearing the crown of France, till satisfied
That fair Queen Isabel, his grandmother,
Was lineal of the Lady Ermengard,
Daughter to Charles the foresaid Duke of Lorraine;
By the which marriage the line of Charles the Great
85 Was reunited to the crown of France.
So that, as clear as is the summer's sun,
King Pepin's title, and Hugh Capet's claim,
King Louis his satisfaction, all appear
To hold in right and title of the female.
90 So do the kings of France unto this day.
Howbeit, they would hold up this Salic law
To bar your highness claiming from the female,
And rather choose to hide them in a net
Than amply to embar their crooked titles
95 Usurp'd from you and your progenitors.
    King
May I with right and conscience make this claim?
    Canterbury
The sin upon my head, dread sovereign,
For in the Book of Numbers is it writ

98 *Book of Numbers*: In the Old Testament the Book of Numbers (27:8) rules that 'If a man die, and hath no son, then ye shall cause his inheritance to pass unto his daughter'.

writ: written.

101 *unwind*: unfurl.

bloody: bloodstained.

103 *great-grandsire*: Edward III.

106–10 The Black Prince defeated the French at the Battle of Crécy in 1346.

108 *Whiles*: whilst.

on a hill: According to Holinshed, the king 'stood aloft on a windmill hill' for the entire duration of the battle.

109 *lion's whelp*: lion cub; see note to line 124.

110 *Forage in*: gorge himself with.

111 *entertain*: cope with.

112 *half*: The English army was arranged in *three* divisions, one of which remained with the king as a reserve force.

114 *for action*: i.e. for lack of action.

'When the man dies, let the inheritance
100 Descend unto the daughter.' Gracious lord,
Stand for your own, unwind your bloody flag,
Look back into your mighty ancestors.
Go, my dread lord, to your great-grandsire's tomb,
From whom you claim. Invoke his warlike spirit,
105 And your great-uncle's, Edward the Black Prince,
Who on the French ground play'd a tragedy,
Making defeat on the full power of France,
Whiles his most mighty father on a hill
Stood smiling to behold his lion's whelp
110 Forage in blood of French nobility.
O noble English, that could entertain
With half their forces the full pride of France,
And let another half stand laughing by,
All out of work and cold for action.

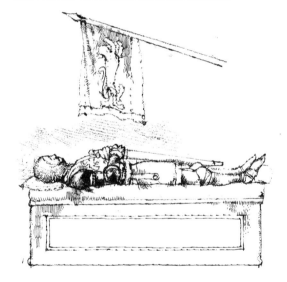

116 *puissant*: powerful.

118 *renowned them*: made them famous.

119 *thrice-puissant*: triply powerful—(1) as heir to the throne; (2) as occupant of the throne; and (3) for his personal prowess. The archbishop reckons up the points he made in lines 117–18.

120 *the very May-morn*: right at the springtime; Henry was in fact 27 years old.

Ely
115 Awake remembrance of these valiant dead,
And with your puissant arm renew their feats.
You are their heir, you sit upon their throne.
The blood and courage that renowned them
Runs in your veins, and my thrice-puissant liege
120 Is in the very May-morn of his youth,
Ripe for exploits and mighty enterprises.

123 *rouse yourself*: come out of your lair.
124 *lions*: The lion, being king among
     beasts, was emblematic of the king
     among men; and heraldic lions charac-
     terize the royal coat-of-arms.

125 *They*: i.e. the French; the stress is on
     the first word of the line.
     cause: legal justification.
126 *So hath your highness*: and indeed you
     do.
129 *pavilion'd*: encamped; '*pavilions*' were
     tents used by the knights in jousting
     tournaments.

Exeter
Your brother kings and monarchs of the earth
Do all expect that you should rouse yourself,
As did the former lions of your blood.
Westmorland
125 They know your grace hath cause, and means, and
        might;
    So hath your highness. Never king of England
    Had nobles richer and more loyal subjects,
    Whose hearts have left their bodies here in England
    And lie pavilion'd in the fields of France.

132 *spirituality*: clergy.
136–9 In Holinshed it is Westmorland, not the king, who raises this issue.
137 *lay down*: estimate.
   proportions: number of troops required.
138 *make road*: attack.
140 *marches*: the border territories; the Lords of the Marches, bordering Scotland and Wales, maintained a military presence until the early seventeenth century.
143 *coursing snatchers*: snatch and grab raiders (who are like greyhounds hunting hares).
144 *main intendment*: general hostile purpose.
145 *still*: always.
   giddy: unstable.
146 *read*: i.e. in history books; the king has learned his lessons—see 1, 1, 41–2.
148 *unfurnish'd*: unprotected.
149 *breach*: break in the sea-wall.
151 *Galling*: wounding.
   gleaned: stripped bare of all resources.
   assays: expeditions, sorties.
152 *Girding*: surrounding.
154 *th'ill neighbourhood*: having such bad neighbours.
155 *fear'd*: frightened.
156 *hear . . . her self*: just consider the precedents in England's past.
157 *chivalry*: knights, men-at-arms.
158 *of*: for.
160 *take . . . stray*: captured and imprisoned like a stray beast which is put in the parish pound (= cattle-pen).
161 King David II, who was captured in 1346 during Edward III's absence in France. A play, *Edward III* (*c.* 1596), shows him being taken to Calais—but this has no basis in fact.
162 *fill*: enlarge.
163 *their chronicle*: the history of England and of Edward III.
   rich with praise: full of praiseworthy deeds.
164 *ooze and bottom*: oozy bottom.
165 *wreck*: wreckage.
   sumless treasuries: inestimable riches.

Canterbury

130 Oh, let their bodies follow, my dear liege,
With blood and sword and fire, to win your right.
In aid whereof we of the spirituality
Will raise your highness such a mighty sum
As never did the clergy at one time
135 Bring in to any of your ancestors.
   King
We must not only arm t'invade the French
But lay down our proportions to defend
Against the Scot, who will make road upon us
With all advantages.
   Canterbury
140 They of those marches, gracious sovereign,
Shall be a wall sufficient to defend
Our England from the pilfering borderers.
   King
We do not mean the coursing snatchers only,
But fear the main intendment of the Scot,
145 Who hath been still a giddy neighbour to us.
For you shall read that my great-grandfather
Never went with his forces into France
But that the Scot on his unfurnish'd kingdom
Came pouring like the tide into a breach
150 With ample and brim fullness of his force,
Galling the gleaned land with hot assays,
Girding with grievous siege castles and towns,
That England, being empty of defence,
Hath shook and trembled at th'ill neighbourhood.
   Canterbury
155 She hath been then more fear'd than harm'd, my liege.
For hear her but exampled by her self:
When all her chivalry hath been in France
And she a mourning widow of her nobles,
She hath herself not only well defended
160 But taken and impounded as a stray
The king of Scots, whom she did send to France
To fill King Edward's fame with prisoner kings,
And make their chronicle as rich with praise
As is the ooze and bottom of the sea
165 With sunken wreck and sumless treasuries.

166–73 It seems reasonable to give this
speech to Westmorland, who was
Warden of northern Marches (see line
140 note). In Q it is given to 'A Lord',
whereas F attributes it to 'Ely'. But it is
unlikely that the Bishop of Ely would
dare dissent in this way to his archbishop's proposals.

169   *in prey*: in pursuit of her prey.

172   Compare, 'While the cat's away, the
mice will play'.

173   *'tame*: attame, break in.
havoc: destroy.

175   *crush'd*: distorted.

177   *pretty*: ingenious.

179   *advised*: prudent.

180–3 Exeter pursues a musical image
throughout these lines.

180   *high and low and lower*: i.e. the verse
notes.

181   *parts*: the separate lines for different
voices or instruments.
one consent: a single harmony.

182   *Congreeing*: agreeing together,
co-operating.
close: the cadence at the end of a
musical phrase.

184   *state*: estate, body politic.
man: humankind.
divers: different.

185   *endeavour*: human effort.

186   *butt*: target.

187   *Obedience*: i.e. to the will of God.

187–204 The use of the bee-hive as an analogy for the well-governed state was very
popular in Elizabethan political theory.
The best-known classical source is Book
IV of Virgil's *Georgics*, lines 152ff.

Westmorland
But there's a saying, very old and true,
'*If that you will France win,*
Then with Scotland first begin.'
For once the eagle England being in prey,
170 To her unguarded nest the weasel Scot
Comes sneaking, and so sucks her princely eggs,
Playing the mouse in absence of the cat
To 'tame and havoc more than she can eat.

Exeter
It follows, then, the cat must stay at home.
175 Yet that is but a crush'd necessity,
Since we have locks to safeguard necessaries
And pretty traps to catch the petty thieves.
While that the armed hand doth fight abroad
Th'advised head defends itself at home.
180 For government, though high and low and lower,
Put into parts, doth keep in one consent,
Congreeing in a full and natural close
Like music.
      Canterbury
                Therefore doth heaven divide
The state of man in diverse functions,
185 Setting endeavour in continual motion,
To which is fixed as an aim or butt
Obedience. For so work the honey bees,
Creatures that by a rule in nature teach
The act of order to a peopled kingdom.
190 They have a king, and officers of sorts,
Where some like magistrates correct at home,
Others like merchants venture trade abroad,
Others like soldiers, armed in their stings,
Make boot upon the summer's velvet buds,
195 Which pillage they with merry march bring home

188 *rule in nature*: instinctive government.
189 *act of order*: orderly action.
    peopled: human.
190 *a king*: the queen bee; Aristotle had
    taught that the head of the hive was
    male, and it was not until the seven-
    teenth century that English scientists
    recognized his error.
    of sorts: of different ranks.
191 *correct*: administer justice.

193 *armed in their stings*: whose weapons are
    their stings.
194 *Make boot*: plunder.
197 *his majesties*: his royal duties; *and* his
    royal splendour.
199 *civil*: orderly, dutiful.
    kneading: moulding.
200 *mechanic*: artisan, labouring.
202 *sad-ey'd justice*: serious-minded
    magistrate.
    hum: the sound of the bee; *and* the
    expression, 'hmm', of the human
    magistrate.
203 *executors pale*: threatening executioners.
205–6 *having . . . consent*: being all related to
    a single common aim.
206 *contrariously*: in opposite ways.
207 *As*: just as.
    loosed several ways: shot from different
    angles.
210 *close*: converge.
    dial: sundial.

211 *afoot*: set on foot, started off.
212 *borne*: sustained.
216 *withal*: with it.
    Gallia: the Latin name for Gaul, the
    ancient France.
218 *the dog*: the dog of war.
219 *worried*: torn to pieces by the dog; *and*
    anxious.
220 *name*: reputation.
    policy: statesmanship.
222 *well resolv'd*: freed from all doubts; *and*
    determined on action.

To the tent royal of their emperor,
Who, busied in his majesties, surveys
The singing masons building roofs of gold,
The civil citizens kneading up the honey,
200 The poor mechanic porters crowding in
Their heavy burdens at his narrow gate,
The sad-ey'd justice with his surly hum
Delivering o'er to executors pale
The lazy yawning drone. I this infer,
205 That many things, having full reference
To one consent, may work contrariously.
As many arrows loosed several ways
Come to one mark; as many ways meet in one town
As many fresh streams meet in one salt sea,
210 As many lines close in the dial's centre,
So may a thousand actions, once afoot
End in one purpose, and be all well borne
Without defeat. Therefore to France, my liege.
Divide your happy England into four,
215 Whereof take you one quarter into France,
And you withal shall make all Gallia shake.
If we with thrice such powers left at home
Cannot defend our own doors from the dog
Let us be worried, and our nation lose
220 The name of hardiness and policy.
      King
Call in the messengers sent from the Dauphin.
                                    [*Exit* Attendant
Now are we well resolv'd, and by God's help
And yours, the noble sinews of our power,
France being ours, we'll bend it to our awe,
225 Or break it all to pieces. Or there we'll sit,
Ruling in large and ample empery
O'er France and all her almost kingly dukedoms,
Or lay these bones in an unworthy urn
Tombless, with no remembrance over them.
230 Either our history shall with full mouth
Speak freely of our acts, or else our grave
Like Turkish mute shall have a tongueless mouth,
Not worshipp'd with a waxen epitaph.

224 *France being ours*: since France belongs
    to the English throne (by right of
    inheritance).
    bend it to our awe: make France recog-
    nize the authority of England.
225–8 *Or . . . Or*: either . . . or.
225 *we'll sit*: i.e. on the throne.
226 *large and ample empery*: complete
    sovereignty.
227 *almost kingly dukedoms*: At the beginning
    of *Act 3* the Chorus refers to the French
    offer of 'some petty and unprofitable
    dukedoms' (line 31).
228 *unworthy urn*: dishonourable grave.
229 *Tombless*: without a monument.
230 *with full mouth*: loudly, with mouth
    widely stretched.
232 *mute*: dumb slave; some Turkish slaves
    had their tongues cut out, to make sure
    they kept the secrets of the royal house-
    hold.
233 *worshipp'd*: venerated.
    waxen: carved in wax, perishable.
234–5 *know . . . Dauphin*: learn what the
    Dauphin has to say.
235 *fair*: honourable; the adjective may be
    applied politely or with sarcasm—as in
    the modern House of Commons.
    cousin: kinsman.
238 *Freely*: directly, in a straightforward
    manner.
    render: deliver.
    what we have in charge: the message we
    have been told to bring.
239 *sparingly . . . far off*: discreetly indicate
    in fairly general terms.
240 'What the Dauphin means and the
    reason for our presence.'
242 *grace*: Christian virtue.
    as subject: as much a subject.
    is: A singular verb with a plural subject
    is not uncommon in Elizabethan usage.
245 *mind*: intention.
    in few: briefly, in a few words.
246 *lately*: recently.
    sending: sending ambassadors.
250–97 Shakespeare here follows Hall's
    account of events, and not that of
    Holinshed.
250 *savour . . . youth*: seem too much like
    the lad you used to be.
251 *be advis'd*: be warned, take care.
252 *galliard*: a lively dance.
253 *revel*: frolic.

Enter Ambassador of France *with*
Attendants

Now are we well prepared to know the pleasure
235 Of our fair cousin Dauphin; for we hear
Your greeting is from him, not from the king.
    Ambassador
May't please your majesty to give us leave
Freely to render what we have in charge,
Or shall we sparingly show you far off
240 The Dauphin's meaning, and our embassy?
    King
We are no tyrant, but a Christian king,
Unto whose grace our passion is as subject
As are our wretches fettered in our prisons.
Therefore with frank and with uncurbed plainness
245 Tell us the Dauphin's mind.
    Ambassador
                Thus then in few:
Your highness lately, sending into France,
Did claim some certain dukedoms, in the right
Of your great predecessor, King Edward the Third.
In answer of which claim the prince our master
250 Says that you savour too much of your youth,
And bids you be advis'd: there's naught in France
That can be with a nimble galliard won;
You cannot revel into dukedoms there.
He therefore sends you, meeter for your spirit,
255 This tun of treasure, and in lieu of this
Desires you let the dukedoms that you claim
Hear no more of you. This the Dauphin speaks.
    King
What treasure, uncle?
    Exeter
              [*Opens tun*] Tennis balls, my liege.
    King
We are glad the Dauphin is so pleasant with us.
260 His present and your pains we thank you for.
When we have match'd our rackets to these balls
We will in France, by God's grace, play a set
Shall strike his father's crown into the hazard.
Tell him he hath made a match with such a wrangler

254 *meeter*: more appropriate.
255 *tun*: large treasure chest or casket.
    lieu of: return for.
258 *Tennis balls*: These were made of leather and stuffed with horsehair. The game of 'royal tennis', from which modern lawn tennis is derived, was very popular with the Elizabethan nobility. It was played on an oblong court, which was paved and enclosed by walls. A rope or low net was stretched between the two longer walls, and the players used rackets, netted with string, to drive their balls from side to side. The two shorter walls were pierced with holes called 'hazards', and points were scored by driving a ball into one of these, or by causing it to bounce twice before it was struck by the opposing player (making a 'chase').
259 *so pleasant with us*: can make such jokes at my expense.
260 *pains*: trouble (in bringing the message).
262 *set*: i.e. of tennis games.
263 *Shall*: that shall.
    into the hazard: See line 258 *note*.
264 *wrangler*: opponent—especially one who disputes in academic exercises.
265 *courts*: (a) royal; (b) tennis; (c) law.
266 *chases*: See line 258 *note*.

267 *comes o'er us*: throws in our face.

269 *seat*: estate, throne.

270 *hence*: away from it.

271 *barbarous licence*: uncivilized freedom.
    common: common practice, common knowledge.
272 *from*: away from.
273 *keep my state*: maintain my royal position.
274 *sail of greatness*: swelling powers of majesty (the image is from the full sails of a galleon).

265 That all the courts of France will be disturb'd
    With chases. And we understand him well,
    How he comes o'er us with our wilder days,
    Not measuring what use we made of them.
    We never valu'd this poor seat of England,
270 And therefore, living hence, did give ourself
    To barbarous licence, as 'tis ever common
    That men are merriest when they are from home.
    But tell the Dauphin I will keep my state,
    Be like a king, and show my sail of greatness

275 *rouse me*: come out of my lair (see line
     123); *and* raise myself up.
     my: King Henry re-asserts his claim.
276 *For that*: because.
     laid by: set aside.
277 *a man for working days*: a common man
     on working days.

281 *pleasant*: jesting.

282 *gun-stones*: cannon balls.

283 *sore charged*: heavily burdened with
     guilt.
     wasteful: destructive.
     vengeance: revenge for the insult.
285 *mock out of*: cheat, deprive of.

287 *ungotten*: not yet begotten.

289 *lies all within*: all depends on.

292 *venge*: avenge.
     as I may: as best I can.
293 *rightful hand*: King Henry constantly
     emphasizes the righteousness of his
     cause and the sacredness of his mission.
     well-hallow'd: most holy.

297 *Convey*: escort.

300 *omit no happy hour*: don't lose any
     convenient occasion.
301 *give furtherance*: advance.

303 'Except for our thoughts about God
     which must go before everything we do.'
304 *proportions*: forces.

307 *God before*: with God to guide us.
308 *chide*: reprove.
     at his father's door: on his home ground.
309 *task his thought*: give his mind to the
     job.
310 *on foot*: in motion.

275 When I do rouse me in my throne of France.
     For that I have laid by my majesty
     And plodded like a man for working days.
     But I will rise there with so full a glory
     That I will dazzle all the eyes of France,
280 Yea, strike the Dauphin blind to look on us.
     And tell the pleasant prince this mock of his
     Hath turn'd his balls to gun-stones, and his soul
     Shall stand sore charged for the wasteful vengeance
     That shall fly with them; for many a thousand
       widows
285 Shall this his mock mock out of their dear husbands,
     Mock mothers from their sons, mock castles down,
     And some are yet ungotten and unborn
     That shall have cause to curse the Dauphin's scorn.
     But this lies all within the will of God,
290 To whom I do appeal, and in whose name
     Tell you the Dauphin I am coming on
     To venge me as I may, and to put forth
     My rightful hand in a well-hallow'd cause.
     So get you hence in peace. And tell the Dauphin
295 His jest will savour but of shallow wit
     When thousands weep more than did laugh at it.
       [*To* Attendants] Convey them with safe conduct.
         Fare you well.
                           [*Exeunt* Ambassador *and* Attendants
       Exeter
     This was a merry message.
       King
     We hope to make the sender blush at it.
300 Therefore, my lords, omit no happy hour
     That may give furtherance to our expedition,
     For we have now no thought in us but France,
     Save those to God that run before our business.
     Therefore let our proportions for these wars
305 Be soon collected, and all things thought upon
     That may with reasonable swiftness add
     More feathers to our wings. For, God before,
     We'll chide this Dauphin at his father's door.
     Therefore let every man now task his thought
310 That this fair action may on foot be brought.
                                   [*Flourish. Exeunt*

Act 2

Chorus

The Chorus tells how the English are preparing to invade France, and how three English lords have been bribed by the French king to betray and murder King Henry. The audience learns that the action of the play will now move from London to Southampton, and from there to France.

2 *silken dalliance . . . lies*: all frivolous behaviour has been set aside like the fine clothes of the courtiers which are left in the dressing-room ('wardrobe').
3 *honour's thought*: the thought of honour.
6 *mirror*: pattern of perfection.
7 Mercury was the messenger and herald of the classical gods; he is usually depicted with wings either on his heels or on his helmet.
8 *sits . . . air*: the air is full of expectation.
9 *a sword . . . point*: The heraldic device of Edward III was a sword ringed by crowns; Shakespeare could have seen a picture of this in his copy of Holinshed's Chronicles.
   hilts: the arms of the cross-piece.

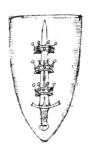

Enter Chorus
Chorus
Now all the youth of England are on fire
And silken dalliance in the wardrobe lies.
Now thrive the armourers, and honour's thought
Reigns solely in the breast of every man.
5 They sell the pasture now to buy the horse,
Following the mirror of all Christian kings
With winged heels, as English Mercuries.
For now sits expectation in the air,
And hides a sword from hilts unto the point
10 With crowns imperial, crowns and coronets
Promised to Harry and his followers.
The French, advis'd by good intelligence
Of this most dreadful preparation,
Shake in their fear, and with pale policy
15 Seek to divert the English purposes.
O England: model to thy inward greatness,
Like little body with a mighty heart,
What mightst thou do, that honour would thee do,
Were all thy children kind and natural?
20 But see, thy fault France hath in thee found out,
A nest of hollow bosoms, which he fills
With treacherous crowns, and three corrupted men—
One, Richard, Earl of Cambridge, and the second
Henry, Lord Scroop of Masham, and the third

10 *crowns imperial, crowns and coronets*: the king's crowns, gold coins (see line 22), and ducal coronets.

12 *advis'd*: warned.
    intelligence: secret reports, espionage.
14 *pale policy*: cowardly intrigue.
15 *divert*: change the course of.
16 *model*: miniature replica.
18 *that . . . do*: that would bring honour to you.
19 *kind and natural*: properly filial and obedient to the law of nature.
20 *fault*: weakness.
    France: the king of France.
21 *hollow*: empty (of proper feelings), false.
    bosoms: hearts; *and also* the clothes worn over the heart, in which money could be hidden.
22 *crowns*: gold coins—the French *écu*.
26 *gilt*: i.e. the crowns.
27 *fearful*: frightened.
28 *grace of kings*: model of kingship.
29 *hold*: keep.
30 *Ere*: before.
31 *Linger . . . on*: be patient.
31-2 *digest . . . distance*: set in order—help you to cope with—the problem of distance.
32 *force perforce*: cram, stuff by force feeding.
34 *is set*: has departed.
35 *gentles*: ladies and gentlemen.
38 *bring you back*: This is usually spoken as a joke.
    charming: i.e. like a magician.
    the narrow seas: the English Channel.
39 *gentle pass*: a good crossing.
    if we may: if we can help it.
40 *offend one stomach*: displease anyone, cause anyone to be seasick.
41 *when the king come*: when the king comes.
41-2 These lines seem to contradict lines 35-6. Here we are told that the action will be set in Southampton *only* when the king appears: the scene that now follows is still set in London.

25 Sir Thomas Gray, knight of Northumberland—
   Have for the gilt of France (oh, guilt indeed)
   Confirm'd conspiracy with fearful France,
   And by their hands this grace of kings must die,
   If hell and treason hold their promises,
30 Ere he take ship for France, and in Southampton.
   Linger your patience on, and we'll digest
   Th'abuse of distance, force perforce a play.
   The sum is paid, the traitors are agreed,
   The king is set from London, and the scene
35 Is now transported, gentles, to Southampton.
   There is the playhouse now, there must you sit,
   And thence to France shall we convey you safe
   And bring you back, charming the narrow seas
   To give you gentle pass, for if we may
40 We'll not offend one stomach with our play.
   But when the king come forth, and not till then,
   Unto Southampton do we shift our scene.   [*Exit*

Act 2   Scene 1

In a London street Bardolph encounters his
mate, Nym, who is depressed because he has
quarrelled with Pistol, another old crony.
When Pistol comes on to the scene with his
newly-married wife, Mistress Quickly, there
is a violent slanging match, conducted in a
mock-heroic style. Bardolph succeeds in
averting bloodshed, and friendship is
restored between the two antagonists when
they are all called to the sickbed of Sir John
Falstaff, the fat old knight who was once
the close friend of Prince Hal, now King
Henry V.

1   *Well met*: A common Elizabethan
    greeting—'Good to see you'.
    Corporal: the officer in charge of one
    quarter of a military company; Nym's is
    the lowest of the three rankings.

2   *morrow*: morning.

3   *Ancient*: a corruption of *ensign* (=
    standard bearer); the rank is mid-way
    between lieutenant and corporal.

4–5 *when time shall serve*: when the time is
    right.

5   *shall be smiles*: I shall be friendly
    enough.

6   *wink*: close my eyes.

7   *iron*: sword.
    simple: cheap.
    what though: so what; Nym's speech is
    usually sprinkled with such meaningless
    expressions.

8   *toast . . . cold*: be useful both as a
    toasting-fork and as a weapon.
    as: as well as.
    another: any other.

9   *there's an end*: that's all there is to it.

10 *bestow a breakfast*: invite you to
    breakfast.

11 *sworn brothers*: joined in a brotherhood
    (usually said of chivalrous knights—or
    thieves).

13 *Faith*: in faith, indeed.
    the certain: for sure.

14–15 *when . . . may*: a proverbial
    expression: 'He that cannot do as he
    would [wants to] must do as he may'.

15 *That is my rest*: that is my final bid—an
    expression borrowed from the game of
    primero.
    rendezvous: last resort.

Scene 1

Enter Corporal Nym *and* Lieutenant
Bardolph

Bardolph
Well met, Corporal Nym.
    Nym
Good morrow, Lieutenant Bardolph.
    Bardolph
What, are Ancient Pistol and you friends yet?
    Nym
For my part, I care not. I say little, but when
5 time shall serve there shall be smiles, but that shall
be as it may. I dare not fight, but I will wink and hold
out mine iron. It is a simple one, but what though?
It will toast cheese, and it will endure cold as another
man's sword will, and there's an end.

    Bardolph
10 I will bestow a breakfast to make you friends, and
we'll be all three sworn brothers to France. Let't be
so, good Corporal Nym.
    Nym
Faith, I will live so long as I may, that's the certain
of it, and when I cannot live any longer I will do as
15 I may. That is my rest, that is the rendezvous of it.
    Bardolph
It is certain, corporal, that he is married to Nell
Quickly, and certainly she did you wrong, for you
were troth-plight to her.
    Nym
I cannot tell. Things must be as they may. Men may
20 sleep, and they may have their throats about them at
that time, and some say knives have edges. It must be
as it may. Though patience be a tired mare, yet she
will plod. There must be conclusions. Well, I cannot
tell.

16–17 *Nell Quickly*: In *Henry IV Part 2* she
    was the hostess of the Boar's Head
    tavern in Eastcheap.
18 *troth-plight*: betrothed; the contract was
    more binding than the modern
    engagement.
22–3 *Though . . . plod*: although it may be
    tedious, patience will get there (i.e.
    succeed) in the end.
23 *conclusions*: some way of sorting things
    out.
27 *host*: Nym's form of address is insulting
    to his superior officer. Pistol became
    the host (= innkeeper) of the tavern
    through his marriage to Mistress
    Quickly, the hostess (= landlady).
28 *tyke*: mongrel, cur.
31 *my troth*: my word.
    not long: Perhaps the lodgers will not
    stay long because the inn has a
    reputation for being a brothel—or
    perhaps it *is* a brothel.
33 *honestly*: respectably.
    by the prick of their needles: as
    seamstresses—but the phrase is capable
    of bawdy innuendo.
34 *bawdy house*: brothel.
    straight: at once.
35 *welladay*: oh dear me.
    Lady: by Our Lady (the Virgin Mary)—
    a mild oath.
35–6 *be not hewn*: is not cut down.
36 *wilful adultery*: A characteristic of the
    Hostess's speech is her mistaking of
    words; here, perhaps, she means
    'rape'—unwilling adultery.
38 *lieutenant*: Shakespeare seems to have
    forgotten that it is Bardolph who is the
    lieutenant—although at *3, 7, 12* Pistol is
    addressed as 'ancient lieutenant'
    (= sub-lieutenant).
    offer nothing: don't start a fight.
40 *Iceland dog*: These were small, hairy lap-
    dogs with pointed ('prick') ears, with a
    reputation for snappish bad-temper.
42 *show thy valour*: This is usually an
    exhortation to fight.
    put up: put away, sheath.
44 *shog off*: go away, clear off.
45 *solus*: alone; the Latin word is often
    used in stage directions.
45–50 Pistol's speech is really an expansion
    of the phrase 'make him eat his words'.

Enter Pistol *and* Quickly

Bardolph
25 Here comes Ancient Pistol and his wife. Good
corporal, be patient here.
    Nym
How now, mine host Pistol?
    Pistol
Base tyke, call'st thou me host? Now by this hand I
swear I scorn the term, nor shall my Nell keep
30 lodgers.
    Hostess
No, by my troth, not long, for we cannot lodge and
board a dozen or fourteen gentlewomen that live
honestly by the prick of their needles but it will be
thought we keep a bawdy house straight. [Nym
35 *draws his sword*] Oh, welladay, Lady, if he be not
hewn now, we shall see wilful adultery and murder
committed.

Pistol draws his sword

    Bardolph
Good lieutenant, good corporal, offer nothing here.
    Nym
Pish.
    Pistol
40 Pish for thee, Iceland dog, thou prick-eared cur of
Iceland.
    Hostess
Good Corporal Nym, show thy valour, and put up
your sword.

They sheathe their swords

    Nym
Will you shog off? [*To* Pistol] I would have you *solus*.
    Pistol
45 *Solus*, egregious dog? O viper vile! The *solus* in thy
most mervailous face, the *solus* in thy teeth, and in
thy throat, and in thy hateful lungs, yea, in thy maw,
perdy, and, which is worse, within thy nasty mouth!
I do retort the *solus* in thy bowels, for I can take, and
50 Pistol's cock is up, and flashing fire will follow!

He visualizes throwing Nym's word back in his face, crushing it against his teeth, and thrusting it down his throat, into his lungs and stomach ('maw'), so that it even comes out by way of his bowels.

46 *mervailous*: marvellous; the accent is on the second syllable.

48 *perdy*: by God (French *par dieu*).
nasty: foul (the word had greater force in Shakespeare's time.

49 *take*: blast, curse.

50 *cock is up*: A gun is ready for firing when it is cocked up; here the sexual innuendo is obvious.

51 *Barbason*: The name is that of a French knight who fought Henry V at the siege of Melun; Nym probably refers to Barbas, a fiend who appeared in the likeness of a raging lion.
conjure: exorcise: Pistol's grandiose speech reminds Nym of the style of a magician.

52 *humour*: urge, whim.
knock: beat.
indifferently well: thoroughly.

53 *grow foul*: discharge your filth.
scour: cleanse.

54 *rapier*: a thin sword; Nym offers to run this through Pistol's body as a rod is drawn through a gun—or blocked-up pipe—for cleaning purposes.
as I may, in fair terms: to put it as decently as I can.
walk off: i.e. come to a more secluded area, away from a main street.

56 *that's the humour of it*: that's how it is.

57 *braggart*: boaster.
wight: person; the word was obsolescent at Shakespeare's time, but it suits Pistol's mock-heroic style.

58 *gape*: open wide.
doting death is near: death is eager to receive you very soon.
exhale: draw forth [your sword].

61 *hilts*: arms protecting the handle of the sword.

62 *mickle*: great.

63 *forefoot*: front paw.

64 *tall*: valiant.

67 *Couple a gorge*: Pistol intends the French *coupez la gorge* (= cut his throat).

Nym
I am not Barbason, you cannot conjure me. I have an humour to knock you indifferently well. If you grow foul with me, Pistol, I will scour you with my rapier, as I may, in fair terms. If you would walk off 55 I would prick your guts a little in good terms, as I may, and that's the humour of it.
Pistol
O braggart vile, and damned furious wight, the grave doth gape and doting death is near. Therefore exhale!
They draw their swords
Bardolph
Hear me, hear me what I say. [*Draws his sword*] He 60 that strikes the first stroke, I'll run him up to the hilts, as I am a soldier.
Pistol
An oath of mickle might, and fury shall abate. Give me thy fist, thy forefoot to me give. Thy spirits are most tall.
Nym
65 I will cut thy throat one time or other in fair terms, that is the humour of it.
Pistol
Couple a gorge, that is the word. I defy thee again! O hound of Crete, thinkst thou my spouse to get? No, to the Spital go, and from the powdering tub of 70 infamy fetch forth the lazar kite of Cressid's kind, Doll Tearsheet, she by name, and her espouse. I have, and I will hold the quondam Quickly for the only she, and *pauca*, there's enough. Go to.

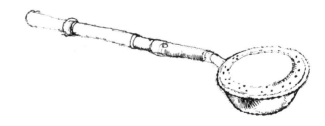

68 *hound of Crete*: Only one reference (in
    Golding's translation of Ovid's
    Metamorphoses) describes Cretan
    hounds as being hairy.
69 *Spital*: hospital, especially for the
    treatment of venereal diseases.
    powdering tub: heated tub generally used
    for salting beef but here specifically
    thought of as a treatment for venereal
    disease.
70 *the . . . kind*: that diseased carrion bird
    of Cressida's family. Medieval stories
    tell how Cressida was false to her lover
    Troilus and, as punishment, was
    afflicted with leprosy (sometimes, by
    the Elizabethans, equated with syphilis).
71 *Doll Tearsheet*: A prostitute in *Henry IV
    Part 2*; at the end of that play she was
    taken away to prison.
    espouse: marry.
71–3 *I have . . . she*: Pistol, newly married,
    remembers the promise he has just
    made in the marriage service, 'to have,
    and to hold [his wife] . . . forsaking all
    other'.
72 *quondam*: former (Latin).
72–3 *the only she*: the only woman in the
    world.
73 *pauca*: few words (Latin).
    Go to: get on with it, get away with you.
74 *my master*: i.e. Sir John Falstaff; the Boy
    is the page given to Falstaff by Prince
    Hal in *Henry IV Part 2*.
75 *would to bed*: wants to go to bed.
76 *thy face*: Bardolph's face was red and
    full of spots or boils; it was the subject
    of many good-humoured jokes in *Henry
    IV Part 1*.
77 *warming pan*: long-handled covered pan
    filled with hot coals used (like the
    modern hot-water bottle) to warm the
    sheets.
79 *yield . . . pudding*: become food for
    birds; the expression was often used to
    predict death by hanging—perhaps the
    Hostess refers to the Boy, although her
    next words speak of Falstaff.
80 *The king . . . heart*: In *Henry IV Part 2*
    the king, immediately after his
    coronation, rejected his former way of
    life and, in particular, his friend Sir
    John Falstaff. The rejection completely
    broke Falstaff's heart, so that he lost all
    pleasure in living; see p. xxxi.

Enter the Boy

Boy
Mine host Pistol, you must come to my master, and
75 your hostess. He is very sick, and would to bed.
Good Bardolph, put thy face between his sheets and
do the office of a warming pan. Faith, he's very ill.
Bardolph
Away, you rogue.
Hostess
By my troth, he'll yield the crow a pudding one of
80 these days. The king has killed his heart. Good
husband, come home presently.
                                        [*Exeunt* Hostess *and* Boy
Bardolph
Come, shall I make you two friends? We must to
France together. Why the devil should we keep
knives to cut one another's throats?
Pistol
85 Let floods o'erswell, and fiends for food howl on!
Nym
You'll pay me the eight shillings I won of you at
betting?
Pistol
Base is the slave that pays.
Nym
That now I will have. That's the humour of it.
Pistol
90 As manhood shall compound. Push home.

They draw their swords

Bardolph
[*Draws his sword*] By this sword, he that makes the
first thrust, I'll kill him, by this sword I will.
Pistol
Sword is an oath, and oaths must have their course.

Sheathes his sword

Bardolph
Corporal Nym, an thou wilt be friends, be
95 friends. An thou wilt not, why then be enemies
with me too. Prithee put up.

81   *presently*: at once.
82   *must*: must go.
85   Pistol's declaration of friendship (which will last until the rivers overflow their banks, and the devils cry out for lack of damned souls to feed on) is as extreme as his professions of enmity had been.
86   *eight shillings*: a considerable sum of money in Elizabethan currency.
      of: from.
87   This seems to be Pistol's version of the saying, 'The poor man always pays'.
90   *manhood*: courage.
      compound: decide.
      Push home: fight for it.
93   *Sword*: i.e. by God's word.
      have their course: be fulfilled.
94   *an*: if.
96   *Prithee*: I pray you.
      put up: sheath your sword.
97   *A noble*: a coin worth six shillings and eight pence; Pistol wants discount for cash.
      present pay: ready money.
99–100   *I'll live . . . by me*: I'll live by the help of a thief, and the thief shall live by my help; Pistol puns on the meaning ('nim' = to steal) of Nym's name.
101   *sutler*: store-keeper, one who sells provisions to the army.
      profits will accrue: i.e. Pistol will make some money for himself.

Nym *sheathes his sword*

Pistol

A noble shalt thou have, and present pay, and liquor likewise will I give to thee, and friendship shall combine, and brotherhood. I'll live by Nym and
100 Nym shall live by me; is not this just? For I shall sutler be unto the camp, and profits will accrue. Give me thy hand.

Nym

I shall have my noble?

Pistol

In cash, most justly paid.

Nym

105 Well, then that's the humour of it.

Enter Hostess *and* Boy

Hostess

As ever you come of women, come in quickly to Sir John. Ah, poor heart, he is so shaked of a burning quotidian tertian that it is most lamentable to behold. Sweet men, come to him.

106   *come of*: are born of—i.e. have human feelings.
108   *quotidian tertian*: The symptoms of the *quotidian* fever occurred daily, while those of the *tertian* appeared on alternate days; the fevers may be combined in Falstaff's sickness—or perhaps the Hostess is confused.

110 *run bad humours*: vented his bad mood
     on Falstaff; or caused Falstaff's
     melancholy.
111 *even*: plain truth.
112 *fracted*: broken.
113 *corroborate*: re-hardened; Pistol's
     Latinate vocabulary has led him into
     some confusion.
115 *passes . . . careers*: indulges some strange
     moods and wild actions; in terms of
     horsemanship, a 'career' is a short
     gallop during which the horse changes
     direction several times.
116 *condole*: sympathize with.
     lambkins: my little ones.
     we will live: i.e. they themselves will go
     on living even though Falstaff is dying.

Act 2   Scene 2

Three counsellors talk about some traitors
whom the king apparently trusts. They are
confident, however, that the treachery will
soon be revealed and that King Henry is
fully in control of the situation. The king
enters, along with three noblemen who speak
in praise of Henry's virtues and of their own
loyalty to him. When asked for their opinions
about a man who has abused the monarch,
they all recommend severe punishment for
him. King Henry confronts them with
evidence of their own conspiracy against
him, reproaching them—especially Lord
Scroop—for their betrayal of his love and
trust. He pronounces sentence of death upon
them all, and then turns his attention to the
war with France.

1 *'Fore*: before, in the name of.
   bold: rash.
2 *apprehended*: arrested.
3 *smooth and even*: confidently.
4 *bosoms*: hearts.
5 *constant*: firm.
7 *By interception*: i.e. their schemes have
   been intercepted and the king has been
   informed.
   dream not of: The conspiracy was
   revealed to the king by the Earl of
   March, the very man who would have
   gained most from its success; see line
   153 *note*.

Nym

110 The king hath run bad humours on the knight;
    that's the even of it.
    Pistol
    Nym, thou hast spoke the right, his heart is fracted
    and corroborate.
    Nym
    The king is a good king, but it must be as it may. He
115 passes some humours and careers.
    Pistol
    Let us condole the knight, for, lambkins, we will live.
    [*Exeunt*

Scene 2

           Enter Exeter, Bedford, *and* Westmorland
    Bedford
    'Fore God, his grace is bold to trust these traitors.
    Exeter
    They shall be apprehended by and by.
    Westmorland
    How smooth and even they do bear themselves,
    As if allegiance in their bosoms sat,
5   Crowned with faith and constant loyalty.
    Bedford
    The king hath note of all that they intend
    By interception which they dream not of.
    Exeter
    Nay, but the man that was his bedfellow,
    Whom he hath dulled and cloyed with gracious
       favours;
10 That he should for a foreign purse so sell
    His sovereign's life to death and treachery!

           Sound trumpets. Enter the King, Scroop,
               Cambridge, Gray, *and* Officers
    King
    Now sits the wind fair, and we will aboard.
    My lord of Cambridge and my kind lord Masham,
    And you my gentle knight, give me your thoughts.

8   *bedfellow*: closest friend—i.e. Lord
Scroop; see lines 91–139. It was very
common for friends to share a bed in
the sixteenth and seventeenth centuries.

9   *dulled and cloyed*: more than satisfied,
even surfeited, his appetite.

10   *foreign purse*: bribes from a foreign
country.

15   *powers*: forces, army.

17   *the execution and the act*: performing the
deed.

18   *in head*: as an army.

20   *well persuaded*: fully believe.

22   *grows . . . consent*: is not in full
agreement.

25   *fear'd and lov'd*: In a well-known book
The Prince, the sixteenth-century
statesman Niccolo Machiavelli
discussed the question of whether a
ruler should be feared more than loved.

27   *heart-grief*: melancholy.

28   *sweet shade*: gentle protection.

30   *steep'd their galls*: drowned their
bitterness.

32   *cause of*: reason for.

33   *forget . . . hand*: forget how to use my
hand. The king's words seem to echo
those of Psalm 137: 'If I forget thee, O
Jerusalem, let my right hand forget her
cunning'.

34   *quittance*: repayment.
     desert: worth.

35   *weight*: value.

36   *service*: each man's service.
     steeled: toughened.

37   *labour*: every man's work.

38   *incessant*: unceasing.

40   *Enlarge*: set free.

41   *rail'd against*: offered verbal abuse to.

42   *set him on*: excited him.

43   *his more advice*: when he has thought
more about it.

44   *security*: over-confidence.

46   *by his sufferance*: by allowing him to go
unpunished.

15 Think you not that the powers we bear with us
Will cut their passage through the force of France,
Doing the execution and the act
For which we have in head assembled them?
    Scroop
No doubt, my liege, if each man do his best.
    King
20 I doubt not that, since we are well persuaded
We carry not a heart with us from hence
That grows not in a fair consent with ours,
Nor leave not one behind that doth not wish
Success and conquest to attend on us.
    Cambridge
25 Never was monarch better fear'd and lov'd
Than is your majesty. There's not I think a subject
That sits in heart-grief and uneasiness
Under the sweet shade of your government.
    Gray
True. Those that were your father's enemies
30 Have steep'd their galls in honey, and do serve you
With hearts create of duty and of zeal.
    King
We therefore have great cause of thankfulness,
And shall forget the office of our hand
Sooner than quittance of desert and merit,
35 According to the weight and worthiness.
    Scroop
So service shall with steeled sinews toil
And labour shall refresh itself with hope,
To do your grace incessant services.
    King
We judge no less. Uncle of Exeter,
40 Enlarge the man committed yesterday
That rail'd against our person. We consider
It was excess of wine that set him on,
And on his more advice we pardon him.
    Scroop
That's mercy, but too much security.
45 Let him be punish'd, sovereign, lest example
Breed by his sufferance more of such a kind.
    King
Oh, let us yet be merciful.

49 *give him life*: allow him to live.

50 *the taste of much correction*: suffering severe punishment.

51 *too much*: very great.

52 *heavy orisons*: pleas that weigh heavily.

53–6 *If . . . us*: if we cannot close our eyes ('wink') to such little faults, how wide must we open ('stretch') them when we see major crimes.

53 *proceeding on distemper*: caused by a disordered state of mind.

55 *capital crimes*: crimes punishable by death.
chew'd, swallow'd, and digested: i.e. very well planned.

58 *preservation*: protection.

60 *late*: recently appointed.
commissioners: regents who will govern the kingdom in the king's absence.

61 *it*: the written commission; from this remark, it becomes evident to the nobles—and to the audience—that Henry has stage-managed this entire business.

Cambridge
So may your highness, and yet punish too.
Gray
Sir, you show great mercy if you give him life
50 After the taste of much correction.
King
Alas, your too much love and care of me
Are heavy orisons 'gainst this poor wretch.
If little faults, proceeding on distemper,
Shall not be wink'd at, how shall we stretch our eye
55 When capital crimes, chew'd, swallow'd, and
digested,
Appear before us? We'll yet enlarge that man,
Though Cambridge, Scroop and Gray, in their dear
care
And tender preservation of our person
Would have him punish'd. And now to our French
causes.
60 Who are the late commissioners?
Cambridge
I one, my lord.
Your highness bade me ask for it today.
Scroop
So did you me, my liege.
Gray
And I, my royal sovereign.
King
Then Richard, Earl of Cambridge, there is yours.
There yours, Lord Scroop of Masham, and sir
knight,
65 Gray of Northumberland, this same is yours.

Gives them papers

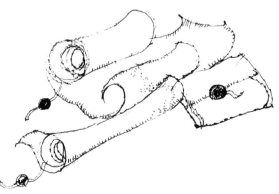

Read them and know I know your worthiness.
My lord of Westmorland and uncle Exeter,
We will aboard tonight. Why, how now, gentlemen?
What see you in those papers, that you lose

70 So much complexion? Look ye how they change.
Their cheeks are paper. Why, what read you there,
That have so cowarded and chas'd your blood
Out of appearance?

Cambridge
      I do confess my fault,
And do submit me to your highness' mercy.

Kneels

Gray and **Scroop**
75 To which we all appeal.

They kneel

King
The mercy that was quick in us but late
By your own counsel is suppress'd and kill'd.
You must not dare for shame to talk of mercy,
For your own reasons turn into your bosoms,

80 As dogs upon their masters, worrying you.
See you, my princes and my noble peers,
These English monsters. My lord of Cambridge here,
You know how apt our love was to accord,
To furnish him with all appurtenants

85 Belonging to his honour, and this man
Hath for a few light crowns lightly conspir'd
And sworn unto the practices of France
To kill us here in Hampton. To the which
This knight, no less for bounty bound to us

90 Than Cambridge is, hath likewise sworn. But oh,
What shall I say to thee, Lord Scroop, thou cruel,
Ingrateful, savage and inhuman creature?
Thou that didst bear the key of all my counsels,
That knew'st the very bottom of my soul,

95 That almost mightst have coined me into gold,
Wouldst thou have practis'd on me for thy use?
May it be possible that foreign hire
Could out of thee extract one spark of evil
That might annoy my finger? 'Tis so strange

---

70 *complexion*: colour from your cheeks.
71 *paper*: the colour—white—of paper.
72 *cowarded*: turned into a coward.
73 *appearance*: sight.

76 *quick*: alive.
 but late: just now.
80 *worrying you*: tearing you to pieces.
82 *English monsters*: Unnatural or deformed creatures, usually said to be of foreign origin, were often on exhibition in Elizabethan fairs.
83 *apt*: ready.
 accord: consent, agree.
84 *appurtenants*: things appropriate.
86 *light crowns*: treacherous money.
 lightly conspir'd: readily plotted.
87 *practices*: schemes.
88 *Hampton*: Southampton.
89 *This knight*: i.e. Lord Gray.
 no less . . . us: was equally obliged to my generosity.
92 *Ingrateful*: ungrateful; the Elizabethan form of the word seems more forceful than the modern one.
93 *bear . . . counsels*: had access to all my secrets.
94 *bottom*: deepest part.
95 *coined me into gold*: used me as the mint; Scroop was Lord Treasurer until 1411.
96 *Wouldst . . . use*: if you had wanted to use your schemes against me for your own purposes.
97 *May*: can.
 hire: bribery.
99 *might annoy*: could hurt.

100–1 *stands off . . . white*: stands out as
     plainly as if it were written in black and
     white.
101 *my eye . . . it*: i.e. I can hardly believe it.
102 *kept*: lived, worked.
103 *yoke-devils*: devils harnessed—yoked—
     together like oxen.
     either's: each other's.
104 *grossly*: obviously.
     natural: i.e. for devils.
105 *That . . . them*: that they raised no
     outcry of amazement.
106 *proportion*: natural order.
109 *preposterously*: unnaturally.
110 *got the voice*: won the vote.
111 *suggest*: tempt.
112–14 *Do . . . piety*: The damnation is less
     perfectly achieved by the other devils
     because the traitor is deceived into
     thinking that he has some virtuous
     reason for what he is doing.
112 *botch*: patch, cobble.
113 *patches*: pretences.
     colours: false pretexts.
     forms: devices.
     fetched: derived.
114 *glistering*: falsely glittering, flashy.
     semblances: appearances.
     piety: loyalty.
115 *he that temper'd thee*: the devil that
     moulded you to fit his cause.
     bade thee stand up: ordered you to rebel.
116 *instance*: reason.
117 *dub*: confer a knighthood (so that
     Scroop would have been 'Sir Traitor').
118 *gull'd*: deceived.
119 *lion gait*: moving like a lion; the king's
     words echo those of the Bible; 'your
     adversary the devil, as a roaring lion,
     walketh about, seeking whom he may
     devour' (1 Peter, 5:8).
120 *vasty Tartar*: the vast depths of Tartarus;
     in classical mythology this was the
     equivalent of hell.
121 *legions*: a Roman legion was composed
     of more than 6,000 soldiers; in the
     Bible the unclean spirit said he was
     called Legion, 'for we are many' (Mark,
     5:9).
123 *jealousy*: suspicion.
124 *affiance*: trust.
     Show men: do men seem.
128 *spare in diet*: moderate in what they eat.

100 That though the truth of it stands off as gross
     As black on white my eye will scarcely see it.
     Treason and murder ever kept together,
     As two yoke-devils sworn to either's purpose,
     Working so grossly in a natural cause
105 That admiration did not whoop at them.
     But thou 'gainst all proportion didst bring in
     Wonder to wait on treason and on murder,
     And whatsoever cunning fiend it was
     That wrought upon thee so preposterously
110 Hath got the voice in hell for excellence.
     All other devils that suggest by treasons
     Do botch and bungle up damnation
     With patches, colours, and with forms being
          fetched
     From glistering semblances of piety;
115 But he that temper'd thee bade thee stand up,
     Gave thee no instance why thou shouldst do
          treason,
     Unless to dub thee with the name of traitor.
     If that same demon that hath gull'd thee thus
     Should with his lion gait walk the whole world
120 He might return to vasty Tartar back
     And tell the legions 'I can never win
     A soul so easy as that Englishman's.'
     Oh, how hast thou with jealousy infected
     The sweetness of affiance? Show men dutiful?
125 Why, so didst thou. Seem they grave and learned?
     Why, so didst thou. Come they of noble family?
     Why, so didst thou. Seem they religious?
     Why, so didst thou. Or are they spare in diet,
     Free from gross passion, or of mirth or anger,
130 Constant in spirit, not swerving with the blood,
     Garnish'd and deck'd in modest complement,
     Not working with the eye without the ear,
     And but in purged judgement trusting neither?
     Such and so finely bolted didst thou seem.
135 And thus thy fall hath left a kind of blot
     To mark the full fraught man, and best endowed
     With some suspicion. I will weep for thee,
     For this revolt of thine, methinks, is like
     Another fall of man. Their faults are open.

129 *or . . . or*: either . . . or.
130 *swerving with the blood*: carried away by passion.
131 *Garnish'd*: adorned.
   complement: outward appearance; *or* personal qualities.
132 *Not . . . ear*: not trusting the evidence of either eye or ear alone.
133 *but*: except.
   purged: purified.
134 *bolted*: sifted (like flour).
136 *full fraught*: fully laden (i.e. with rich experience and wisdom); the words usually describe merchant ships.
   best endowed: endowed with the best qualities.
139 *fall of man*: The first fall of man was brought about when Satan tempted Adam and Eve (Genesis chs. 2–3).
   open: manifest.
140 *answer of the law*: answer charges brought by the law.
141 *practices*: scheming.
147 *purposes*: schemes.
151 *For me*: as far as I am concerned.
152 *admit*: accept.
153 *effect*: accomplish.
   what I intended: Cambridge was part of a conspiracy to put Edmund Mortimer, the Earl of March, on the English throne (see 'Family Tree', p. x).
155 *in sufferance*: in enduring the penalty.
159 *joy o'er myself*: rejoice over the discovery of my own treachery.
162 *quit*: forgive.

165 *earnest*: part-payment in advance.

170 *Touching*: as regards.
171 *tender*: cherish.

175 *taste*: suffering.

140 Arrest them to the answer of the law,
     And God acquit them of their practices.
          Exeter
     I arrest thee of high treason, by the name of Richard
     Earl of Cambridge. I arrest thee of high treason, by
     the name of Henry, Lord Scroop of Masham. I
145 arrest thee of high treason, by the name of Thomas
     Gray, knight of Northumberland.
          Scroop
     Our purposes God justly hath discover'd,
     And I repent my fault more than my death,
     Which I beseech your highness to forgive,
150 Although my body pay the price of it.
          Cambridge
     For me, the gold of France did not seduce
     Although I did admit it as a motive
     The sooner to effect what I intended.
     But God be thanked for prevention,
155 Which I in sufferance heartily will rejoice,
     Beseeching God and you to pardon me.
          Gray
     Never did faithful subject more rejoice
     At the discovery of most dangerous treason
     Than I do at this hour joy o'er myself,
160 Prevented from a damned enterprise.
     My fault, but not my body, pardon, sovereign.
          King
     God quit you in His mercy. Hear your sentence.
     You have conspir'd against our royal person,
     Join'd with an enemy proclaim'd, and from his coffers
165 Receiv'd the golden earnest of our death;
     Wherein you would have sold your king to slaughter,
     His princes and his peers to servitude,
     His subjects to oppression and contempt,
     And his whole kingdom into desolation.
170 Touching our person seek we no revenge,
     But we our kingdom's safety must so tender,
     Whose ruin you have sought, that to her laws
     We do deliver you. Get you therefore hence,
     Poor miserable wretches, to your death,
175 The taste whereof God of His mercy give

177 *dear*: costing dearly.

179 *like*: equally.

184 *rub*: obstacle.
186 *puissance*: power, forces.
187 *straight*: immediately.
       in expedition: in motion.
188 *Cheerly*: cheerfully.
       signs: ensigns, standards.
       advance: raise.
189s.d. *Flourish*: trumpet call.

You patience to endure, and true repentance
Of all your dear offences. Bear them hence.
           Exeunt Cambridge, Scroop, Gray *and*
           Officers
Now lords, for France, the enterprise whereof
Shall be to you as us, like glorious.
180 We doubt not of a fair and lucky war,
Since God so graciously hath brought to light
This dangerous treason lurking in our way
To hinder our beginnings. We doubt not now
But every rub is smoothed on our way.
185 Then forth, dear countrymen. Let us deliver
Our puissance into the hand of God,
Putting it straight in expedition.
Cheerly to sea, the signs of war advance.
No king of England if not king of France!
           [*Flourish. Exeur*

Act 2   Scene 3

Sir John Falstaff is dead. His friends grieve,
telling how he died, and remembering details
of his life. At last the men set off to go to
France with the king's army, leaving the
Hostess behind to look after things at home.

2 *Staines*: a town about twenty miles from
    London on the road to Southampton.
3 *yearn*: grieve, mourn.
4 *vaunting veins*: swaggering spirits.
    bristle: rouse.
5–6 *we . . . therefore*: consequently we shall
    have to provide for ourselves; Falstaff
    was also a source of cash for his
    followers.
7 *Would*: I wish.
    wheresome're: wheresoever.
9 *Arthur's bosom*: The Hostess confuses
    King Arthur, the legendary ruler of the
    Knights of the Round Table and the
    model of English chivalry, with the
    Biblical patriarch, Abraham. The
    parable of Dives and Lazarus (Luke
    16:19–31) tells how Dives, the rich man,
    died and went to hell, whereas the
    beggar Lazarus was carried away to
    heaven—'Abraham's bosom'.

Scene 3

           Enter Pistol, Nym, Bardolph, Boy *and*
           Hostess

     Hostess
Prithee, honey-sweet husband, let me bring thee t
Staines.
     Pistol
No, for my manly heart doth yearn. Bardolph, b
blithe. Nym, rouse thy vaunting veins. Boy, bristl
5 thy courage up, for Falstaff he is dead, and we mus
earn therefore.
     Bardolph
Would I were with him, wheresome're he is, eithe
in heaven or in hell.
     Hostess
Nay, sure, he's not in hell. He's in Arthur's boso
10 if ever man went to Arthur's bosom. A made a fin
end, and went away an it had been any christor
child. A parted e'en just between twelve and on
e'en at the turning o'the tide, for after I saw hi
fumble with the sheets, and play with flowers, an

10 *A*: he.

11 *went away*: died.
    an: as if.

11–12 *christom child*: newly christened baby.
    For the first month after baptism the
    infant was dressed in a white robe
    called a 'chrism-cloth' ('chrism' = the
    oil then used for anointing at baptism).

12–13 *A parted . . . tide*: he died between
    midnight and one o'clock, just as the
    tide was turning. It was a very old
    superstition that the life of a dying man
    ebbed away with the ebbing of the tide.

14–16 *fumble . . . pen*: These were said to
    be classical signs of impending death.

16 *a pen*: a sharpened goose quill.

17 *a babbled*: This is one of the most
    famous of textual problems; F reads 'a
    Table', but an eighteenth-century
    editor, Lewis Theobald, emended to
    the present reading.
    green fields: Falstaff may have been
    remembering the 'green pastures' of
    Psalm 23.

22 *bade*: told (the past tense of 'bid').

25 *up-peered*: upward; this may be an
    attempt to indicate the Hostess's
    dialectal pronunciation.

27 *of sack*: against drinking sack; this
    Spanish wine was Falstaff's favourite
    drink in *Henry IV Part 1*.

29 *of women*: against women.

31 *incarnate*: made flesh; but the Hostess
    misunderstands.

32 *carnation*: Sixteenth-century carnations
    were pink—an appropriate colour for
    devils.

36 *handle*: talk about.

37 *rheumatic*: The Hostess would stress the
    first syllable; she probably means
    'lunatic' (= confused, deranged).

37–38 *Whore of Babylon*: the 'scarlet
    woman' of the Book of Revelation
    (17:4–5); the term was often applied by
    English Protestants to the pope and
    hence to the Roman Catholic Church.
    The Hostess's speech moves by
    association from 'incarnate' and
    'carnation' and perhaps from
    'rheumatic' to 'Rome' (which was then
    pronounced 'Room').

15 smile upon his finger's end, I knew there was but
one way. For his nose was as sharp as a pen, and a
babbled of green fields. 'How now, Sir John,' quoth
I, 'what man, be o' good cheer!' So a cried out 'God,
God, God' three or four times. Now I, to comfort
20 him, bid him a should not think of God; I hoped
there was no need to trouble himself with any such
thoughts yet. So a bade me lay more clothes on his
feet. I put my hand into the bed, and felt them, and
they were as cold as any stone. Then I felt to his
25 knees, and so up-peered and upward, and all was as
cold as any stone.

Nym

They say he cried out of sack.

Hostess

Ay, that a did.

Bardolph

And of women.

Hostess

30 Nay, that a did not.

Boy

Yes, that a did, and said they were devils incarnate.

Hostess

A could never abide carnation, 'twas a colour he
never liked.

Boy

A said once, the Devil would have him about
35 women.

Hostess

A did in some sort, indeed, handle women. But then
he was rheumatic, and talked of the Whore of
Babylon.

Boy

Do you not remember a saw a flea stick upon
40 Bardolph's nose, and a said it was a black soul
burning in hell?

42 *fuel*: i.e. the drink paid for by Falstaff.

44 *shog*: get on our way.

46–7 *Look to . . . moveables*: look after everything I have (which could be stolen).
47 *Let senses rule*: keep on the alert.
48 *pitch and pay*: cash down, no credit.
49 *straws*: no stronger than straws.
wafer cakes: promises are like thin cakes (compare the proverb 'Promises and pie-crusts are made to be broken').
49–50 *Hold-fast . . . dog*: There was a proverbial saying, 'Brag is a good dog, but Holdfast is a better'; both 'brag' and 'dog' were names for nails, and a 'holdfast' was a clamp.
50 *caveto*: beware.
51 *clear thy crystals*: wipe your eyes.
51–2 *Yoke-fellows in arms*: fellow-soldiers.
54 *unwholesome food*: Culinary writers advised that the blood of beasts and fowl was indigestible.

58 *let housewifery appear*: show yourself to be a careful housewife.
Keep close: keep yourself occupied in the house.

Bardolph
Well, the fuel is gone that maintained that fire
That's all the riches I got in his service.
  Nym
Shall we shog? The king will be gone from
45 Southampton.
  Pistol
Come, let's away. My love, give me thy lips. Look to
my chattels and my moveables. Let senses rule: the
word is, pitch and pay. Trust none, for oaths are
straws, men's faiths are wafer cakes, and Hold-fast is
50 the only dog, my duck. Therefore *caveto* be thy
counsellor. Go, clear thy crystals. Yoke-fellows in
arms, let us to France, like horseleeches, my boys, to
suck, to suck, the very blood to suck!
  Boy
And that's but unwholesome food, they say.
  Pistol
55 Touch her soft mouth, and march.
  Bardolph
Farewell, hostess.

          Kisses her

  Nym
I cannot kiss, that is the humour of it, but adieu.
  Pistol
Let housewifery appear. Keep close, I thee
command.
  Hostess
60 Farewell, adieu.
                              [*Exeunt*

Act 2   Scene 4

The King of France recognizes the need to defend his country against the English invasion. The Dauphin speaks scathingly of King Henry, but the Constable, who has been impressed by the Ambassador's report of his reception at the English court, reproves the Dauphin. The embassy from England arrives, led by the Duke of Exeter who delivers King Henry's challenge. The French king is warned that there will be war if he does not surrender his crown.

Scene 4

          Flourish. Enter the French King, *the*
          Dauphin, *the* Dukes of Berri *and*
          Bourbon, *the* Constable *and other* Lords

  French King
Thus comes the English with full power upon us,
And more than carefully it us concerns
To answer royally in our defences.
Therefore the Dukes of Berri and of Bourbon,

os.d. *Constable*: The Lord Constable was head of the royal household, and commander of the army.

2 *more than . . . concerns*: we must be more than usually concerned.

3 *To . . . defences*: to defend ourselves with all our royal power.

5 *make forth*: set out.

6 *swift despatch*: with all haste.

7 *line*: reinforce.

8 *means defendant*: defensive equipment.

9 *England*: the King of England.

10 *gulf*: whirlpool.

11 *fits*: befits, is necessary.

12 *late examples*: recent example—i.e. the Battles of Crécy (1346) and Poitiers (1356).

13 *fatal and neglected*: fatally underrated.

14 *fields*: battlefields.
    redoubted: respected.

15 *meet*: proper.

16 *dull*: make lazy.

17 *Though*: even though.
    known: particular, declared.

18 *musters*: armies.

19 *maintain'd . . . collected*: The verbs correspond in order to the nouns of line 18.

5 Of Brabant and of Orléans, shall make forth,
   And you, Prince Dauphin, with all swift despatch
   To line and new repair our towns of war
   With men of courage and with means defendant,
   For England his approaches makes as fierce
10 As waters to the sucking of a gulf.
   It fits us then to be as provident
   As fear may teach us, out of late examples
   Left by the fatal and neglected English
   Upon our fields.
        Dauphin
                  My most redoubted father,
15 It is most meet we arm us 'gainst the foe,
   For peace itself should not so dull a kingdom,
   Though war nor no known quarrel were in question,
   But that defences, musters, preparations
   Should be maintain'd, assembled and collected
20 As were a war in expectation.
   Therefore I say 'tis meet we all go forth
   To view the sick and feeble parts of France.
   And let us do it with no show of fear,
   No, with no more than if we heard that England
25 Were busied with a Whitsun morris dance.

25 *Whitsun morris dance*: The traditional
   morris dance, often performed at
   Whitsuntide, sometimes featured a
   comic king and queen who were
   attended by the dancers with bells and
   wooden swords; the Dauphin compares
   England to the morris queen, with King
   Henry as her comic king.
26 *idly king'd*: foolishly ruled.
27 *sceptre . . . borne*: her royal power so
   absurdly exercised.
28 *giddy*: unstable.
   humorous: whimsical.
29 *attends*: accompanies.
31 *the late ambassadors*: i.e. those who have
   just returned from England.
32 *great state*: dignity.
   embassy: ambassadorial message.
34 *in exception*: in raising objections.
   withal: altogether.
35 *in constant resolution*: in his firm
   determination.
36 *vanities, forespent*: former frivolousness,
   now exhausted.
37 *outside . . . Brutus*: Lucius Junius Brutus
   (not the Brutus who murdered Julius
   Caesar) gave the appearance of
   stupidity in order to preserve his life
   from the Roman tyrant Tarquin—whom
   he later helped to expel from Rome.
38 *coat of folly*: the fool's costume, worn at
   the morris dance.
39 *ordure*: mulch, compost.
42 *though*: even if.
43 *weigh*: esteem.
45 *So . . . fill'd*: in this way all possible
   means of defence will be provided.
46 *projection*: estimated scale.
47 *scanting*: begrudging, trying to
   economize on.
48 *Think we*: let us think.
50 *The kindred of him*: his ancestors.
   flesh'd: trained in warfare (the image is
   from the training of hawks and hounds,
   which are fed with the flesh of the
   quarries they must hunt).
51 *bloody strain*: bloodthirsty breed.
52 *haunted . . . paths*: pursued us on our
   home ground.
54 *When Crécy . . . struck*: when the Battle
   of Crécy was fought and we were
   defeated.
55 *captiv'd*: taken captive.

For, my good liege, she is so idly king'd,
Her sceptre so fantastically borne,
By a vain, giddy, shallow, humorous youth,
That fear attends her not.
Constable
                    Oh peace, Prince Dauphin
30 You are too much mistaken in this king.
Question, your grace, the late ambassadors,
With what great state he heard their embassy,
How well supplied with noble counsellors,
How modest in exception, and withal
35 How terrible in constant resolution,
And you shall find his vanities, forespent,
Were but the outside of the Roman Brutus,
Covering discretion with a coat of folly,
As gardeners do with ordure hide those roots
40 That shall first spring and be most delicate.
Dauphin
Well, 'tis not so, my Lord High Constable.
But though we think it so, it is no matter.
In cases of defence, 'tis best to weigh
The enemy more mighty than he seems,
45 So the proportions of defence are fill'd,
Which of a weak and niggardly projection
Doth like a miser spoil his coat, with scanting
A little cloth.
French King
                    Think we King Harry strong,
And, princes, look you strongly arm to meet him.
50 The kindred of him hath been flesh'd upon us,
And he is bred out of that bloody strain
That haunted us in our familiar paths.
Witness our too-much memorable shame
When Crécy battle fatally was struck,
55 And all our princes captiv'd, by the hand
Of that black name, Edward, black Prince of Wales,
Whilst that his mountant sire, on mountain
   standing,
Up in the air, crown'd with the golden sun,
Saw his heroical seed, and smil'd to see him
60 Mangle the work of nature and deface
The patterns that by God and by French fathers

56 *black*: evil (from the French point of view); the French king speaks as though the Prince of Wales had been a devil.

57 *mountant*: in the ascendant, climbing up to the peak of success; early texts have 'mountain'.
   on mountain standing: See *1, 2, 108 note*.

59 *seed*: offspring.

61 *patterns*: models.

62 *stem*: offshoot.

63 *stock*: root.

64 *The native . . . him*: the great destiny to which he was born.

67 *give . . . audience*: hear them immediately.

69 *this chase*: The king picks up the hunting imagery from line 50.

70 *Turn head*: turn to face them (like a stag at bay; 'head' = antlers).

71 *spend their mouths*: give tongue, bark loudly.

73 *short*: abruptly.

76 *brother*: brother king.

78 *wills*: desires.

79 *divest*: strip off.

80-1 *by gift . . . of nations*: by all laws—divine, natural, and human. Divine law (which could only be learned through revelation) controlled all things; working within this was the law of nature (whose scientific truths were discoverable by human reasoning powers); and subordinate to these were the laws of nations (which were often decided by custom).

81 *'longs*: belongs.

83 *all . . . pertain*: every title that derives, no matter how remotely, from this.

84 *ordinance of times*: established practice, tradition.

85 *That*: in order that.

86 *sinister*: irregular; in heraldry, the 'bend sinister' on a shield indicated the bearer's illegitimacy of birth.
   awkward: oblique, illegitimate.

87 *Pick'd . . . worm-holes*: found with much research into worm-eaten manuscripts.

88 *from . . . rak'd*: from raking amongst the dust of things that have been forgotten for years.

89 *line*: i.e. of the family tree (see p. x).

Had twenty years been made. This is a stem
Of that victorious stock, and let us fear
The native mightiness and fate of him.

Enter a Messenger

Messenger
65 Ambassadors from Harry, king of England,
Do crave admittance to your majesty.
        French King
We'll give them present audience.
Go, and bring them.   [*Exit* Messenger
You see this chase is hotly follow'd, friends.
        Dauphin
70 Turn head and stop pursuit, for coward dogs
Most spend their mouths when what they seem to
        threaten
Runs far before them. Good my sovereign,
Take up the English short, and let them know
Of what a monarchy you are the head.
75 Self love, my liege, is not so vile a sin
As self neglecting.

Enter Exeter

        French King
                From our brother of England?
        Exeter
From him, and thus he greets your majesty:
He wills you in the name of God almighty
That you divest yourself, and lay apart
80 The borrow'd glories that by gift of heaven,
By law of nature and of nations, 'longs
To him and to his heirs, namely, the crown,
And all wide-stretched honours that pertain
By custom and the ordinance of times
85 Unto the crown of France. That you may know
'Tis no sinister nor no awkward claim
Pick'd from the wormholes of long vanish'd days,
Nor from the dust of old oblivion rak'd,
He sends you this most memorable line

Delivers scroll

90   In every branch truly demonstrative,
       Willing you overlook this pedigree,
       And when you find him evenly deriv'd
       From his most fam'd of famous ancestors,
       Edward the Third, he bids you then resign
95   Your crown and kingdom, indirectly held
       From him, the native and true challenger.

French King

Or else what follows?

Exeter

Bloody constraint, for if you hide the crown
Even in your hearts, there will he rake for it.
100   Therefore in fierce tempest is he coming,
       In thunder and in earthquake, like a Jove,
       That if requiring fail, he will compel,
       And bids you, in the bowels of the Lord,
       Deliver up the crown, and to take mercy
105   On the poor souls for whom this hungry war
       Opens his vasty jaws, and on your head
       Turning the widow's tears, the orphan's cries,
       The dead men's blood, the prived maiden's groans,
       For husbands, fathers, and betrothed lovers
110   That shall be swallow'd in this controversy.
       This is his claim, his threatening, and my message—
       Unless the Dauphin be in presence here,
       To whom expressly I bring greeting to.

French King

For us, we will consider of this further.
115   Tomorrow shall you bear our full intent
       Back to our brother of England.

91   *Willing you overlook*: desiring you to read through.
92   *evenly deriv'd*: directly descended.
95   *indirectly*: wrongfully, illegitimately.
96   *native*: natural by right of birth.
       challenger: claimant.
98   *constraint*: compulsion, force.
99   *rake*: search for.

100–1 *coming . . . in earthquake*: In the Bible (Isaiah 29:6) it is prophesied that Jehovah, the Lord of Hosts, will come to earth in this manner.
101   *Jove*: Jupiter, king of the Roman gods; he is often depicted with a thunderbolt.
102   *requiring*: requesting.
103   *in the bowels of the Lord*: in all compassion; the phrase was biblical (see Philippians 1:8, 'in the bowels of Jesus Christ').
106   *vasty*: immense.
106–7 *on your head Turning*: taking the guilt on yourself.
108   *prived*: deprived.
110   *swallow'd*: i.e. by the 'vasty jaws of war'.
112   *in presence*: in the presence chamber.
113   *expressly*: particularly.

115   *full intent*: considered reply.

117 *stand here*: represent.

118 *slight regard*: disdain.

119 *misbecome*: be inappropriate.

120 *prize*: reckon, rate.

121 *and if*: An intensive form of 'if'.

122 *in grant . . . at large*: satisfying all my
demands in full.

125 *womby vaultages*: hollow caverns.

127 *second accent*: echo.
ordinance: artillery.

128 *fair return*: polite response.

130 *odds*: quarrel.

131 *matching to*: appropriate for, *and* making
a match with.
vanity: shallowness.

132 *Paris balls*: tennis balls; the French ones
were particularly lightweight.

133 *Louvre*: the Royal Court of France; the
word was pronounced 'Lover'—which
leads to word-play in the next line.

134 *mistress-court*: chief court.

137 *greener*: more immature.

138 *masters*: possesses.

139 *utmost grain*: last grain of sand in the
hour-glass.
read: recognize; perhaps there is also a
pun with 'rede' (= regret).

141 *at full*: completely.
Flourish: The trumpets sound as the king
rises and prepares to depart; but Exeter
boldly interrupts. The trumpeters might
renew or repeat their 'flourish' when the
king leaves the stage after line 147.

142 *Dispatch us*: send us away.
our king: the king of England. Exeter's
pronoun emphasizes that the King of
France is subject to King Henry just as
much as he himself.

144 *footed . . . already*: In historical fact,
Exeter's embassy was in February 1415,
and the king did not land in France until
August of that year.

146 *small breath*: little breathing-space.

Dauphin
                                    For the Dauphin,
I stand here for him. What to him from England?
    Exeter
Scorn and defiance, slight regard, contempt,
And anything that may not misbecome
120 The mighty sender, doth he prize you at.
Thus says my king, and if your father's highness
Do not, in grant of all demands at large,
Sweeten the bitter mock you sent his majesty,
He'll call you to so hot an answer of it
125 That caves and womby vaultages of France
Shall chide your trespass and return your mock
In second accent of his ordinance.
    Dauphin
Say, if my father render fair return
It is against my will, for I desire
130 Nothing but odds with England. To that end,
As matching to his youth and vanity,
I did present him with the Paris balls.
    Exeter
He'll make your Paris Louvre shake for it,
Were it the mistress-court of mighty Europe.
135 And be assur'd, you'll find a difference,
As we his subjects have in wonder found,
Between the promise of his greener days
And these he masters now. Now he weighs time
Even to the utmost grain. That you shall read
140 In your own losses, if he stay in France.
    French King
Tomorrow shall you know our mind at full.

                Flourish

    Exeter
Dispatch us with all speed, lest that our king
Come here himself to question our delay,
For he is footed in this land already.
    French King
145 You shall be soon dispatch'd, with fair conditions.
A night is but small breath and little pause
To answer matters of this consequence.
                        [*Flourish. Exeunt*

Act 3

The Chorus continues to exhort the audience that they must make full use of their imaginations. They must visualize the scene at Southampton as the king embarks his troops, and then conjure up for themselves the sight of all the ships crossing the English Channel. And then they must picture the scene when the army is besieging Harfleur. The French king's attempt at appeasement has been rejected, and the fighting is about to start.

1 *imagin'd wing*: wing of imagination.
  scene: setting, locality.
2–3 *In . . . thought*: as quick as thought.
4 *well-appointed*: well-equipped.
  Hampton: Southampton.
5 *royalty*: majesty—himself and his entourage.
  brave: spectacular.
6 *streamers*: banners.
  young Phoebus feigning: looking like the rising sun (Phoebus Apollo was the classical god of the sun).
7 *Play with your fancies*: exercise your imaginations.
8 *hempen tackle*: rigging, the ship's ropes.

Enter Chorus

Chorus
Thus with imagin'd wing our swift scene flies
In motion of no less celerity
Than that of thought. Suppose that you have seen
The well-appointed king at Hampton Pier
5 Embark his royalty, and his brave fleet
With silken streamers the young Phoebus feigning.
Play with your fancies, and in them behold
Upon the hempen tackle ship-boys climbing.

9   *whistle*: i.e. the one blown by the
    master-mariner to communicate with
    the ship-boys.
10 *threaden*: stitched with strengthening
    cords, or, strung on the 'hempen
    tackle'.
12 *bottoms*: vessels.
14 *rivage*: shore.
15 *inconstant*: unsteady, heaving.
17 *holding due course to Harfleur*: headed
    directly for Harfleur (see map, p. 55).
18 *Grapple*: hook on, fasten with grappling
    irons.
    sternage: the rear ends.
19 *as . . . still*: as silent as midnight.
20 *grandsires*: grandfathers.
21 *to pith and puissance*: at strength and full
    power.
22 *but*: only.
24 *cull'd and choice-drawn cavaliers*: hand-
    picked and specially selected knights.
26 *ordnance on their carriages*: guns
    mounted on their carriages.
27 *fatal mouths*: deadly muzzles.
    girded: fortified.
28 *Suppose*: imagine.
30 *to dowry*: for a dowry.
31 *petty and unprofitable dukedoms*: The
    Chorus now scorns what were once
    called 'almost kingly dukedoms'. (*1, 2,
    227*). In historical fact, these offers were
    made about two months before Henry
    landed in France.
32 *likes not*: does not please.
    nimble: adroit, agile.
33 *linstock*: stick holding the gunner's
    match.
    devilish: fireworks were usually
    associated with devils (especially on the
    Elizabethan stage).
33s.d. *Alarm*: trumpet signal ordering battle
    to commence.
    chambers: small cannons; in the theatre
    these would be positioned above the
    stage.
35 *eke*: fill, complete.
    mind: invention.

Hear the shrill whistle, which doth order give
10 To sounds confus'd. Behold the threaden sails,
Borne with the invisible and creeping wind,
Draw the huge bottoms through the furrow'd sea,
Breasting the lofty surge. O do but think
You stand upon the rivage, and behold
15 A city on th'inconstant billows dancing,
For so appears this fleet majestical,
Holding due course to Harfleur. Follow, follow!
Grapple your minds to sternage of this navy,
And leave your England as dead midnight, still,
20 Guarded with grandsires, babies and old women,
Either past or not arriv'd to pith and puissance.
For who is he whose chin is but enrich'd
With one appearing hair that will not follow
These cull'd and choice-drawn cavaliers to France?
25 Work, work your thoughts, and therein see a siege.
Behold the ordnance on their carriages
With fatal mouths gaping on girded Harfleur.
Suppose th'ambassador from the French comes
    back,
Tells Harry that the king doth offer him
30 Katherine his daughter, and with her to dowry
Some petty and unprofitable dukedoms.
The offer likes not, and the nimble gunner
With linstock now the devilish cannon touches
    Alarm, and chambers go off
And down goes all before them. Still be kind,
35 And eke out our performance with your mind.
                                                    [*Exit*

Act 3   Scene 1

A single speech from King Henry. The English army has burst open part of the city wall surrounding Harfleur, but the soldiers are now in retreat. The king urges his troops to make just one more assault. He calls upon their loyalty, patriotism, and their sense of honour; and at last he sounds the battle-cry.

os.d. *scaling ladders*: apparently the cannon shots have destroyed part of the parapets, thus enabling the soldiers to climb over ('scale') the city wall.

1 *breach*: break in the wall made by the cannon.

2 *the wall*: i.e. the 'breach'.

4 *stillness*: quietness.

7 *conjure up the blood*: call up your vital spirits; the Elizabethans believed that these resided in the blood, and gave rise to all manly actions.

8 *fair nature*: naturally attractive appearance.
  hard-favour'd: grim-featured.

9 *aspect*: expression; the word is stressed on the second syllable.

10 *pry*: peer.
  portage: portholes.

11 *o'erwhelm it*: over-hang the threatening glare of the eyes, frown.

12 *galled rock*: cliff which is being washed away.

13 *jutty*: jut out over.
  confounded: eroded.

14 *Swill'd*: violently washed.

16–17 *bend up . . . full height*: The image is of a bow, bent until the bowstring is taut.

Scene 1

Enter the King, Exeter, Bedford, *and* Gloucester

Alarm. Enter soldiers *with scaling ladders at Harfleur*

King

Once more unto the breach, dear friends, once more,
Or close the wall up with our English dead!
In peace there's nothing so becomes a man
As modest stillness and humility.
5 But when the blast of war blows in our ears,
Then imitate the action of the tiger:
Stiffen the sinews, conjure up the blood,
Disguise fair nature with hard-favour'd rage.
Then lend the eye a terrible aspect,
10 Let it pry through the portage of the head,
Like the brass cannon. Let the brow o'erwhelm it
As fearfully as doth a galled rock
O'erhang and jutty his confounded base,
Swill'd with the wild and wasteful ocean.
15 Now set the teeth and stretch the nostril wide,
Hold hard the breath, and bend up every spirit

17 *his*: its.
18 *fet*: fetched, inherited.
   war-proof: tested and experienced in war.
19 *Alexander*: Alexander the Great, who is said to have lamented that there were no more worlds for him to conquer.
20 *from morn till even*: from morning to night; King Henry's language becomes momentarily romantic and 'poetic'.
21 *argument*: opposition.
22 *Dishonour not your mothers*: i.e. by casting doubt on your paternity.
   attest: bear witness, prove.
24 *copy*: example.
   grosser: thicker, less refined.
25 *war*: fight.
   yeomen: countrymen who fought as foot-soldiers, particularly archers; their service was especially distinguished at Crécy, Poitiers, and Agincourt.
27 *mettle of your pasture*: quality of the land which bred you.
28 *worth your breeding*: deserve all that it has cost to bring you up.
29 *mean and base*: however humble and lowly by birth.
31 *slips*: leashes.
32 *Straining upon the start*: eager to get started.
   The game's afoot: the quarry—the hare that greyhounds would chase—has set off.
33 *upon this charge*: as you charge.
34 *Saint George*: the patron saint of England, to whom Henry was especially devoted. The name was pronounced to rhyme with 'charge'.
34s.d. *Alarm . . . off*: The trumpet signals the fresh assault, and the cannons are fired again.

To his full height. On, on, you noble English,
Whose blood is fet from fathers of war-proof,
Fathers that like so many Alexanders
20 Have in these parts from morn till even fought,
And sheath'd their swords for lack of argument.
Dishonour not your mothers. Now attest
That those whom you call'd fathers did beget you.
Be copy now to men of grosser blood,
25 And teach them how to war. And you, good yeomen,
Whose limbs were made in England, show us here
The mettle of your pasture. Let us swear
That you are worth your breeding, which I doubt not,
For there is none of you so mean and base
30 That hath not noble lustre in your eyes.
I see you stand like greyhounds in the slips,
Straining upon the start. The game's afoot.
Follow your spirit, and upon this charge
Cry 'God for Harry, England and Saint George!'
         [*Alarm, and chambers go off. Exeunt*

Act 3   Scene 2

Four characters whom we last saw in the
London tavern re-appear on the battlefields
of France. They sing to keep up their spirits
before the soldiers return to the fight, leaving
the Boy alone on the stage to speak
confidentially to the audience.

2   *corporal*: Bardolph seems to have been
    demoted from his rank (2, 1, 2) of
    lieutenant.
    knocks: fighting.
3   *I . . . lives*: I've only got one life; a 'case'
    is a set of two pistols.
4   *humour*: temper; the word has many
    different senses, allowing for easy word-
    play—as in line 6.
    the very plain-song: the simple truth; in
    music, plain-song is the air without
    variations.
6   *most just*: right word (French *mot juste*).
    humours: bad airs, mists; there would
    even be smoke in the playhouse—as on
    the battlefield—caused by the cannon.
7   *vassals*: servants.
9–20 Pistol and the Boy sing fragments of
    old songs.
11 *Doth*: Shakespeare often mixes singular
    and plural verbs and nouns.
12 *Would*: I wish.
15 *prevail with*: succeed.
17 *hie*: go quickly.
18 *duly*: accurately.
19 *truly*: honourably.

21 *preach*: breach (= break in the wall); the
    p/b substitution is one of Shakespeare's
    indications of the character's Welsh
    accent.
    Avaunt: get away.
    cullions: rascals.
22 *duke*: leader (from the Latin *dux*).
    men of mould: men of earth, mere
    mortals.
24 *bawcock*: fine fellow.
    bate: abate.
    use lenity: be lenient.
25 *chuck*: good lad.
26–7 *These . . . humours*: this is a fine
    change of mood.
26 *wins*: conquers.

Scene 2

Enter Nym, Bardolph, Pistol, *and* Boy

Bardolph
On, on, on, on, on, to the breach, to the breach!
　　Nym
Pray thee, corporal, stay. The knocks are too hot,
and for mine own part I have not a case of lives. The
humour of it is too hot, that is the very plain-song
5 of it.
　　Pistol
'The plain-song' is most just, for humours do
abound. Knocks go and come, God's vassals drop
and die,
　　　　[*Sings*] And sword and shield,
10　　　　In bloody field,
　　　　Doth win immortal fame.
　　Boy
Would I were in an ale-house in London. I would
give all my fame for a pot of ale, and safety.
　　Pistol
And I.
15　　　　[*Sings*] If wishes would prevail with me,
　　　　My purpose should not fail with me,
　　　　But thither would I hie.
　　Boy
　　　　[*Sings*] As duly
　　　　But not as truly
20　　　　As bird doth sing on bough.

Enter Llewellyn

　　Llewellyn
Up to the preach, you dogs! Avaunt, you cullions!
　　Pistol
Be merciful, great duke, to men of mould! Abate thy
rage, abate thy manly rage! Abate thy rage, great
duke! Good bawcock, bate thy rage. Use lenity,
25 sweet chuck.
　　Nym
These be good humours! Your honour wins bad
humours!
　　　　[*Exeunt* Pistol, Bardolph, *and* Nym,
　　　　pursued by Llewellyn

29 *swashers*: swaggerers.
    boy to: (a) servant to; (b) younger than.
31 *man to me*: (a) my manservant; (b) more manly than I am.
    antics: clowns.
32 *white-livered*: bloodless, cowardly (the liver was thought to be the seat of courage).
33 *red-faced*: courageous in appearance—but Bardolph's face was covered in spots and boils (see *2, 1, 74 note*).
    a: he.
34 *killing tongue*: foul mouth.
35–6 *breaks words*: fights verbal battles, *and* does not keep his promises.
37 *men . . . best men*: Nym must have heard the proverbial saying: *vir sapit qui pauca loquitur*—it's a wise man who doesn't talk much.
43 *purchase*: fair exchange.
44 *league*: a French mile (equivalent to three English miles).
45 *filching*: pilfering.
46 *Calais*: At this time Calais was an English property.
46–7 *piece of service*: little job.
47 *carry coals*: do any degrading work, *and*, be damned in hell.
48 *as familiar*: as often on the inside.
49–50 *makes much . . . manhood*: greatly offends my self-respect.
51–2 *pocketing up of wrongs*: (a) putting up with insults; *and* (b) receiving stolen goods.
53 *goes against*: upsets.
54 *cast it up*: throw—or vomit—it back again, give up this employment.

Boy

As young as I am, I have observed these three swashers. I am boy to them all three, but all
30 they three, though they would serve me, could not be man to me, for indeed three such antics do not amount to a man. For Bardolph, he is white-livered and red-faced, by the means whereof a faces it out but fights not. For Pistol, he hath a killing tongue
35 and a quiet sword, by the means whereof a breaks words and keeps whole weapons. For Nym, he hath heard that men of few words are the best men, and therefore he scorns to say his prayers lest a should be thought a coward, but his few bad words are
40 matched with as few good deeds, for a never broke any man's head but his own, and that was against a post when he was drunk. They will steal anything and call it purchase. Bardolph stole a lute-case, bore it twelve leagues and sold it for three halfpence. Nym
45 and Bardolph are sworn brothers in filching, and in Calais they stole a fire-shovel. I knew by that piece of service the men would carry coals. They would have me as familiar with men's pockets as their gloves or their handkerchiefs, which makes much against my
50 manhood if I should take from another's pocket to put into mine, for it is plain pocketing up of wrongs. I must leave them and seek some better service. Their villainy goes against my weak stomach, and therefore I must cast it up.

[*Exit*

Act 3   Scene 3

Three army officers—a Scotsman, a Welshman, and an Irishman—engage in cautious nationalistic sparring. The English captain stands neutral.

1 *presently*: immediately.
2 *mines*: tunnels dug underneath fortifications for the purpose of laying explosives.
5 *look you*: An emphatic phrase which, like the p/b confusion (*3, 2, 21*), indicates Llewellyn's Welsh accent.

Scene 3

Enter Gower *and* Llewellyn

Gower

Captain Llewellyn, you must come presently to the mines. The Duke of Gloucester would speak with you.

Llewellyn

To the mines? Tell you the duke it is not so good
5 to come to the mines, for, look you, the mines is not

6 *disciplines of war*: conventions of warfare.

6–7 *the . . . sufficient*: Llewellyn means that there is not enough space in the tunnels for the explosives to be effective.

8 *athversary*: the enemy.
discuss unto: inform.

9–10 *is . . . countermines*: has dug countermines for himself four yards underneath our mines.

10 *Cheshu*: Jesus.
plow: blow.

11 *directions*: instructions.

12 *order*: management.

14 *gentleman*: The captains in the play are all referred to as 'gentlemen', a social rank between the nobles and the yeomen.

18 *verify . . . beard*: prove it to his face.

20 *Roman disciplines*: These were thought to be superior to any modern theories of warfare; Llewellyn clearly thinks that the Irishman will be ignorant of such refinements.
is: has.

23 *falorous*: valorous.

24 *expedition*: quick-thinking.

25 *anchient*: ancient.

28 *pristine*: faultless, perfectly conducted.

30 *guidday*: good day—Shakespeare now attempts to suggest a Scottish accent.

31 *Goodden*: God give you good day.

33 *pioneers*: sappers.

34 *law*: This is an intensifier for the oath, not quite 'lord'.
'tish: 'tis; Shakespeare tries to suggest Irish speech.

35 *retreat*: order to retreat.

according to the disciplines of the war, the concavities of it is not sufficient. For, look you, th'athversary, you may discuss unto the duke, look you, is digged himself, four yard under, the
10 countermines! By Cheshu, I think a will plow up all, if there is not better directions.

Gower
The Duke of Gloucester, to whom the order of the siege is given, is altogether directed by an Irishman, a very valiant gentleman, i'faith.

Llewellyn
15 It is Captain Macmorris, is it not?

Gower
I think it be.

Llewellyn
By Cheshu, he is an ass, as in the world. I will verify as much in his beard. He has no more directions in the true disciplines of the wars, look
20 you, of the Roman disciplines, than is a puppy dog.

Enter Macmorris *and* Captain Jamy

Gower
Here a comes, and the Scots captain, Captain Jamy, with him.

Llewellyn
Captain Jamy is a marvellous falorous gentleman, that is certain, and of great expedition and
25 knowledge in th'anchient wars, upon my particular knowledge of his directions. By Cheshu, he will maintain his argument as well as any military man in the world, in the disciplines of the pristine wars of the Romans.

Jamy
30 I say guidday, Captain Llewellyn.

Llewellyn
Goodden to your worship, good Captain James.

Gower
How now, Captain Macmorris, have you quit the mines? Have the pioneers given o'er?

Macmorris
By Chrish law, 'tish ill done. The work ish give over,
35 the trumpet sound the retreat. By my hand I swear,

38 *law*: Macmorris intensifies his oath.

and my father's soul, the work ish ill done. It ish give over. I would have blowed up the town, so Chrish save me law, in an hour. O, 'tish ill done, 'tish ill done. By my hand, 'tish ill done.

Llewellyn

40 Captain Macmorris, I beseech you now, will you vouchsafe me, look you, a few disputations with you, as partly touching or concerning the disciplines of the war, the Roman wars, in the way of argument, look you, and friendly communication? Partly to sat-

45 isfy my opinion, and partly for the satisfaction, look you, of my mind, as touching the direction of the military discipline, that is the point.

42 *touching*: regarding.

Jamy

It sall be vary guid, guid faith, guid captains baith, and I sall 'quite you with guid leave, as I may pick

50 occasion, that sall I, marry.

49 *'quite*: requite, answer.

Macmorris

It is no time to discourse, so Chrish save me. The day is hot, and the weather, and the wars, and the king, and the dukes. It is no time to discourse, the town is besieched! An the trumpet call us to the

55 breach, and we talk and be Chrish do nothing, 'tis shame for us all! So God sa' me, 'tis shame to stand still, it is shame, by my hand. And there is throats to be cut, and works to be done, and there ish nothing done, so Christ sa' me law.

54 *besieched*: besieged.
55 *be*: by.

Jamy

60 By the mess, ere these eyes of mine take themselves to slumber I'll dee guid service, or I'll lig i'the grund for it. I owe Got a death, and I'll pay't as valorously as I may, that sal I surely do, that is the breff and the long. Marry, I wad full fain hear some question

65 'tween you twae.

59 *sa'*: save.

60 *By the mess*: The Protestant Elizabethans would find it acceptable for Jamy, being a Roman Catholic Scot, to swear by the mass.
61 *lig*: lie.
    grund: ground.
63 *the breff*: short (brief).
64 *wad full fain*: would very much like to.
    some question: discussion, argument.
65 *twae*: two.

Llewellyn

Captain Macmorris, I think, look you, under your correction, there is not many of your nation—

Macmorris

Of my nation? What ish my nation? Ish a villain, and a bastard, and a knave, and a rascal. What ish my

70 nation? Who talks of my nation?

68 *Of my nation*: Macmorris is sensitive about his nationality. The Elizabethans had special martial rules to prevent this kind of quarrelling in camps.

Llewellyn

Look you, if you take the matter otherwise than is
meant, Captain Macmorris, peradventure I shall
think you do not use me with that affability as in
discretion you ought to use me, look you, being as
75 good a man as yourself, both in the disciplines of
war, and in the derivation of my birth, and in other
particularities.

Macmorris

I do not know you so good a man as myself. So
Chrish save me, I will cut off your head!

Gower

80 Gentlemen both, you will mistake each other.

Jamy

Ah, that's a foul fault.

A parley

Gower

The town sounds a parley.

Llewellyn

Captain Macmorris, when there is more better
opportunity to be required, look you, I will be so
85 bold as to tell you I know the disciplines of war,
and there is an end.

[*Exeunt*

72 *peradventure*: it may be.

73 *use*: treat.

80 *you will mistake*: you persist in
misunderstanding.

81s.d. *parley*: trumpet-call signalling a
cease-fire for the two sides to begin
negotiations.

84 *to be required*: presents itself.

Scene 4

Enter the King, Exeter, *and all his train
before the gates*

King

How yet resolves the governor of the town?
This is the latest parle we will admit,
Therefore to our best mercy give yourselves,
Or like to men proud of destruction
5 Defy us to our worst. For as I am a soldier,
A name that in my thoughts becomes me best,
If I begin the battery once again
I will not leave the half-achiev'd Harfleur
Till in her ashes she lie buried.
10 The gates of mercy shall be all shut up

Act 3   Scene 4

Outside Harfleur, King Henry addresses the
enemy soldiers who are drawn up on the city
walls. He demands the surrender of the city,
painting a graphic picture of the sufferings
that must be endured by its citizens if they
refuse to submit. The Governor
acknowledges the superiority of the English
power, and yields up Harfleur.

1 *resolves*: decides.

2 *latest parle*: final attempt at negotiation.

4 *proud of*: excited by, glorying in.

5 *to our worst*: to do our worst.

6 *in my thoughts*: in my opinion.
becomes: suits.

7 *battery*: assaults.

8 *half-achiev'd*: already half-conquered.

10 'We shall show no compassion.'

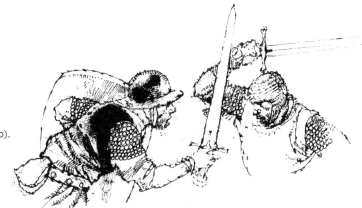

11 *flesh'd*: trained in slaughter (see *2*, 4, 50).
12 *In liberty*: given complete freedom.
    range: go anywhere.
13 *With . . . hell*: with a conscience that
    will accommodate all hellish deeds.
15 *impious war*: civil war (Latin *bellum
    impium*). It could be so described
    because Harfleur was supposed to be
    English, and the Governor was
    withholding the city from its rightful
    ruler.
16 *prince of fiends*: Lucifer, the leading devil
    in hell; he was also the bringer of light
    (and fire).
17 *smirch'd*: blackened (with gunpowder).
    fell feats: cruel deeds.
18 *Enlink'd*: connected with, linked
    together (as by a chain); a 'link' was
    also a flaming torch used to light
    travellers in dark streets.
19 *you yourselves*: i.e. because (from King
    Henry's point of view) they are fighting
    against their lawful sovereign.
23 *career*: headlong gallop.
24 *bootless*: unrewarding.
    vain: futile.
25 *spoil*: looting.
26 *precepts*: written summons; the word is
    stressed on the second syllable.
    the Leviathan: the whale; its massive
    strength was described for the
    Elizabethans in the Book of Job chap. 41.
30 *grace*: human kindness.
31 *filthy . . . clouds*: i.e. the storm and
    smoke of battle.
32 *heady*: intoxicating.
33 *look*: expect.
34 *blind*: reckless.
    bloody: bloodthirsty.
35 *Defile the locks*: tear the hair, *and also*
    ravish the chastity.
38 *spitted*: pierced on spits (like roasting
    pigs).

And the flesh'd soldier, rough and hard of heart,
In liberty of bloody hand shall range
With conscience wide as hell, mowing like grass
Your fresh fair virgins and your flowering infants.
15 What is it then to me if impious war,
Array'd in flames like to the prince of fiends,
Do with his smirch'd complexion all fell feats
Enlink'd to waste and desolation?
What is't to me, when you yourselves are cause,
20 If your pure maidens fall into the hand
Of hot and forcing violation?
What rein can hold licentious wickedness
When down the hill he holds his fierce career?
We may as bootless spend our vain command
25 Upon th'enraged soldiers in their spoil
As send precepts to the Leviathan
To come ashore. Therefore, you men of Harfleur,
Take pity of your town and of your people
Whiles yet my soldiers are in my command,
30 Whiles yet the cool and temperate wind of grace
O'erblows the filthy and contagious clouds
Of heady murder, spoil and villainy.
If not, why, in a moment look to see
The blind and bloody soldier with foul hand
35 Defile the locks of your shrill-shrieking daughters,
Your fathers taken by the silver beards,
And their most reverend heads dash'd to the walls,
Your naked infants spitted upon pikes

40-1 *wives . . . slaughtermen*: Jewish
mothers were wild with grief when
Herod (the King of Israel—'Jewry'),
hearing of the birth of Jesus Christ,
commanded the slaughter of all male
babies (see Matthew 2: 16–18).

43 *in defence*: because you are defending
the city from its rightful king.

43s.d. *above*: i.e. on the stage balcony,
representing the city walls.

Whiles the mad mothers with their howls confus'd
40 Do break the clouds, as did the wives of Jewry
At Herod's bloody-hunting slaughtermen.
What say you? Will you yield, and this avoid?
Or guilty in defence be thus destroy'd?

Enter Governor *above*

Governor
Our expectation hath this day an end.

45 *of succours*: for aid.

46 *Returns us*: sends back the reply.
yet not: still not.

45 The Dauphin, whom of succours we entreated,
Returns us that his powers are yet not ready
To raise so great a siege. Therefore, great king,
We yield our town and lives to thy soft mercy.
Enter our gates, dispose of us and ours,
50 For we no longer are defensible.

50 *defensible*: capable of being defended.

King
Open your gates. Come, uncle Exeter,
                                                    [*Exit* Governor *above*
Go you and enter Harfleur. There remain
And fortify it strongly 'gainst the French.
Use mercy to them all. For us, dear uncle,

54 *Use mercy*: show mercy; according to
Holinshed, the town was cruelly sacked.

55   *sickness*: The English army was suffering badly from dysentery.

58   *address'd*: prepared.
58s.d. *Flourish*: The trumpets herald the king's entry into Harfleur.

55 The winter coming on, and sickness growing
Upon our soldiers, we will retire to Calais.
Tonight in Harfleur we will be your guest,
Tomorrow for the march we are address'd.

[*Flourish, and enter the town*

Act 3   Scene 5

A scene of quiet comedy follows the bloody violence threatened outside Harfleur as Princess Katherine takes her first lesson in English.

1–2 *tu . . . langage*: you have been in England and you speak the language well.
3   *Un peu*: a little.
4–5 *Je te . . . anglais*: I beg you, teach me; I've got to learn to speak it. How do you say 'hand' in English?

6   *Elle est appelée de hand*: It is called *de hand*.

7   *Et les doigts*: And the 'fingers'?

8–10 *Les . . . fingres*: The 'fingers'? Oh my word, I forgot 'fingers', but I'll remember, the 'fingers'. I think they are called *de fingres*. Yes, *de fingres*.

11–13 *Je . . . ongles*: I think I'm a good pupil. I have learned two words of English very quickly. What do you call the 'nails'?

14 *nous . . . nails*: we call them '*de nails*'.

15 *Ecoutez . . . bien*: Listen! Tell me if I speak correctly.

17 *C'est . . . anglais*: That's well spoken, madam. It is very good English.

Scene 5

Enter Katherine *and* Alice, *an old gentlewoman*

Katherine
Alice, tu as été en Angleterre, et tu bien parles le langage.
Alice
Un peu, madame.
Katherine
Je te prie, m'enseignez. Il faut que j'apprenne à
5 parler. Comment appelez-vous la main en anglais?
Alice
La main. Elle est appelée *de hand*.
Katherine
De hand. Et les doigts?
Alice
Les doigts, ma foi, j'ai oublié les doigts, mais je me souviendrai les doigts. Je pense qu'ils sont appelés *de*
10 *fingres*. Oui, *de fingres*.
Katherine
La main, *de hand*. Les doigts, les *fingres*. Je pense que je suis le bon écolier. J'ai gagné deux mots d'anglais vitement. Comment appelez-vous les ongles?
Alice
Les ongles, nous les appelons *de nails*.
Katherine
15 *De nails*. Écoutez! Dites-moi si je parle bien: *de hand, de fingres*, et *de nails*.
Alice
C'est bien dit, madame. Il est fort bon anglais.

18 *Dites . . . bras*: Tell me the English for the 'arm'.

22–3 *Je m'en fais . . . présent*: I'm going to repeat all the words that you have taught me so far.

24 *Il est . . . pense*: It's too difficult, madam, I think.

25 *Excusez-moi*: not at all.
Écoutez: listen.

26 *bilbow*: The bilbow was a short sword, or a bar shackling the legs of prisoners.

28 *O Seigneur Dieu*: oh good heavens.
je m'en oublié: I have forgotten.

28–9 *Comment . . . le col*: What do you call the 'neck'. Both *nick* and *cul* were slang names for the vulva.

34–5 *Sauf . . . d'Angleterre*: If it please your honour, you really do pronounce the words just as well as the natives of England.

36–7 *Je . . . temps*: I've no doubt I shall be able to learn it with God's help, and very quickly.

38–9 *N'avez . . . enseigné*: Haven't you already forgotten what I have taught you?

40 *Non . . . promptement*: No, I'll recite it to you straightaway.

Katherine

Dites-moi l'anglais pour le bras.

Alice

De arm, madame.

Katherine

20 Et le coude.

Alice

D'elbow.

Katherine

D'elbow. Je m'en fais la répétition de tous les mots que vous m'avez appris dès à présent.

Alice

Il est trop difficile, madame, comme je pense.

Katherine

25 Excusez-moi, Alice. Écoutez, *d'hand, de fingres, de nails, d'arma, de bilbow.*

Alice

D'elbow, madame.

Katherine

O Seigneur Dieu, je m'en oublié *d'elbow*! Comment appelez-vous le col?

Alice

30 *De nick*, madame.

Katherine

De nick. Et le menton?

Alice

De chin.

Katherine

De sin. Le col, *de nick.* Le menton, *de sin.*

Alice

Oui. Sauf votre honneur, en vérité vous prononcez
35 les mots aussi droit que les natifs d'Angleterre.

Katherine

Je ne doute point d'apprendre, par la grâce de Dieu,
et en peu de temps.

Alice

N'avez-vous pas déjà oublié ce que je vous ai
enseigné?

Katherine

40 Non, et je réciterai à vous promptement: *d'hand, de
fingre, de mailés*—

44 *Sauf votre honneur*: If it please your
    honour.

45 *Ainsi dis-je*: That's what I said.

48 Katherine hears Alice's words as the
    French *foutre* (= to fuck) and *con*
    (= cunt).
48–54 *ils sont . . . ensemble*: these words
    sound wicked, corrupting, obscene and
    rude, and not to be spoken by ladies of
    honour. I would not like to utter these
    words in front of French gentlemen for
    all the world. Ugh! the 'foot' and the
    'count'! All the same, I will recite my
    lesson once more, altogether.

57 *C'est . . . dîner*: That's enough for one
    time. Let's go in to dinner.

Alice

De nails, madame.

Katherine

De nails, de arma, de ilbow—

Alice

Sauf votre honneur, *de elbow.*

Katherine

45 Ainsi dis-je. *D'elbow, de nick,* et *de sin.* Comment
    appelez-vous les pieds et la robe?

Alice

De foot, madame, et *de count.*

Katherine

De foot et *de count?* O Seigneur Dieu, ils sont les mots
    de son mauvais, corruptible, gros et impudique, et
50 non pour les dames d'honneur d'user! Je ne voudrais
    prononcer ces mots devant les seigneurs de France
    pour tout le monde! Foh! *De foot* et *de count!*
    Néanmoins, je réciterai une autre fois ma leçon
    ensemble: *de hand, de fingre, de nails, d'arma, d'elbow,*
55 *de nick, de sin, de foot,* le *count.*

Alice

Excellent, madame!

Katherine

C'est assez pour une fois. Allons-nous à dîner.

[*Exeunt*

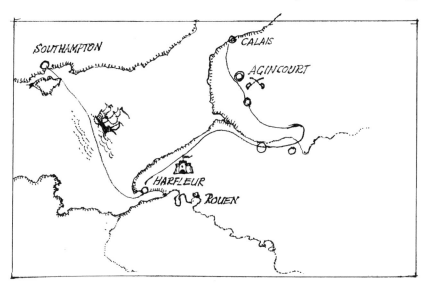

Act 3   Scene 6

The French king, dismayed by the English success at Harfleur, urges his nobles to make greater efforts to expel King Henry from their country.

1 *pass'd the River Somme*: i.e. on the retreat to Calais (see *3, 3, 35*); the river is half-way between Calais and Harfleur—see map above.

2 *And if*: An intensive form of 'if'.
withal: with.

3 *quit*: to give up.

5 *O Dieu vivant*: Oh living God.
sprays of us: of our bastards; the English are descendants—'offshoots'—of the Normans who invaded England in 1066.

6 *The emptying*: that which was emptied out.
luxury: lust.

7 *scions*: sprigs for grafting.
stock: the parent plants on to which the shoots are grafted.

8 *Spurt*: sprout.

9 *overlook*: grow bigger than, dominate.
grafters: plants from which the grafts were originally taken.

Scene 6

Enter the King of France, *the* Dauphin, *the* Constable *of France, the* Duke of Bourbon, *and others*

French King
'Tis certain he hath pass'd the River Somme.
  Constable
And if he be not fought withal, my lord,
Let us not live in France. Let us quit all
And give our vineyards to a barbarous people.
  Dauphin
5 *O Dieu vivant!* Shall a few sprays of us,
The emptying of our fathers' luxury,
Our scions, put in wild and savage stock,
Spurt up so suddenly into the clouds
And overlook their grafters?

11 *Mort de ma vie*: death of my life.
13 *slobbery*: wet and slimy.
14 *nook-shotten*: full of corners—the reference is to England's jagged coastline.
Albion: an old name (deriving from the white—Latin *alba*—cliffs) for the kingdoms of England, Scotland, and Wales.
15 *Dieu de batailles*: God of battles.
have . . . mettle: do they get this spirit.
17 *as in despite*: as though in scorn.
18–19 *sodden . . . broth*: The Constable scorns the English beer as being no stronger than boiled water, suitable only as a medicine for over-ridden horses.
20 *Decoct*: infuse, warm up.
21 *quick*: lively.
23 *roping*: hanging down.
25 *drops of gallant youth*: i.e. the blood shed in fighting.
26 *'Poor' . . . lords*: we should call our land poor, not rich, because its nobles are so feeble.
28 *madams*: fashionable ladies.
29 *bred out*: exhausted.
31 *new-store*: restock.
32 *bid us . . . dancing-schools*: tell us to become dancing-teachers to the English.
33 *lavoltas*: dances with jumping and leaping steps.
corantos: dances with swift running steps.
34 *grace*: elegant movement, skill.
heels: dancing, *and* running away.
35 *lofty runaways*: high born (*or* accomplished, high leaping) deserters.

Bourbon

10 Normans, but bastard Normans, Norman bastards!
Mort de ma vie, if they march along
Unfought withal, but I will sell my dukedom
To buy a slobbery and a dirty farm
In that nook-shotten isle of Albion.

Constable

15 *Dieu de batailles*, where have they this mettle?
Is not their climate foggy, raw and dull,
On whom, as in despite, the sun looks pale,
Killing their fruit with frowns? Can sodden water,
A drench for sur-reined jades, their barley-broth,
20 Decoct their cold blood to such valiant heat?
And shall our quick blood, spirited with wine,
Seem frosty? Oh, for honour of our land
Let us not hang like roping icicles
Upon our houses' thatch whiles a more frosty people
25 Sweat drops of gallant youth in our rich fields!
'Poor' may we call them, in their native lords!

Dauphin

By faith and honour,
Our madams mock at us and plainly say
Our mettle is bred out, and they will give
30 Their bodies to the lust of English youth
To new-store France with bastard warriors.

Bourbon

They bid us to the English dancing-schools,
And teach lavoltas high and swift corantos,
Saying our grace is only in our heels,
35 And that we are most lofty runaways.

French King
Where is Montjoy the herald? Speed him hence,
Let him greet England with our sharp defiance.
Up, princes, and with spirit of honour edg'd
More sharper than your swords hie to the field.
40 Charles Delabret, High Constable of France,
You Dukes of Orléans, Bourbon and of Berri,
Alençon, Brabant, Bar and Burgundy,
Jacques Châtillon, Rambures, Vaudemont,
Beaumont, Grandpré, Roussi and Fauconbridge,
45 Foix, Lestrelles, Boucicault and Charolais,
High dukes, great princes, barons, lords and
    knights,
For your great seats, now quit you of great shames.
Bar Harry England that sweeps through our land
With pennons painted in the blood of Harfleur.
50 Rush on his host as doth the melted snow
Upon the valleys, whose low vassal seat
The Alps doth spit and void his rheum upon.
Go down upon him. You have power enough,
And in a captive chariot into Rouen
55 Bring him our prisoner.
Constable
                    This becomes the great.
Sorry am I his numbers are so few,
His soldiers sick, and famish'd in their march,
For I am sure when he shall see our army
He'll drop his heart into the sink of fear
60 And for achievement offer us his ransom.
French King
Therefore, Lord Constable, haste on Montjoy,
And let him say to England that we send
To know what willing ransom he will give.
Prince Dauphin, you shall stay with us in Rouen.
Dauphin
65 Not so, I do beseech your majesty.
French King
Be patient, for you shall remain with us.
Now forth, Lord Constable and princes all,
And quickly bring us word of England's fall.
                                    [*Exeunt*

39 *hie*: go quickly.
40–5 These names, all except Berri and
    Charolais, are from Holinshed's list of
    those slain at Agincourt.
47 *For*: for the sake of.
    seats: positions, family-seats.
    quit you of: clear yourselves of.
48 *Bar*: block the path of.
    Harry England: Henry king of England.
49 *pennons*: streamers carried on cavalry
    lances.

50 *host*: army.
51 *vassal*: servile.
52 *The Alps . . . rheum*: The king describes
    an avalanche of white snow from the
    Alps (spoken of as a single mountain).
    void: empty.
    rheum: phlegm.
54 *captive chariot*: i.e. a triumphal chariot
    designed to show off the captive.
55 *becomes*: is appropriate for.
59 *sink*: pit.
60 *for achievement*: to settle the business
    (rather than engage in honourable
    encounter).
61 *haste on*: hasten, tell him to hurry.
63 *know*: learn.
    willing . . . give: he is willing to give.
66 *shall*: must.

Act 3   Scene 7

Llewellyn has been at the battle-front and
can report the successful capture of a
strategic bridge. But Bardolph has got
himself into serious trouble, and Pistol
pleads for his life. Llewellyn is unmoved: the
disciplines of war must be maintained. King
Henry supports Llewellyn. Montjoy brings a
message from the French king which is both
boastful and threatening. Henry hears with
patience, and returns a courteous but defiant
answer.

2   *the bridge*: A detachment of English
     soldiers was sent ahead to capture the
     bridge over the Ternoise at Blangy; the
     main army crossed over on 24 October,
     the night before the battle of Agincourt.
3   *services*: exploits.
5   *Exeter*: According to the historians, he
     was not at the bridge—but Shakespeare
     has work for him in this scene!
6   *magnanimous*: great in heart.
7   *Agamemnon*: the leader of the Greek
     expedition in the Trojan war.
11   *woreld*: world—an attempt to indicate
     Welsh pronunciation.
     keeps: is in control of.
12   *anchient lieutenant*: ensign (= first, or
     sub-) lieutenant.
14   *Mark Antony*: The Roman hero, friend
     of Julius Caesar; Llewellyn seems to
     have forgotten his earlier encounter
     with Pistol (*Act 3*, Scene 2).
15   *estimation*: reputation.

26   *buxom*: sturdy.

Scene 7

> *Enter* Captains, *English and Welsh,* [Gower
> *and* Llewellyn]

Gower
How now, Captain Llewellyn, come you from the
bridge?

Llewellyn
I assure you there is very excellent service
committed at the bridge.

Gower
5 Is the Duke of Exeter safe?

Llewellyn
The Duke of Exeter is as magnanimous as
Agamemnon, and a man that I love and honour
with my soul, and my heart, and my duty, and my
life, and my living, and my uttermost power. He is
10 not, God be praised and blessed, any hurt in the
woreld, but keeps the pridge most valiantly with
excellent discipline. There is an anchient lieutenant
there at the pridge. I think in my very conscience he
is as valiant a man as Mark Antony, and he is a man
15 of no estimation in the world, but I did see him do
as gallant service.

Gower
What do you call him?

Llewellyn
He is called Anchient Pistol.

Gower
I know him not.

> *Enter* Pistol

Llewellyn
20 Here is the man.

Pistol
Captain, I thee beseech to do me favours. The Duke
of Exeter doth love thee well.

Llewellyn
Ay, I praise God, and I have merited some love at his
hands.

Pistol
25 Bardolph, a soldier firm and sound of heart, and of
buxom valour, hath by cruel fate and gidd

27 *Fortune's . . . wheel*: Pistol confuses two icons of the blind goddess: in one she holds a wheel, and in the other she balances precariously on a rolling stone. Llewellyn expounds the iconography in lines 29–35.
furious: cruel.

37 *moral*: message, emblem.
38 *Fortune . . . him*: Pistol paraphrases a popular song, 'Fortune my foe, why dost thou frown on me?'.
39 *pax*: a small metal plate with a crucifix impressed on it, which was kissed by the communicants at mass.
a: he.
40 *dog*: Dogs and cats were regularly hanged for misdemeanours.
41 *hemp*: the hangman's rope.
42 *given . . . death*: The king had decreed that any man caught stealing from a church should be hanged immediately.
44 *vital thread*: thread of life which (in classical mythology) was cut by one of the three Fates.
45 *vile reproach*: reproach of being despicable.
46 *requite*: repay.
47 *partly understand*: Llewellyn understands that he is being offered a bribe.

53 *used*: maintained.

Fortune's furious fickle wheel, that goddess blind
that stands upon the rolling restless stone—
Llewellyn
By your patience, Anchient Pistol, Fortune is
30 painted plind, with a muffler afore her eyes to signify
to you that Fortune is plind. And she is painted also
with a wheel to signify to you, which is the moral of
it, that she is turning and inconstant and mutability
and variation. And her foot, look you, is fixed upon
35 a spherical stone, which rolls and rolls and rolls. In
good truth, the poet makes a most excellent
description of it. Fortune is an excellent moral.
Pistol
Fortune is Bardolph's foe, and frowns on him. For
he hath stolen a pax, and hanged must a be. A
40 damned death! Let gallows gape for dog, let man go
free, and let not hemp his windpipe suffocate! But
Exeter hath given the doom of death, for pax of little
price. Therefore go speak. The duke will hear thy
voice, and let not Bardolph's vital thread be cut with
45 edge of penny cord and vile reproach! Speak,
captain, for his life, and I will thee requite.

Llewellyn
Anchient Pistol, I do partly understand your
meaning.
Pistol
Why then, rejoice therefore.
Llewellyn
50 Certainly, anchient, it is not a thing to rejoice at. For
if, look you, he were my brother I would desire the
duke to use his good pleasure and put him to
execution. For discipline ought to be used.

54 *fico*: a term of contemptuous dismissal, usually accompanied by an obscene gesture in which the thumb was thrust between two fingers, or into the mouth.

56 *fig of Spain*: a more emphatic insult.

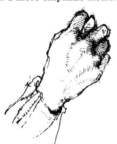

58 *arrant*: utter.
    counterfeit: cheating.
59 *bawd*: brothel-keeper.
    cutpurse: petty thief, pickpocket.
60 *prave words*: Llewellyn has been deceived by the bombast of Pistol's language.
63 *when time is serve*: Llewellyn will be revenged at some opportune moment.
64 *gull*: stupid oaf.
65 *grace*: dignify.
67 *perfect . . . names*: know the names of all senior officers.
68 *learn you by rote*: learn by heart from themselves; the 'you' is merely intensive.
68–9 *services were done*: there was action.
69 *sconce*: fortification.
70 *convoy*: military escort.
    came off bravely: acquitted himself well.
71 *terms*: conditions for surrender.
71–2 *stood on*: accepted.
72 *con*: study.
    the phrase of war: military language.
73 *trick up*: dress up, embellish.
    new-tuned: freshly-coined.
74 *of the general's cut*: trimmed in the same fashion of the general's beard.
74–5 *horrid suit of the camp*: fearsome battle-dress.
77 *slanders of the age*: those who bring disgrace on their times.
80 *make show*: pretend.
81 *find . . . coat*: A proverbial expression meaning 'find a weak spot', 'take him at a disadvantage'.
82s.d. *within*: off-stage.
84 *from*: about.

Pistol
Die and be damned, and *fico* for thy friendship!
    Llewellyn
55 It is well.
    Pistol
The fig of Spain!   [*Exi*
    Llewellyn
Very good.
    Gower
Why, this is an arrant counterfeit rascal. I remember
him now: a bawd, a cutpurse.
    Llewellyn
60 I'll assure you, a uttered as prave words at the pridge
as you shall see in a summer's day. But it is very well.
What he has spoke to me, that is well, I warrant you,
when time is serve.
    Gower
Why, 'tis a gull, a fool, a rogue, that now and then
65 goes to the wars, to grace himself at his return into
London under the form of a soldier. And such
fellows are perfect in the great commanders' names,
and they will learn you by rote where services were
done—at such and such a sconce, at such a breach,
70 at such a convoy; who came off bravely, who was
shot, who disgraced, what terms the enemy stood
on. And this they con perfectly in the phrase of war,
which they trick up with new-tuned oaths. And what
a beard of the general's cut and a horrid suit of the
75 camp will do among foaming bottles and ale-washed
wits is wonderful to be thought on. But you must
learn to know such slanders of the age, or else you
may be marvellously mistook.
    Llewellyn
I tell you what, Captain Gower: I do perceive he is
80 not the man that he would gladly make show to the
woreld he is. If I find a hole in his coat I will tell him
my mind.

A drum within

Hark you, the king is coming, and I must speak with
him from the pridge.

84s.d. *colours*: banners, heading the royal
  procession.
90 *passages*: i.e. of arms, fighting.
  was have: did have.
95 *perdition*: losses.
97 *never a man*: not a single man.
  like: likely.
99 *bubuckles*: Llewellyn conflates 'bubo' (=
  abscess) and 'carbukles' (= carbuncles).
100 *whelks*: pimples.
100–1 *lips . . . nose*: i.e. his lips protruded
  under his nose.
102–3 *nose is executed*: A thief's nose was slit
  before he was executed.
103 *his*: its.
105–8 *give . . . language*: The sentence is
  repeated exactly from Holinshed and
  Hall.
105 *express charge*: specific orders.
106 *compelled*: extorted.
108 *upbraided*: reviled.
109 *play*: i.e. with dice.
110 *gamester*: gambler.
110s.d. *Tucket*: trumpet-call.
  Montjoy: the name given to the chief
  herald of France.

111 *habit*: uniform: the herald wore a tabard
  emblazoned with the arms of the
  authority he represented. Montjoy's
  address is curt—almost insolent—and
  King Henry replies in the same manner.
112 *know of*: learn from.

Drum and colours. Enter the King,
Gloucester *and his poor soldiers*

Llewellyn
85 God pless your majesty.
King
How now, Llewellyn? Camest thou from the bridge?
Llewellyn
Ay, so please your majesty. The Duke of Exeter has
very gallantly maintained the pridge. The French is
gone off, look you, and there is gallant and most
90 prave passages. Marry, th'athversary was have
possession of the pridge, but he is enforced to retire,
and the Duke of Exeter is master of the pridge. I
can tell your majesty, the duke is a prave man.
King
What men have you lost, Llewellyn?
Llewellyn
95 The perdition of th'athversary hath been very great,
reasonable great. Marry, for my part I think the duke
hath lost never a man, but one that is like to be
executed for robbing a church, one Bardolph, if your
majesty know the man. His face is all bubuckles and
100 whelks, and knobs, and flames o'fire, and his lips
blows at his nose, and it is like a coal of fire,
sometimes plue and sometimes red. But his nose is
executed and his fire's out.
King
We would have all such offenders so cut off, and we
105 give express charge that in our marches through the
country there be nothing compelled from the
villages, nothing taken but paid for, none of the
French upbraided or abused in disdainful language.
For when lenity and cruelty play for a kingdom, the
110 gentler gamester is the soonest winner.

Tucket. Enter Montjoy

Montjoy
You know me by my habit.
King
Well then, I know thee. What shall I know of thee?
Montjoy
My master's mind.

117 *Advantage*: seizing the right opportunity.

119 *bruise an injury*: squeeze an abscess.
120 *speak upon our cue*: i.e. like an actor.
121 *England*: the king of England.
122 *admire our sufferance*: wonder at our patience.
123 *consider of*: think about.
124 *proportion*: balance.
125 *digested*: endured.
125–6 *in weight . . . re-answer*: to make complete compensation.
126 *pettiness*: meagre strength.
127 *exchequer*: entire wealth.
128 *effusion*: pouring out.
     muster: whole roll-call of soldiers.

132 *betrayed*: The subject of a king's responsibility for his soldiers is debated in *Act 4*, Scene 1.
133 *condemnation*: who are condemned to death.
134 *office*: duty as herald.
135 *quality*: professional ability.

139 *could be willing*: would like to.
140 *impeachment*: hindrance.
     say the sooth: tell you the truth.
142 *of craft and vantage*: who is cunning and who has superior strength.

147–8 *upon . . . Frenchmen*: i.e. one Englishman was equal to three Frenchmen.
149 *brag*: boast.
     air: weather; the French were conventionally regarded as braggarts (and cowards). There is also a pun on 'heir' (to the throne)—i.e. the Dauphin.

King
Unfold it.

Montjoy

115 Thus says my king: 'Say thou to Harry of England,
though we seemed dead, we did but sleep.
Advantage is a better soldier than rashness. Tell him
we could have rebuked him at Harfleur, but that we
thought not good to bruise an injury till it were full

120 ripe. Now we speak upon our cue, and our voice is
imperial. England shall repent his folly, see his
weakness and admire our sufferance. Bid him
therefore consider of his ransom, which must
proportion the losses we have borne, the subjects we

125 have lost, the disgrace we have digested, which in
weight to re-answer, his pettiness would bow under.
For our losses, his exchequer is too poor. For
th'effusion of our blood, the muster of his kingdom
too faint a number. And for our disgrace, his own

130 person kneeling at our feet but a weak and worthless
satisfaction. To this add defiance, and tell him for
conclusion, he hath betrayed his followers, whose
condemnation is pronounced.' So far my king and
master, so much my office.

King

135 What is thy name? I know thy quality.

Montjoy
Montjoy.

King
Thou dost thy office fairly. Turn thee back
And tell thy king I do not seek him now,
But could be willing to march on to Calais

140 Without impeachment. For to say the sooth,
Though 'tis no wisdom to confess so much
Unto an enemy of craft and vantage,
My people are with sickness much enfeebled,
My numbers lessen'd, and those few I have

145 Almost no better than so many French,
Who when they were in health, I tell thee, herald,
I thought upon one pair of English legs
Did march three Frenchmen. Yet forgive me, God,
That I do brag thus. This your air of France

150 Hath blown that vice in me. I must repent.

152 *this . . . trunk*: his body (and not a
     trunk full of treasure).

155 *France himself*: the king of France.

156 *There's for thy labour*: Both Holinshed
     and Hall report that Henry gave the
     herald a generous reward.

157–60 Holinshed used the same words: 'yet
     I wish not any of you so unadvised as to
     be the occasion that I dye your tawny
     ground with your red blood'.

157 *well advise himself*: take good warning.

162 *would not*: do not want to.

166 *come upon*: attack.

Go therefore, tell thy master here I am.
My ransom is this frail and worthless trunk,
My army but a weak and sickly guard.
Yet, God before, tell him we will come on
155 Though France himself and such another
        neighbour
Stand in our way. There's for thy labour, Montjoy.
Go, bid thy master well advise himself.
If we may pass, we will. If we be hinder'd,
We shall your tawny ground with your red blood
160 Discolour. And so, Montjoy, fare you well.
The sum of all our answer is but this:
We would not seek a battle as we are,
Nor as we are we say we will not shun it.
So tell your master.
       Montjoy
165 I shall deliver so. Thanks to your highness.   [*Exit*
       Gloucester
I hope they will not come upon us now.
       King
We are in God's hand, brother, not in theirs.
March to the bridge. It now draws toward night.
Beyond the river we'll encamp ourselves,
170 And on tomorrow. Bid them march away.
                                            [*Exeunt*

Act 3   Scene 8

The French lords are impatient as they wait for the dawn, when battle can commence. The Lord Bourbon has extravagant praise for his horse, and the other lords tease him about his rhapsodies. Bourbon departs to get his armour, leaving the other lords to joke idly until a messenger brings news of the English approach.

os.d. *Bourbon*: In the Folio text it is the Dauphin who enters now and who speaks the lines here assigned to Bourbon, *but* in historical fact the Dauphin was not present at the battle of Agincourt, and in *Act 3*, Scene 5 of the play Shakespeare's character was expressly ordered to remain in Rouen.

1   *armour*: suit of armour.

4   *his due*: the credit he deserves (compare the saying, 'Give the devil his due').

9   *provided of*: equipped with.

11–42 Bourbon's speech is in the form of an exercise in rhetoric which takes a theme—here, 'my horse'—and develops it with variations (as in music) which include references, quotations, and illustrations. A comparable description of a warhorse is in the Bible, Job 39: 19–25.

12   *pasterns*: the part of a horse's leg between the fetlock and the hoof. *Ch'ha*: Bourbon imitates his horse's neigh; see Job 39:25, 'he saith among the trumpets, "Ha ha"'.

13   *as if . . . hairs*: as though he were stuffed with hair (like a tennis ball).

14   *Pegasus*: the flying horse ('*le cheval volant*') of Greek mythology. When Perseus cut off the head of the Gorgon Medusa, Pegasus rose up from the monster's blood. The horse's hoof, striking the earth, caused Hippocrene (the fountain of the Muses and source of all poetic inspiration) to spring up on Mount Helicon.
qui a les narines de feu: which has nostrils of fire: see Job 39:20, 'the glory of his nostrils is terrible'.

15–16 *trots the air*: trots on air.

17   *basest horn*: lowest part of *both* the hoof *and* the hunting-horn.

18   *Hermes*: the Greek god who invented the lyre and the reed pipe.

Scene 8

Enter the Constable *of France, the* Lord Rambures, Orléans, Bourbon, *with others*

Constable

Tut, I have the best armour of the world! Would it were day.

Orléans

You have an excellent armour, but let my horse have his due.

Constable

5   It is the best horse of Europe.

Orléans

Will it never be morning?

Bourbon

My lord of Orléans, and my lord High Constable, you talk of horse and armour?

Orléans

You are as well provided of both as any prince in the
10 world.

Bourbon

What a long night is this! I will not change my horse with any that treads but on four pasterns. *Ch'ha!* He bounds from the earth as if his entrails were hairs— *le cheval volant*, the Pegasus, *qui a les narines de feu*.

15 When I bestride him I soar, I am a hawk! He trots the air. The earth sings when he touches it. The basest horn of his hoof is more musical than the pipe of Hermes.

19 *nutmeg*: i.e. mid-brown. Orléans seems to offer a criticism of the horse, since it was commonly believed that colour was an indication of temperament—which was determined in every creature by the mixture of the four elements, earth, air, fire, and water.

24 *jades*: poor nags.
25 *beasts*: i.e. not worthy of the name of 'horse'.
26 *absolute*: perfect.

28 *palfreys*: A 'poetic' word for the horses ridden by heroic knights in chivalric romance.

32–3 *rising . . . lamb*: morning until night.
33 *vary*: speak variations on a theme (as he himself is now doing).
34 *fluent*: flowing, eloquent.
35 *Turn . . . tongues*: i.e. if there were as many orators as the sands of the sea.
36 *argument*: subject matter.
   subject: theme, *and* subordinate.
37 *reason*: discourse.
39 *particular*: individual.
40 *writ*: wrote.

44 *courser*: horse ('poetic').

45 *bears well*: carries the rider *and* (of a female) breeds.
46 *prescript*: prescribed.
47 *particular*: belonging to one man only.
48 *shrewdly*: sharply, like a shrew (= a nagging woman; shrews could be punished with bridles to keep their mouths closed).

Orléans
He's of the colour of the nutmeg.
Bourbon
20 And of the heat of the ginger. It is a beast for Perseus. He is pure air and fire, and the dull elements of earth and water never appear in him but only in patient stillness while his rider mounts him. He is indeed a horse, and all other jades you may call
25 beasts.
Constable
Indeed, my lord, it is a most absolute and excellent horse.
Bourbon
It is the prince of palfreys. His neigh is like the bidding of a monarch, and his countenance enforces
30 homage.
Orléans
No more, cousin.
Bourbon
Nay, the man hath no wit that cannot from the rising of the lark to the lodging of the lamb vary deserved praise on my palfrey. It is a theme as fluent as the
35 sea. Turn the sands into eloquent tongues and my horse is argument for them all. 'Tis a subject for a sovereign to reason on, and for a sovereign's sovereign to ride on, and for the world, familiar to us and unknown, to lay apart their particular functions
40 and wonder at him. I once writ a sonnet in his praise, and began thus: 'Wonder of nature! . . . '
Orléans
I have heard a sonnet begin so to one's mistress.
Bourbon
Then did they imitate that which I composed to my courser, for my horse is my mistress.
Orléans
45 Your mistress bears well.
Bourbon
Me well, which is the prescript praise and perfection of a good and particular mistress.
Constable
Nay, for methought yesterday your mistress shrewdly shook your back.

Bourbon

50 So perhaps did yours.

Constable

Mine was not bridled.

Bourbon

Oh, then belike she was old and gentle, and you rode like a kern of Ireland, your French hose off, and in your strait strossers.

Constable

55 You have good judgement in horsemanship.

Bourbon

Be warned by me, then. They that ride so and ride not warily fall into foul bogs. I had rather have my horse to my mistress.

Constable

I had as lief have my mistress a jade.

Bourbon

60 I tell thee, Constable, my mistress wears his own hair.

Constable

I could make as true a boast as that, if I had a sow to my mistress.

Bourbon

'Le chien est retourné à son propre vomissement, et la 65 truie lavée au bourbier.' Thou makest use of anything

Constable

Yet do I not use my horse for my mistress, or any such proverb so little kin to the purpose.

Rambures

My lord Constable, the armour that I saw in your tent tonight, are those stars or suns upon it?

Constable

70 Stars, my lord.

Bourbon

Some of them will fall tomorrow, I hope.

Constable

And yet my sky shall not want.

Bourbon

That may be, for you bear a many superfluously, and 'twere more honour some were away.

Constable

75 Even as your horse bears your praises, who would trot as well were some of your brags dismounted.

---

51 *bridled*: i.e. like a horse or shrew.

53 *kern of Ireland*: barefoot Irish peasant soldier.
    French hose: loose-fitting breeches.
54 *strait strossers*: tight trousers, leggings (but Bourbon probably means 'bare-legged').
55 *horsemanship*: The Constable puns on 'whoresmanship'.
57 *foul bogs*: dirty places—in Ireland *and* with whores.

59 *as lief*: would rather.
    jade: female (or horse) of inferior quality.
60–1 *wears his own hair*: Bourbon implies that the Constable's mistress wears a wig, presumably because her own hair has been lost through venereal disease.

64–5 *Le chien . . . bourbier*: 'The dog is turned to his own vomit again, and the sow that was washed to her wallowing in the mire', 2 Peter 2:22.
65 *use*: i.e. sexually.
67 *kin*: related, relevant.

69 *stars or suns*: i.e. as decoration; Rambures tries to change the subject.

72 *want*: be deficient.

73 *a many superfluously*: far many more than you need.
74 *away*: taken off.

76 *brags*: boasts.

77 *would*: I wish.
desert: what he deserves.

80–1 *faced . . . way*: put to shame; *and* turned away.

81–2 *fain . . . English*: would like to get on with fighting the English.

83 *go to hazard*: make a bet.

84 *go . . . hazard*: put yourself in danger.

89 *eat all he kills*: i.e. none of them.

90 *prince*: nobleman.

91 *tread out*: stamp out.

92 *simply*: absolutely.

93 *Doing*: fornicating.
still: always.

Bourbon

Would I were able to load him with his desert. Will it never be day? I will trot tomorrow a mile, and my way shall be paved with English faces.

Constable

80 I will not say so, for fear I should be faced out of my way. But I would it were morning, for I would fain be about the ears of the English.

Rambures

Who will go to hazard with me for twenty prisoners?

Constable

You must first go yourself to hazard, ere you have
85 them.

Bourbon

'Tis midnight. I'll go arm myself.   [*Exit*

Orléans

The Duke of Bourbon longs for morning.

Rambures

He longs to eat the English.

Constable

I think he will eat all he kills.

Orléans

90 By the white hand of my lady, he's a gallant prince.

Constable

Swear by her foot, that she may tread out the oath.

Orléans

He is simply the most active gentleman of France.

Constable

Doing is activity, and he will still be doing.

Orléans

He never did harm that I heard of.

Constable

95 Nor will do none tomorrow. He will keep that good name still.

Orléans

I know him to be valiant.

Constable

I was told that, by one that knows him better than you.

Orléans

100 What's he?

Constable

Marry, he told me so himself, and he said he cared not who knew it.

Orléans

He needs not, it is no hidden virtue in him.

Constable

105 By my faith, sir, but it is. Never anybody saw it but his lackey. 'Tis a hooded valour, and when it appears it will bate.

Orléans

Ill will never said well.

Constable

I will cap that proverb with 'There is flattery in friendship'.

Orléans

110 And I will take up that with 'Give the devil his due'.

Constable

Well placed. There stands your friend for the devil. Have at the very eye of that proverb with 'A pox of the devil'.

Orléans

You are the better at proverbs, by how much 'a fool's 115 bolt is soon shot'.

Constable

You have shot over.

Orléans

'Tis not the first time you were overshot.

Enter a Messenger

Messenger

My lord High Constable, the English lie within fifteen hundred paces of your tents.

Constable

120 Who hath measured the ground?

Messenger

The lord Grandpré.

Constable

A valiant and most expert gentleman. Would it were day! Alas, poor Harry of England! He longs not for the dawning as we do.

---

105 *lackey*: stable-lad (the only one he dared to beat).

105–6 *hooded . . . bate*: The image is from falconry: hawks were blindfolded until the quarry was in sight, and then the hood was removed so that the trained bird would fly in pursuit. But an untrained bird would 'bate' (= flap its wings wildly and ineffectually).

107 *Ill . . . well*: The lords begin a game of swapping proverbs with each other.

111 *placed*: answered.
stands . . . for: stands in the position of.

112 *have at the very eye*: let me aim right at the heart.

115 *bolt*: arrow.

116 *shot over*: missed the target.

117 *overshot*: mistaken, *and* drunk.

119 *fifteen hundred paces*: According to Holinshed, the armies were 250 paces apart (a 'pace' = 75cm or 30 inches).

120 *measured the ground*: estimated the distance.

125 *peevish*: tiresome.

126 *mope*: blunder aimlessly about.
fat-brained: brainless.

128 *apprehension*: understanding,
appreciation of the situation.

132 *headpieces*: helmets; if the English had
any sense, they would not be fighting at
all.

134 *mastiffs*: huge fighting-dogs, comparable
to the modern pit bull-terrier.

135 *winking*: with their eyes shut.

139 *sympathize with*: behave like.
140 *robustious*: wildly energetic.
coming on: attack.

144 *shrewdly*: cruelly.

146 *stomachs*: appetites.
147 *about it*: get on with it.

Orléans

125 What a wretched and peevish fellow is this king of
England, to mope with his fat-brained followers so
far out of his knowledge.

Constable

If the English had any apprehension they would run
away.

Orléans

130 That they lack, for if their heads had any intellectual
armour they could never wear such heavy
headpieces.

Rambures

That island of England breeds very valiant creatures.
Their mastiffs are of unmatchable courage.

Orléans

135 Foolish curs, that run winking into the mouth of a
Russian bear and have their heads crushed like
rotten apples. You may as well say that's a valiant flea
that dare eat his breakfast on the lip of a lion.

Constable

Just, just. And the men do sympathize with the
140 mastiffs in robustious and rough coming on, leaving
their wits with their wives. And then, give them great
meals of beef and iron and steel, they will eat like
wolves and fight like devils.

Orléans

Ay, but these English are shrewdly out of beef.

Constable

145 Then shall we find tomorrow they have only
stomachs to eat and none to fight. Now is it time to
arm. Come, shall we about it?

Orléans

It is now two o'clock. But let me see, by ten
We shall have each a hundred Englishmen!

[*Exeunt*

Act 4

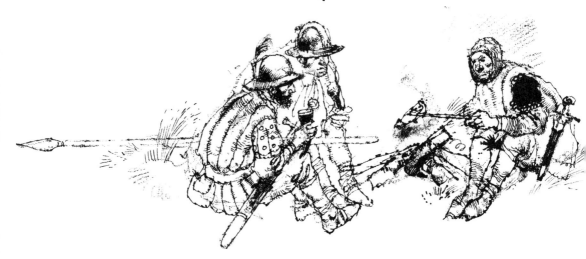

Act 4 Chorus

The Chorus now exhorts the audience to
move, in imagination, from the tent of the
French lords across to the English camp,
where the knights are arming for the next
day's battle. The common soldiers are
waiting restlessly by their camp-fires, and the
figure of the king can be discerned as he goes
from one fire to another.

1 *entertain conjecture*: open your minds to
  the imagination.
2 *creeping . . . dark*: The soldiers are
  creeping and whispering, straining their
  eyes to see in the darkness.
3 *wide vessel*: hollow vault.
4 *foul womb*: Night is personified as a
  witch (line 21) who gives birth to foul
  things—both nightmares, and the next
  day's hideous battle.
5 *either army*: both the armies.
  stilly: quietly *and* constantly—*and also* in
  the still of the night.
6 *fix'd sentinels*: guards who do not leave
  the posts at which they have been
  positioned.
7 *each other's watch*: the other side's
  guard; the night is so silent (and the
  armies so close) that they can hear each
  other.

Enter Chorus

Chorus

Now entertain conjecture of a time
When creeping murmur and the poring dark
Fills the wide vessel of the universe.
From camp to camp, through the foul womb of
    night,
5 The hum of either army stilly sounds,
That the fix'd sentinels almost receive
The secret whispers of each other's watch.
Fire answers fire, and through their paly flames
Each battle sees the other's umber'd face.
10 Steed threatens steed, in high and boastful neighs,
Piercing the night's dull ear. And from the tents
The armourers accomplishing the knights
With busy hammers closing rivets up
Give dreadful note of preparation.
15 The country cocks do crow, the clocks do toll,
And the third hour of drowsy morning name.
Proud of their numbers and secure in soul
The confident and over-lusty French
Do the low-rated English play at dice,
20 And chide the cripple tardy-gaited night
Who like a foul and ugly witch doth limp

8 *answers*: reflects.
  paly: pale and flickering.
9 *battle*: army already drawn up to fight—
  i.e. in battle order.
  umber'd: orange-brown, fire-lit.
11 *dull*: unresponsive.
12 *accomplishing the knights*: fitting the
  knights into their armour.
14 *note*: sound, notice.
17 *secure in soul*: over-confident in their
  minds.
18 *over-lusty*: excessively merry.
19 *low-rated*: despised, under-estimated.
  play: gamble for.
20 *tardy-gaited*: slow-paced.
23 *watchful fires*: watch-fires; it is the
  soldiers who are 'watchful'.
24 *inly*: inwardly.
25 *gesture*: bearing, 'body-language'.
26 *Investing*: pervading.
  lank-lean: drawn and hollow.
28 *so many*: like so many.
  horrid: horrifying.
  who will behold: who wishes to imagine.
30 *watch*: watch-fire.
32 *host*: army.
33 *good morrow*: good morning.
35 *note*: sign.
36 *enrounded*: surrounded.
37–8 *nor . . . night*: and he does not look at
  all pale for this tiring and sleepless
  night.
39 *overbears attaint*: overcomes all physical
  and mental strain.
40 *semblance*: appearance.
  sweet majesty: gracious royal bearing.
43 *A largess . . . sun*: a bounty as generous
  as that of the sun.
45 *mean and gentle*: humble and noble by
  birth.
46 *as . . . define*: what I might humbly
  describe as.
47 *A . . . night*: some little feeling tonight
  of what our king is really like.
48 *our scene*: this stage production.
50 *vile and ragged foils*: crude and blunted
  swords.
51 *Right ill dispos'd*: most clumsily handled.
53 *Minding*: calling to mind, 'entertain[ing]
  conjecture'.
  mockeries: imitations.

So tediously away. The poor condemned English,
Like sacrifices, by their watchful fires
Sit patiently and inly ruminate
25 The morning's danger; and their gesture sad,
Investing lank-lean cheeks and war-worn coats,
Presented them unto the gazing moon
So many horrid ghosts. O now, who will behold
The royal captain of this ruin'd band
30 Walking from watch to watch, from tent to tent?
Let him cry 'Praise and glory on his head!'
For forth he goes and visits all his host,
Bids them good morrow with a modest smile,
And calls them brothers, friends, and countrymen.
35 Upon his royal face there is no note
How dread an army hath enrounded him,
Nor doth he dedicate one jot of colour
Unto the weary and all-watched night,
But freshly looks and overbears attaint
40 With cheerful semblance and sweet majesty,
That every wretch, pining and pale before,
Beholding him, plucks comfort from his looks.
A largess universal like the sun
His liberal eye doth give to everyone,
45 Thawing cold fear, that mean and gentle all
Behold, as may unworthiness define,
'A little touch of Harry in the night'.
And so our scene must to the battle fly,
Where (O for pity!) we shall much disgrace,
50 With four or five most vile and ragged foils
Right ill dispos'd in brawl ridiculous,
The name of Agincourt. Yet sit and see,
Minding true things by what their mockeries be.
                                                    [*Exit*

Act 4   Scene 1

As the Chorus promised, we now see King Henry doing the rounds of the English camp, and speaking (in disguise) to all the different ranks of soldiers. He hears their complaints, and he tries to answer their questions. Finally he remains alone on the stage, meditating on the moral responsibilities of a king.

os.d. *another door*: i.e. from different sides of the stage.
5   *observingly*: by taking notice.
     distil it out: extract it.
6   *stirrers*: risers; the expression was proverbial.
7   *husbandry*: management, economy.
10 *dress . . . end*: get dressed properly for the work we have to do; *and also*, prepare ourselves spiritually to meet our deaths.
11 *gather . . . weed*: find some good in everything: a proverbial saying.
12 *make a moral of*: learn a lesson from.

15 *churlish*: rough, unfriendly.

16 *likes me*: suits me.

18–23 *'Tis . . . legerity*: Probably King Henry keeps these thoughts to himself, speaking them 'aside' to the play's audience.
19 *Upon example so*: with such an example [as Sir Thomas Erpingham].
20 *quickened*: stirred, brought to life.
21 *organs*: bodily functions, limbs.
     defunct: lifeless.
22 *Break . . . grave*: awaken from sleep (as though bursting out of a tomb).
23 *with casted slough*: having shaken off their despondency (like snakes shedding their old skins).
     legerity: quickness, nimbleness.
26 *do my good morrow*: say 'good morning' to them for me.
     anon: shortly.
27 *Desire . . . to*: ask them to come.
     pavilion: tent.

Scene 1

Enter the King *and* Gloucester *and* Bedford *by another door*

King
Gloucester, 'tis true that we are in great danger.
The greater therefore should our courage be.
Good morrow, brother Bedford. God almighty,
There is some soul of goodness in things evil
5 Would men observingly distil it out.
For our bad neighbour makes us early stirrers,
Which is both healthful and good husbandry.
Besides, they are our outward consciences
And preachers to us all, admonishing
10 That we should dress us fairly for our end.
Thus may we gather honey from the weed
And make a moral of the devil himself.

Enter Erpingham

Good morrow, old Sir Thomas Erpingham.
A good soft pillow for that good white head
15 Were better than a churlish turf of France.
Erpingham
Not so, my liege. This lodging likes me better
Since I may say 'now lie I like a king'.
King
'Tis good for men to love their present pains.
Upon example so the spirit is eased,
20 And when the mind is quickened, out of doubt
The organs, though defunct and dead before,
Break up their drowsy grave and newly move
With casted slough and fresh legerity.
Lend me thy cloak, Sir Thomas. Brothers both,
25 Commend me to the princes in our camp.
Do my good morrow to them, and anon
Desire them all to my pavilion.
Gloucester
We shall, my liege.
Erpingham
Shall I attend your grace?
King
                                    No, my good knight.

31   *bosom*: heart.
32   *would*: want.

34   *a*: have.

35   *Qui vous là?*: Pistol's French is not very
        good: he wants to say '*Qui va là?*'
        (= who goes there?).

37   *Discuss*: explain.
37–8 *base, common and popular*: of low
        degree, a common soldier, and an
        ordinary man.
39   *gentleman of a company*: non-
        commissioned officer.
40   *Trail'st . . . pike*: i.e. are you in the
        infantry. The pike ('puissant' =
        powerful) was a wooden staff, at least
        12 feet (4 metres) long, with multi-
        bladed spearhead—see illustration,
        p. 70.
42   *As . . . emperor*: a proverbial
        comparison.

44   *bawcock*: good lad.
45   *imp of fame*: lucky young devil.
46   *heartstring*: bottom of my heart.
47   *lovely bully*: splendid chap.

48   *le roi*: the king.

49   *crew*: mob, crowd.

30   Go with my brothers to my lords of England.
     I and my bosom must debate awhile,
     And then I would no other company.
          Erpingham
     The Lord in heaven bless thee, noble Harry.
                              [*Exeunt all but* King
          King
     God a mercy, old heart, thou speak'st cheerfully.

                    Enter Pistol

          Pistol
35   *Qui vous là?*
          King
     A friend.
          Pistol
     Discuss unto me, art thou officer, or art thou base,
     common and popular?
          King
     I am a gentleman of a company.
          Pistol
40   Trail'st thou the puissant pike?
          King
     Even so. What are you?
          Pistol
     As good a gentleman as the emperor.
          King
     Then you are better than the king.
          Pistol
     The king's a bawcock and a heart of gold, a lad of
45   life, an imp of fame, of parents good, of fist most
     valiant. I kiss his dirty shoe, and from heartstring I
     love the lovely bully. What is thy name?
          King
     Harry *le roi*.
          Pistol
     Leroy? A Cornish name. Art thou of Cornish crew?
          King
50   No, I am a Welshman.
          Pistol
     Knowest thou Llewellyn?
          King
     Yes.

53 *leek*: the emblem of Wales, worn (and
    eaten) by all Welshmen on St David's
    Day, 1st March.
    pate: head.

59 *The fico*: a term of contemptuous
    dismissal; see *3, 7, 54 note*.

62 *sorts*: fits.

63s.d. *separate doors*: different sides of the
        stage.

64 *speak fewer*: don't talk so loud.
65 *admiration*: amazing thing.
66 *ancient prerogatives*: traditional rights.

68 *Pompey the Great*: A distinguished
    Roman general (d. 48 BC).
69–70 *tiddle taddle . . . pibble babble*:
       chattering and babbling.

72 *sobriety*: seriousness.
73 *modesty*: decency.

75–6 *prating coxcomb*: prattling idiot.
76 *meet*: right, suitable.

Pistol

Tell him I'll knock his leek about his pate upon St
Davy's day.

King

55 Do not you wear your dagger in your cap that day,
lest he knock that about yours.

Pistol

Art thou his friend?

King

And his kinsman too.

Pistol

The *fico* for thee, then.

King

60 I thank you. God be with you.

Pistol

My name is Pistol called.   [*Exit*

King

It sorts well with your fierceness.

> *Enter* Llewellyn *and* Gower *by separate*
> *doors*

Gower

Captain Llewellyn!

Llewellyn

So! In the name of Jesu Christ, speak fewer. It is the
65 greatest admiration in the universal woreld when the
true and ancient prerogatives and laws of the wars is
not kept. If you would take the pains but to examine
the wars of Pompey the Great you shall find, I
warrant you, that there is no tiddle taddle nor pibble
70 pabble in Pompey's camp. I warrant you, you shall
find the ceremonies of the wars, and the cares of it,
and the forms of it, and the sobriety of it, and the
modesty of it, to be otherwise.

Gower

Why, the enemy is loud. You hear him all night.

Llewellyn

75 If the enemy is an ass and a fool and a prating
coxcomb, is it meet, think you, that we should also,
look you, be an ass and a fool and a prating
coxcomb, in your own conscience, now?

Gower

I will speak lower.

Llewellyn

80 I pray you, and beseech you, that you will.

[*Exeunt* Gower *and* Llewellyn

King

Though it appear a little out of fashion,

There is much care and valour in this Welshman.

Enter three soldiers, John Bates, Alexander
Court *and* Michael Williams

Court

Brother John Bates, is not that the morning which
breaks yonder?

Bates

85 I think it be. But we have no great cause to desire
the approach of day.

Williams

We see yonder the beginning of the day, but I think
we shall never see the end of it. Who goes there?

King

A friend.

Williams

90 Under what captain serve you?

King

Under Sir Thomas Erpingham.

Williams

A good old commander, and a most kind gentleman.
I pray you, what thinks he of our estate?

King

Even as men wrecked upon a sand, that look to be
95 washed off the next tide.

Bates

He hath not told his thought to the king?

King

No. Nor it is not meet he should. For though I speak
it to you, I think the king is but a man as I am. The
violet smells to him as it doth to me. The element
100 shows to him as it doth to me. All his senses have but
human conditions. His ceremonies laid by, in his
nakedness he appears but a man; and though his
affections are higher mounted than ours, yet when

81   *out of fashion*: old fashioned,
unconventional.

93   *estate*: situation, chances.
94   *wrecked upon a sand*: shipwrecked on a
sandbank.
look: expect.
97–8   *though . . . you*: I'll tell you in
confidence.
99–100   *element shows*: sky appears.
101   *conditions*: qualities.
ceremonies: symbols of royalty.
laid by: set aside, apart.

103   *affections*: emotions.
higher mounted: set on higher things,
soar higher (the metaphor is from
hawking).

104 *stoop*: plunge down, drop (like a hawk).
104 *like*: same.

106 *relish*: taste, appreciation.
107 *possess him with*: put on himself.

112 *I would*: I wish.

113 *at all adventures*: at any price.
      so . . . here: as long as we were out of
      this.
114 *By my troth*: by my word, in truth.
      speak my conscience: say what I really
      believe to be true.

117 *So*: in that way.
118 *a-many*: a lot of.

121–2 *howsoever . . . minds*: whatever you
      may say in order to find out what others
      are thinking.
123–4 *his . . . just*: so long as his legal case is
      sound.

126 *seek after*: enquire into.

131 *heavy . . . make*: a serious charge to
      answer, a big account to settle.
131–3 *when . . . day*: It was believed that on
      the Day of Judgement ('the latter day')
      the dead would rise again, and all lost
      limbs would be re-united with their
      bodies.
137 *rawly left*: unprovided for.
      afeard: afraid.
      die well: i.e. spiritually prepared for
      death.
138 *charitably dispose*: settle in a proper
      Christian manner.

they stoop they stoop with the like wing. Therefore
105 when he sees reason of fears as we do, his fears, out
of doubt, be of the same relish as ours are. Yet in
reason no man should possess him with any
appearance of fear, lest he by showing it should
dishearten his army.

Bates
110 He may show what outward courage he will, but I
believe, as cold a night as 'tis, he could wish himself
in Thames up to the neck. And so I would he were,
and I by him, at all adventures, so we were quit here.

King
By my troth, I will speak my conscience of the king.
115 I think he would not wish himself anywhere but
where he is.

Bates
Then I would he were here alone. So should he be
sure to be ransomed and a-many poor men's lives
saved.

King
120 I dare say you love him not so ill to wish him here
alone, howsoever you speak this to feel other men's
minds. Methinks I could not die anywhere so
contented as in the king's company, his cause being
just and his quarrel honourable.

Williams
125 That's more than we know.

Bates
Ay, or more than we should seek after, for we know
enough if we know we are the king's subjects. If his
cause be wrong our obedience to the king wipes the
crime of it out of us.

Williams
130 But if the cause be not good the king himself hath a
heavy reckoning to make, when all those legs and
arms and heads chopped off in a battle shall join
together at the latter day and cry all 'We died at such
a place', some swearing, some crying for a surgeon,
135 some upon their wives left poor behind them, some
upon the debts they owe, some upon their children
rawly left. I am afeard there are few die well that die
in a battle, for how can they charitably dispose of

139 *blood is their argument*: killing is their business.

142 *proportion of subjection*: rightful duties of a subject.

144 *sinfully miscarry*: die in a state of sin.

145 *imputation of*: blame, responsibility, for.
by your rule: according to your interpretation.

148–9 *in . . . iniquities*: with many unrepented sins.

150 *the author of*: the one responsible for.

152 *answer*: take responsibility for.
particular: individual.

154 *purpose*: intend.

156–7 *arbitrament of swords*: decision by battle.

157 *try*: fight.
unspotted: sinless.

158 *peradventure*: perhaps.

159 *contrived*: plotted, intentional.

160 *beguiling*: cheating.
seals of perjury: promises of marriage.

161 *bulwark*: defence.

162 *gored*: wounded.

163 *defeated*: cheated.

164 *outrun*: run away from.
native punishment: punishment at home, in their native land.

166 *beadle*: policeman, agent of the law.

167 *before-breach*: a previous breach.

168–70 *Where . . . perish*: they ran for life to escape punishment for their crimes, but where they hoped to be safe (i.e. in the army) they were killed.

171 *unprovided*: not spiritually prepared.

173 *visited*: punished.

174 *the king's*: to the king.

175 *his own*: i.e. his own responsibility.

176 *mote*: blemish, stain of sin.

177 *so*: in this way—i.e. purged of all sin.

177–8 *death . . . advantage*: For a Christian, death is the beginning of eternal life: see Philippians 1:21, 'For Christ is to me life, and death is to me advantage'.

178 *lost*: spent.

anything when blood is their argument? Now if these
140 men do not die well it will be a black matter for the
king that led them to it, who to disobey were against
all proportion of subjection.

King

So if a son that is by his father sent about
merchandise do sinfully miscarry upon the sea, the
145 imputation of his wickedness, by your rule, should
be imposed upon his father that sent him. Or if a
servant, under his master's command transporting a
sum of money, be assailed by robbers and die in
many irreconciled iniquities, you may call the
150 business of the master the author of the servant's
damnation. But this is not so. The king is not bound
to answer the particular endings of his soldiers, the
father of his son, nor the master of his servant, for
they purpose not their death when they purpose
155 their services. Besides, there is no king, be his
cause never so spotless, if it come to the arbitrament
of swords can try it out with all unspotted soldiers.
Some, peradventure, have on them the guilt of
premeditated and contrived murder, some of
160 beguiling virgins with the broken seals of perjury,
some, making the wars their bulwark, that have
before gored the gentle bosom of peace with pillage
and robbery. Now, if these men have defeated the
law and outrun native punishment, though they can
165 outstrip men they have no wings to fly from God.
War is His beadle, war is His vengeance, so that here
men are punished for before-breach of the king's
laws in now the king's quarrel. Where they feared the
death they have borne life away, and where they
170 would be safe they perish. Then, if they die
unprovided, no more is the king guilty of their
damnation than he was before guilty of those
impieties for the which they are now visited. Every
subject's duty is the king's, but every subject's soul is
175 his own. Therefore should every soldier in the wars
do as every sick man in his bed, wash every mote out
of his conscience. And dying so, death is to him
advantage; or, not dying, the time was blessedly lost
wherein such preparation was gained. And in him

180 *it were not sin*: it would not be sinful.
181 *free*: generous.

184 *dies ill*: in a state of sin.
    the ill: the sin.

194 *pay him*: make him pay, punish him.
195 *elder gun*: pop-gun, made from
    hollowed-out stick of elder.
    a poor . . . displeasure: the grievance of a
    humble individual.
197 *his face*: i.e. the sun's face.

200 *round*: blunt.

202 *quarrel*: bone of contention.
205 *gage*: pledge, glove thrown down in
    challenge.

206 *bonnet*: cap.
207 *make it*: recognize it as.

---

180 that escapes it were not sin to think that, making
God so free an offer, He let him outlive that day to
see His greatness, and to teach others how they
should prepare.

Williams
'Tis certain, every man that dies ill, the ill upon his
185 own head; the king is not to answer it.

Bates
I do not desire he should answer for me, and yet I
determine to fight lustily for him.

King
I myself heard the king say he would not be
ransomed.

Williams
190 Ay, he said so to make us fight cheerfully, but when
our throats are cut he may be ransomed and we ne'er
the wiser.

King
If I live to see it, I will never trust his word after.

Williams
You pay him then! That's a perilous shot out of an
195 elder gun, that a poor and a private displeasure can
do against a monarch. You may as well go about to
turn the sun to ice with fanning in his face with a
peacock's feather. You'll never trust his word after!
Come, 'tis a foolish saying.

King
200 Your reproof is something too round. I should be
angry with you if the time were convenient.

Williams
Let it be a quarrel between us, if you live.

King
I embrace it.

Williams
How shall I know thee again?

King
205 Give me any gage of thine and I will wear it in my
bonnet. Then, if ever thou darest acknowledge it, I
will make it my quarrel.

Williams
Here's my glove. Give me another of thine.

King
There.

They exchange gloves

Williams
210 This will I also wear in my cap. If ever thou come to
me and say, after tomorrow, 'This is my glove', by
this hand I will take thee a box on the ear.

King
If ever I live to see it, I will challenge it.

Williams
Thou darest as well be hanged.

King
215 Well, I will do it, though I take thee in the king's
company.

Williams
Keep thy word. Fare thee well.

Bates
Be friends, you English fools, be friends! We have
French quarrels enough if you could tell how to
220 reckon.

King
Indeed, the French may lay twenty French crowns to
one they will beat us, for they bear them on their
shoulders. But it is no English treason to cut French
crowns, and tomorrow the king himself will be a
225 clipper.   [*Exeunt* Soldiers
Upon the king! 'Let us our lives, our souls, our
debts, our careful wives, our children and our sins,
lay on the king.'
We must bear all.
230 O hard condition, twin-born with greatness,
Subject to the breath of every fool, whose sense
No more can feel but his own wringing.
What infinite heart's ease must kings neglect
That private men enjoy?
235 And what have kings that privates have not too,
Save ceremony, save general ceremony?
And what art thou, thou idol ceremony?
What kind of god art thou, that suffer'st more
Of mortal griefs than do thy worshippers?
240 What are thy rents? What are thy comings-in?
O ceremony, show me but thy worth!

---

212 *I will take*: I will give.

215 *I take thee*: I find you.

220 *reckon*: count.

221 *lay*: bet.
crowns: heads; *and also* gold coins (*écus*).

224 *crowns*: heads *and* coins; it was a
treasonable act to clip the edges of
English coins (in order to steal the
gold).
225 *clipper*: one of those clipping the French
crowns.
227 *careful*: anxious, full of care.
229–58 The king muses on the difference
between kings and their subjects. He
apostrophizes the 'idol ceremony' (lines
237–248), then addresses himself (lines
248–54), and finally (lines 254–81)
denounces 'ceremony'.
230 *twin-born with*: born the twin of—i.e. an
inevitable accompaniment.
231 *breath*: utterance, words.
sense: understanding, awareness.
232 *his own wringing*: his own stomach-
ache—i.e. only his own pains.
233 *neglect*: renounce, deprive themselves of.
234 *private*: ordinary.
240 *comings-in*: income, benefits.
241 *show me but*: just show me.

242 *Is . . . adoration*: are you nothing more
than adoration.
243 *place*: public position.
degree: social rank.
form: ritual.

248 *great greatness*: King Henry is sarcastic
as he speaks to himself.

251 *blown from adulation*: fanned (*and*
flyblown, corrupted) by flattery.
252 *it*: i.e. the fever.
give place: yield.
flexure and low bending: kneeling and
bowing (by flattering courtiers).
254 *proud dream*: The king addresses
'ceremony' again.
256 *find*: expose, judge.
257 *balm*: holy oil with which the king is
annointed at his coronation.
ball: orb.

259 *intertissued*: interwoven.
260 *farced title*: pompous, long-winded titles
with which the king is addressed.
261 *tide of pomp*: The king envisages grand
ceremonial proceedings as a high tide
whose waves swell up to the cliffs.
267 *distressful bread*: food he has laboured
for.
268 *horrid*: full of horrors; see Chorus 4,
line 4.
269 *lackey*: footman running beside a
chariot.
270 *the eye of Phoebus*: under the gaze of
Phoebus Apollo, the sun-god—i.e. in
the heat of the sun.
271 *Elysium*: the 'heaven' of Greek
mythology, and home of Phoebus the
sun-god.
272 *Hyperion*: the oldest god of the sun: the
peasant is up before sunrise to help the
god harness his horses.

What? Is thy soul of adoration?
Art thou ought else but place, degree and form,
Creating awe and fear in other men,
245 Wherein thou art less happy being fear'd
Than they in fearing?
What drink'st thou oft, instead of homage sweet,
But poison'd flattery? Oh, be sick, great greatness,
And bid thy ceremony give thee cure.
250 Thinkst thou the fiery fever will go out
With titles blown from adulation?
Will it give place to flexure and low bending?
Canst thou, when thou command'st the beggar's
knee,
Command the health of it? No, thou proud dream,
255 That playst so subtly with a king's repose.
I am a king that find thee, and I know
'Tis not the balm, the sceptre and the ball,
The sword, the mace, the crown imperial,
The intertissued robe of gold and pearl,
260 The farced title running 'fore the king,
The throne he sits on, nor the tide of pomp
That beats upon the high shore of this world;
No, not all these, thrice-gorgeous ceremony,
Not all these, laid in bed majestical,
265 Can sleep so soundly as the wretched slave
Who, with a body fill'd and vacant mind,
Gets him to rest, cramm'd with distressful bread;
Never sees horrid night, the child of hell,
But like a lackey from the rise to set
270 Sweats in the eye of Phoebus, and all night
Sleeps in Elysium; next day after dawn
Doth rise and help Hyperion to his horse

And follows so the ever-running year
With profitable labour to his grave.
275 And but for ceremony such a wretch,
Winding up days with toil and nights with sleep,
Had the forehand and vantage of a king.
The slave, a member of the country's peace,
Enjoys it, but in gross brain little wots
280 What watch the king keeps to maintain the peace,
Whose hours the peasant best advantages.

Enter Erpingham

Erpingham
My lord, your nobles, jealous of your absence,
Seek through your camp to find you.
King
Good old knight,
285 Collect them all together at my tent.
I'll be before thee.
Erpingham
I shall do't, my lord.   [*Exit*
King
O God of battles, steel my soldiers' hearts.
Possess them not with fear. Take from them now
290 The sense of reckoning ere th'opposed numbers
Pluck their hearts from them. Not today, O Lord,
Oh, not today, think not upon the fault
My father made in compassing the crown.
I Richard's body have interred new,
295 And on it have bestow'd more contrite tears
Than from it issued forced drops of blood.
Five hundred poor I have in yearly pay
Who twice a day their wither'd hands hold up
Toward heaven to pardon blood. And I have built
300 Two chantries where the sad and solemn priests
Sing still for Richard's soul. More will I do,
Though all that I can do is nothing worth
Since that my penitence comes after all,
Imploring pardon.

276 *Winding up*: completely occupied with.
277 *forehand*: superior hold in wrestling.
   vantage of: advantage over.
278 *member . . . peace*: limb of the body politic, one who shares in the peace of the nation.
279 *gross*: dull, thick.
   wots: knows.
280 *watch*: wakefulness.
281 *best advantages*: gets most benefit from.
282 *jealous of*: worried about.

288 *steel*: harden, strengthen.
289 *possess . . . fear*: do not let them be afraid.
290 *reckoning*: counting, adding up.
   opposed numbers: numbers of soldiers on the opposite side.
292 *fault*: sin.
293 *My father*: See p. v.
   compassing: obtaining.
294 *interred new*: At the beginning of his reign, Henry caused the body of Richard II to be brought to London and buried in Westminster Abbey.
296 *forced*: i.e. in the act of murder.
298 *who . . . hold up*: i.e. in prayer.
299 *blood*: bloodshed.
300 *chantries*: chapels where requiem masses could be sung every day.
   sad: grave.
301 *sing*: i.e. sing requiem masses.
   still: always.
302 *all . . . worth*: i.e. because not even good deeds are valuable (in the sight of God) without faith.
303 *after all*: Repentance should come *before* atonement.

Enter Gloucester

Gloucester

305 305 My liege.

King

My brother Gloucester's voice? Ay,
I know thy errand. I will go with thee.
308 The day, my friends, and all things stay for me.

[*Exeun*

305 *liege*: royal lord.

308 *stay*: wait for.

Act 4   Scene 2

The French lords, anticipating an easy
victory, gloat over the miserable little English
army.

Scene 2

Enter Bourbon, Orléans, Rambures *and*
Beaumont

Orléans

The sun doth gild our armour. Up, my lords!

Bourbon

Montez à cheval! My horse, varlet lackey! Ha!

Orléans

Oh, brave spirit!

Bourbon

Via les eaux et terres!

Orléans

5 5 *Rien puis l'air et feu?*

Bourbon

Cieux, cousin Orléans!

Enter Constable

Now, my lord Constable?

Constable

Hark how our steeds for present service neigh.

Bourbon

Mount them, and make incision in their hides
10 10 That their hot blood may spin in English eyes
And dout them with superfluous courage! Ha!

Rambures

What, will you have them weep our horses' blood?
How shall we then behold their natural tears?

2 *Montez à cheval*: to horse, mount up.
varlet lackey: you wretched groom.

4 *Via . . . terres*: go across water and land.

5 *Rien . . . feu*: not air and fire then
(Orléans is sarcastic).

6 *Cieux*: heavens.

8 *present service*: immediate action.

9 *make . . . hides*: spur them on.
10 *spin*: spray.
11 *dout*: douse, quench.

Enter Messenger

Messenger
The English are embattled, you French peers.
Constable
15 To horse, you gallant princes, straight to horse!
Do but behold yon poor and starved band
And your fair show shall suck away their souls,
Leaving them but the shells and husks of men.
There is not work enough for all our hands,
20 Scarce blood enough in all their sickly veins
To give each naked curtal-axe a stain,
That our French gallants shall today draw out
And sheathe for lack of sport. Let us but blow on them,
The vapour of our valour will o'erturn them.
25 'Tis positive 'gainst all exceptions, lords,
That our superfluous lackeys and our peasants
Who in unnecessary action swarm
About our squares of battle were enough
To purge this field of such a hilding foe,
30 Though we upon this mountain's basis by
Took stand for idle speculation,
But that our honours must not. What's to say?
A very little little let us do
And all is done. Then let the trumpets sound
35 The tucket sonance and the note to mount,
For our approach shall so much dare the field
That England shall couch down in fear, and yield.

14   *embattled*: drawn up in fighting line.

15   *straight*: at once.

17   *your . . . souls*: the impressive appearance will take away their hearts.

21   *curtal-axe*: cutlass—a short, broad-bladed, sword (for chopping).

25   *'gainst all exceptions*: without any question.
28   *squares of battle*: military formations of soldiers.
29   *hilding*: contemptible.
30–1 *Though . . . speculation*: even though we ourselves stood by as mere spectators: the Constable refers to the French king's description of Edward III 'on mountain standing' at the battle of Crécy (*2, 4, 55–62*).
35   *The tucket sonance*: trumpet call for the infantry to march.
     note to mount: order for the cavalry to mount their horses.
36   *dare*: terrify.
37   *couch*: lie.

Enter Grandpré

Grandpré
Why do you stay so long, my lords of France?
Yon island carrions, desperate of their bones,
40 Ill-favouredly become the morning field.
Their ragged curtains poorly are let loose
And our air shakes them passing scornfully.
Big Mars seems bankrupt in their beggar'd host,
And faintly through a rusty beaver peeps.
45 The horsemen sit like fixed candlesticks
With torch staves in their hand, and their poor jades
Lob down their heads, dropping the hides and hips,
The gum down-roping from their pale dead eyes,
And in their pale dull mouths the gemell'd bit
50 Lies foul with chew'd-grass, still and motionless.
And their executors the knavish crows
Fly o'er them all, impatient for their hour.
Description cannot suit itself in words
To demonstrate the life of such a battle,
55 In life so lifeless, as it shows itself.
Constable
They have said their prayers, and they stay for death.
Bourbon
Shall we go send them dinners and fresh suits
And give their fasting horses provender,
And after fight with them?
Constable
60 I stay but for my guidon. To the field!
I will the banner from a trumpet take
And use it for my haste. Come, come, away!
The sun is high and we outwear the day.

[*Exeunt*

39 *island*: i.e. from the British Isles.
    carrions: corpses, food for carrion birds.
    desperate of: careless about.
40 *Ill-favouredly become*: look unsightly.
41 *curtains*: i.e. military banners.
    let loose: unfolded.
42 *passing*: exceedingly.
43 *Big Mars . . . host*: all the spirit of fighting seems to be exhausted in this worn-out army; *Mars* was the Roman god of war—to whom Henry was compared in the Prologue (line 6).
44 *faintly*: timidly.
    beaver: visor, the face-piece of a helmet.
45 *fixed candlesticks*: i.e. suits of armour placed (e.g. at the foot of a great staircase) to look like knights holding torches or candles.
46 *torch staves*: candle holders.
    jades: nags.
47 *Lob*: droop down.
48 *down-roping*: hanging down.
49 *gemell'd*: jointed.
51 *executors*: those who dispose of what the dead leave behind them—in this case, the bodies.
54 *demonstrate*: depict.
    the life of: to the life.
    battle: army drawn up ready to fight.
56 *stay*: wait.
58 *provender*: hay, horse-food.

60 *guidon*: standard, pennant.
61 *trumpet*: trumpeter.
62 *for my haste*: so that I can get moving.
63 *outwear*: waste.

Act 4   Scene 3

The English lords are gloomy about their chances in the battle now imminent. King Henry invigorates them with a rousing speech, and seems undaunted even with the arrival of the French herald asking questions about ransom money.

2   *is rode*: has ridden.
   battle: formal battle-array.

3   *full*: at least; historians vary in their accounts of the actual number of troops involved in the fighting (Shakespeare gives Holinshed's estimate), but all agree that the English were desperately out-numbered.

6   *wi'*: with.
   charge: division.

10   *kind kinsman*: Westmorland's son was married to Salisbury's daughter.

13   *mind*: remind.
14   *fram'd*: composed.

16s.d.   The king probably enters unobserved—perhaps still disguised in Erpingham's cloak.

17   *one ten thousand*: one in every ten thousand.

20   *mark'd*: chosen, doomed.
21   *To . . . loss*: for our country to lose.

Scene 3

Enter Gloucester, Bedford, Exeter, Erpingham *with all his host*, Salisbury *and* Westmorland

Gloucester
Where is the king?
    Bedford
The king himself is rode to view their battle.
    Westmorland
Of fighting men they have full threescore thousand.
    Exeter
There's five to one. Besides, they all are fresh.
    Salisbury
5 God's arm strike with us! 'Tis a fearful odds.
God be wi'you, princes all. I'll to my charge.
If we no more meet till we meet in heaven
Then joyfully, my noble lord of Bedford,
My dear lord Gloucester and my good lord Exeter,
10 And my kind kinsman, warriors all, adieu.
    Bedford
Farewell, good Salisbury, and good luck go with
    thee.
    Exeter
Farewell, kind lord. Fight valiantly today.
                    [*Exit* Salisbury
And yet I do thee wrong to mind thee of it,
For thou art fram'd of the firm truth of valour.
    Bedford
15 He is as full of valour as of kindness,
Princely in both.

    Enter the King

    Westmorland
            O that we now had here
But one ten thousand of those men in England
That do no work today.
    King
            What's he that wishes so?
My cousin Westmorland. No, my fair cousin.
20 If we are mark'd to die, we are enough
To do our country loss. And if to live,

24 *Jove*: Almighty God: the Old Testament
Jehovah, or Jupiter in classical
mythology.
25 *feed upon my cost*: live at my expense.
26 *yearns*: grieves.
28 *a sin to covet*: Covetousness is forbidden
in the tenth commandment of Moses.

30 *coz*: cousin, kinsman.

32 *share from me*: reduce my share of.
33 *best hope*: i.e. of spiritual salvation.

34 *host*: army.
35 *stomach to*: appetite—courage—for.
36 *passport*: letter giving right of passage
through a foreign country.
37 *crowns for convoy*: money to pay for his
journey.
38 *We would*: we do not want to; King
Henry uses the royal plural pronoun—
but he also implies that all those present
share his opinion.
39 *fellowship*: brotherhood.
40 *Feast of Crispian*: 25 October; two
brothers, Crispinus and Crispianus,
were martyred together in AD 287.
44 *live old age*: live to be an old man.
45 *vigil*: eve.

50 *with advantages*: adding some
exaggeration.

55 *flowing cups*: celebratory drinking.

57 *Crispin Crispian*: see line 40 note.

62 *vile*: lowly born.

The fewer men, the greater share of honour.
God's will, I pray thee wish not one man more.
By Jove, I am not covetous for gold,
25 Nor care I who doth feed upon my cost.
It yearns me not if men my garments wear.
Such outward things dwell not in my desires.
But if it be a sin to covet honour,
I am the most offending soul alive.
30 No, faith, my coz, wish not a man from England.
God's peace, I would not lose so great an honour
As one man more, methinks, would share from me,
For the best hope I have. Oh, do not wish one
    more!
Rather proclaim it, Westmorland, through my host
35 That he which hath no stomach to this fight
Let him depart. His passport shall be made,
And crowns for convoy put into his purse.
We would not die in that man's company
That fears his fellowship to die with us.
40 This day is called the Feast of Crispian.
He that outlives this day and comes safe home
Will stand a-tiptoe when this day is nam'd,
And rouse him at the name of Crispian.
He that shall see this day and live old age
45 Will yearly on the vigil feast his neighbours,
And say 'Tomorrow is Saint Crispian.'
Then will he strip his sleeve and show his scars,
And say 'These wounds I had on Crispin's day.'
Old men forget, yet all shall be forgot
50 But he'll remember, with advantages,
What feats he did that day. Then shall our names,
Familiar in his mouth as household words,
Harry the king, Bedford and Exeter,
Warwick and Talbot, Salisbury and Gloucester,
55 Be in their flowing cups freshly remember'd.
This story shall the good man teach his son,
And Crispin Crispian shall ne'er go by
From this day to the ending of the world
But we in it shall be remembered.
60 We few, we happy few, we band of brothers—
For he today that sheds his blood with me
Shall be my brother; be he ne'er so vile

63 *gentle his condition*: raise his social status to that of 'gentleman'.

64 *now abed*: On the battlefield it is only just after dawn.

66 *hold . . . cheap*: be ashamed, think themselves cowards.

This day shall gentle his condition—
And gentlemen in England, now abed,
65 Shall think themselves accurs'd they were not here,
And hold their manhoods cheap whiles any speaks
That fought with us upon Saint Crispin's Day.

Enter Salisbury

Salisbury
My sovereign lord, bestow yourself with speed.
The French are bravely in their battles set,

68 *bestow*: prepare, arm.

69 *bravely*: boldly; *and also* flauntingly, splendidly.
their battles: fighting positions.

70 *expedience*: expedition, convenient speed.

70 And will with all expedience charge on us.
King
All things are ready, if our minds be so.
Westmorland
Perish the man whose mind is backward now!
King
Thou dost not wish more help from England, coz?
Westmorland
God's will, my liege, would you and I alone,
75 Without more help, could fight this royal battle!
King
Why, now thou hast unwish'd five thousand men,
Which likes me better than to wish us one.
You know your places. God be with you all.

72 *backward*: hesitant.

74 *liege*: royal lord.
would: I wish.

76 *unwish'd*: undone.

77 *likes me*: pleases me.

78s.d. *Tucket*: This interruption is not the trumpet call to charge, but that which sounded at *3, 7, 110* to introduce the French herald.

79 *know of*: learn from.

80 *compound*: make a bargain.

Tucket. Enter Montjoy

Montjoy
Once more I come to know of thee, King Harry,
80 If for thy ransom thou wilt now compound
Before thy most assured overthrow.
For certainly thou art so near the gulf
Thou needs must be englutted. Besides, in mercy,
The Constable desires thee thou wilt mind
85 Thy followers of repentance, that their souls
May make a peaceful and a sweet retire
From off these fields where, wretches, their poor bodies
Must lie and fester.
King
                        Who hath sent thee now?
Montjoy
The Constable of France.

82 *gulf*: brink, edge (of danger).

83 *englutted*: swallowed up.

84 *mind*: remind.

86 *retire*: withdrawal.

91 *achieve*: capture.

93 *the man*: Aesop tells this fable about a man who tried to sell a bearskin before he had caught the bear; here the royal lion is the quarry.

95 *A many*: most.

96 *native*: where they were born—i.e. in England.

97 *witness live in brass*: memorial engraved in brass (e.g. on funeral monuments).

100 *fam'd*: made famous.

100-1 *the sun . . . heaven*: their honour is immortal and will rise up to heaven, just as the sun draws vapours steaming ('reeking') from the dunghill.

102 *clime*: region.

104 *abounding*: abundant.

105 *crazing*: rebounding, in ricochet.

106 *mischief*: damage.

107 *relapse of mortality*: whilst they themselves have fallen in death.

109 *for the working day*: whilst we are working.

110 *besmirch'd*: muddied.

111 *rainy marching*: marching in the rain. *painful field*: battlefield.

112 *piece of feather*: helmet-plume.

113 *Good . . . fly*: Henry offers a wry jest.

114 *slovenry*: scruffiness.

115 *in the trim*: in perfect condition.

116 *ere*: before.

117-19 *pluck . . . service*: take away their fine uniforms and dismiss the French soldiers from the battle, just as a servant was stripped of his master's livery when he was given the sack.

121 *soon*: easily (because the soldiers will have taken possession of the French treasure).

King

90 I pray thee bear my former answer back.
    Bid them achieve me, and then sell my bones.
    Good God, why should they mock poor fellows thus?
    The man that once did sell the lion's skin
    While the beast liv'd, was kill'd with hunting him.
95 A many of our bodies shall no doubt
    Find native graves, upon the which, I trust,
    Shall witness live in brass of this day's work.
    And those that leave their valiant bones in France,
    Dying like men, though buried in your dunghills,
100 They shall be fam'd, for there the sun shall greet them
    And draw their honours reeking up to heaven,
    Leaving their earthly parts to choke your clime,
    The smell whereof shall breed a plague in France.
    Mark then abounding valour in our English,
105 That being dead, like to the bullet's crazing
    Break out into a second course of mischief
    Killing in relapse of mortality.
    Let me speak proudly. Tell the Constable
    We are but warriors for the working day.
110 Our gayness and our gilt are all besmirch'd
    With rainy marching in the painful field.
    There's not a piece of feather in our host
    (Good argument, I hope, we will not fly)
    And time hath worn us into slovenry.
115 But by the mass, our hearts are in the trim,
    And my poor soldiers tell me yet ere night
    They'll be in fresher robes, or they will pluck
    The gay new coats o'er the French soldiers' heads
    And turn them out of service. If they do this—
120 As, if God please, they shall—my ransom then
    Will soon be levied. Herald, save thou thy labour.
    Come thou no more for ransom, gentle herald.
    They shall have none, I swear, but these my joints,
    Which if they have, as I will leave 'em them,
125 Shall yield them little. Tell the Constable.

Montjoy

    I shall, King Harry. And so fare thee well.
    Thou never shalt hear herald any more.   [*Exit*

28–9 *I fear . . . ransom*: Henry's prose
'aside' voices fears that he will not
openly admit.

28s.d. This is York's only appearance in the
play, but it prepares for the report of his
death at *4, 6, 11–32* and *4, 8, 100*; York is
named by Holinshed as asking to lead the
'vaward', being of 'an haughty corage'.

King
[*Aside*] I fear thou wilt once more come again for a
ransom.

   Enter York

York
My lord, most humbly on my knee I beg
130 The leading of the vanguard.

King
Take it, brave York. Now soldiers, march away,
And how Thou pleasest, God, dispose the day.

          [*Exeunt*

Act 4   Scene 4

Pistol has taken a prisoner, and the Boy
acts as interpreter for the pleas, the
threats—and the ransom bargaining.

s.d. *Alarm*: drum rolls.
 Excursions: signs of action—e.g. soldiers
running over the stage—to indicate
battle in progress.

Scene 4

 Alarm. Excursions. Enter Pistol, French
Soldier, Boy

Pistol
Yield, cur!

French Soldier

Je pense que vous êtes le gentilhomme de bon qualité.

Pistol

Quality? 'Colin o custure me'. Art thou a gentleman
What is thy name? Discuss.

French Soldier

5 *O Seigneur Dieu!*

Pistol

O Seigneur Due should be a gentleman. Perpend m
words, O Seigneur Due, and mark: O Seigneur Due
thou diest on point of fox, except, O Seigneur, tho
do give to me egregious ransom.

French Soldier

10 *Oh, prenez miséricorde! Ayez pitié de moi!*

Pistol

Moy shall not serve. I will have forty moys, or I wi
fetch thy rim out at thy throat, in drops of crimso
blood.

French Soldier

Est-il impossible d'échapper la force de ton bras?

Pistol

15 Brass, cur? Thou damned and luxurious mountai
goat, offer'st me brass?

French Soldier

Oh, pardonnez-moi!

Pistol

Sayest thou me so? Is that a tun of moys? Com
hither, boy. Ask me this slave in French what
20 his name.

Boy

Écoutez. Comment êtes-vous appelé?

French Soldier

Monsieur le Fer.

Boy

He says his name is Mr Fer.

Pistol

Mr Fer. I'll fer him, and firk him, and ferret him
25 Discuss the same in French unto him.

Boy

I do not know the French for fer and ferret and fir

Pistol

Bid him prepare, for I will cut his throat.

---

2 *Je . . . qualité*: I think you are a gentleman of high rank.

3 *Colin . . . me*: This has been identified as an anglicization of 'callin og o' stor', the refrain of a popular Irish song, 'Maiden, my treasure'. It may have been suggested to Pistol by similarity of sound with '*qualité*'—or perhaps he is rejoicing at his prize.

5 *Seigneur Dieu*: Lord God.

6 *Due*: i.e. proper, just.
   perpend: hearken, understand (a mock-pompous term).

8 *fox*: broadsword.

9 *egregious*: exceptional.

10 *prenez . . . moi*: be merciful, take pity on me.

11 *Moy*: Pistol thinks he hears 'moiety' (= a share, half).

12 *rim*: guts, diaphragm.

14 *Est-il . . . bras*: Is it impossible to escape the power of your arm?

15 *luxurious*: lecherous—thought to be a particular quality of goats.

17 *pardonnez-moi*: excuse me.

18 *tun of moys*: treasure chest of half-coins.

21 *Ecoutez . . . appelé*: Listen to me. What's your name?

22 *le Fer*: In French the name means 'iron'.

24 *I'll . . . ferret*: I'll give him 'fer', and clobber him, and sort him out.

27 *prepare*: i.e. for death.

28 *Que dit-il*: what is he saying.

29–31 *Il . . . gorge*: He is ordering me to tell you that you must make yourself ready to die, because this soldier here is inclined to cut your throat right now.

35–7 *Je . . . écus*: Oh, I beg you, for the love of God, forgive me. I am a gentleman from a good family. Save my life and I will give you two hundred crowns.

40 *house*: The Boy translates '*maison*' literally.

44 *Petit . . . il*: Little gentleman, what does he say?

45–8 *Encore . . . franchisement*: Again that it is contrary to his oath to take mercy on any prisoner. Nevertheless, because of the crowns you have promised him, he is content to give you your liberty, your freedom.

49–52 *Sur . . . Angleterre*: On my knees I give you a thousand thanks, and I think myself fortunate to have fallen into the hands of a gentleman—I think the bravest, most valiant, and very distinguished nobleman of England.

French Soldier
Que dit-il, monsieur?
    Boy
Il me commande à vous dire que vous faites-vous prêt,
30 *car ce soldat ici est disposé tout à cette heure de couper votre gorge.*
    Pistol
Oui, coupe la gorge, par ma foi, peasant, unless thou give me crowns, brave crowns, or mangled shalt thou be by this my sword.
    French Soldier
35 [*Kneels*] *Oh! Je vous supplie, pour l'amour de Dieu, me pardonner! Je suis le gentilhomme de bonne maison. Gardez ma vie, et je vous donnerai deux cents écus.*
    Pistol
What are his words?
    Boy
He prays you to save his life. He is a gentleman of a
40 good house, and for his ransom he will give you two hundred crowns.
    Pistol
Tell him my fury shall abate, and I the crowns will take.
    French Soldier
Petit monsieur, que dit-il?
    Boy
45 *Encore qu'il est contre son jurement de pardonner aucun prisonnier. Néanmoins, pour les écus que vous l'ayez promis, il est content à vous donner la liberté, le franchisement.*
    French Soldier
Sur mes genoux je vous donne mille remerciements, et je
50 *m'estime heureux que je suis tombé entre les mains d'un chevalier—je pense le plus brave, vaillant, et très distingué seigneur d'Angleterre.*
    Pistol
Expound unto me, boy.
    Boy
He gives you upon his knees a thousand thanks, and
55 he esteems himself happy that he hath fallen into the hands of one (as he thinks) the most brave, valorous and thrice-worthy seigneur of England.

58 *suck blood*: i.e. as a leech.
59 *Suivez . . . capitaine*: Follow the great captain.
60 *so full . . . heart*: such loud boasts from so great a coward (compare the proverb, 'Empty vessels make the most noise').
63–5 *roaring . . . dagger*: The Boy alludes to one of the regular stage routines of the Morality Plays, in which the long-clawed devil was beaten until he roared with the Vice's wooden dagger.
64 *pare*: trim.
65 *both hanged*: We heard of Bardolph's execution in *Act 3, Scene 7*, but we know nothing of Nym's fate.
67 *lackeys*: lads.
    luggage: heavy baggage.

Pistol
As I suck blood, I will some mercy show. Follow me
    Boy
Suivez-vous le grand capitaine.
                    [*Exeunt* Pistol *and* French Soldie␣
60 I did never know so full a voice issue from so empt␣
    a heart. But the saying is true, the empty vesse␣
    makes the greatest sound. Bardolph and Nym had te␣
    times more valour than this roaring devil i'th'ol␣
    play, that everyone may pare his nails with a woode␣
65 dagger, and they are both hanged, and so would thi␣
    be if he durst steal anything adventurously. I mus␣
    stay with the lackeys with the luggage of our camp␣
    The French might have a good prey of us if he kne␣
    of it, for there is none to guard it but boys.   [*Ex␣

Scene 5

Act 4   Scene 5
The French lords are appalled to see the overthrow of their vast army, but they resolve to return to the fray.

1 *O diable*: Oh hell.

2 *O . . . perdu*: Oh God! The day is lost, everything is lost.

3 *Mort de ma vie*: death of my life.

5 *plumes*: helmet plumes (which were the outward representation of the French pride).

Enter Constable, Orléans, Bourbon, *and*
Rambures

    Constable
O diable!
    Orléans
O Seigneur! Le jour est perdu, tout est perdu!
    Bourbon
Mort de ma vie, all is confounded, all!
Reproach and everlasting shame
5 Sits mocking in our plumes.

5s.d *alarm*: call to renew fighting.

6 *méchante fortune*: evil chance.

8 *perdurable*: everlasting.

15 *pander*: bawd, pimp.

16 *slave*: peasant.
no gentler: no better bred.

17 *contaminate*: polluted, violated.

18 *spoil'd*: ruined.
friend: befriend.

19 *on heaps*: in complete disorder.

21 *in our throngs*: by our numbers.

24 *Let . . . long*: A variation of the proverb,
'It is better to die with honour than to
live with shame'.

A short alarm

O méchante fortune! Do not run away.
Constable
Why, all our ranks are broke.
Bourbon
O perdurable shame, let's stab ourselves.
Be these the wretches that we play'd at dice for?
Orléans
10 Is this the king we sent to for his ransom?
Bourbon
Shame, and eternal shame, nothing but shame!
Let us die! In once more, back again,
And he that will not follow Bourbon now
Let him go hence, and with his cap in hand
15 Like a base pander hold the chamber door,
Whilst by a slave, no gentler than my dog,
His fairest daughter is contaminate.
Constable
Disorder, that hath spoil'd us, friend us now.
Let us on heaps go offer up our lives.
Orléans
20 We are enough yet living in the field
To smother up the English in our throngs,
If any order might be thought upon.
Bourbon
The devil take the order now, I'll to the throng.
Let life be short, else shame will be too long.
[*Exeunt*

Over on the English side, King Henry (who believes that the French are undefeated) hears of the death of the noble Duke of York. When the enemy's trumpet calls to a renewed onslaught, the king orders his soldiers to kill their prisoners.

2 *keep the field*: are winning.

3 *commends him*: sends his compliments.

8 *Larding*: enriching.
9 *Yoke-fellow*: equal partner.
   honour-owing: honourable, honour-owning.
11 *all haggled over*: hacked all over.
12 *insteep'd*: soaked.

14 *yawn*: gape open.

Scene 6

Alarm. Enter the King *and his train, with prisoners*

King
Well have we done, thrice-valiant countrymen.
But all's not done, yet keep the French the field.

Enter Exeter *by another door*

Exeter
The Duke of York commends him to your majesty.
King
Lives he, good uncle? Thrice within this hour
5 I saw him down, thrice up again and fighting.
From helmet to the spur all blood he was.
Exeter
In which array, brave soldier, doth he lie
Larding the plain; and by his bloody side,
Yoke-fellow to his honour-owing wounds,
10 The noble Earl of Suffolk also lies.
Suffolk first died, and York, all haggled over,
Comes to him where in gore he lay insteep'd,
And takes him by the beard, kisses the gashes
That bloodily did yawn upon his face.

15 *Tarry*: wait.

19 *kept*: lived.
chivalry: knightly conduct.
20 *cheer'd him up*: gave him encouragement.
21 *raught*: reached out.
22 *grip*: grasp.

26 *espous'd*: engaged (i.e. as in marriage).
27 *testament*: will (which is usually sealed with wax, but here with blood).
28 *pretty and sweet*: gentle and patient.

30 *man*: masculine stoicism.
31 *all my mother*: all the tender feelings that I inherited from my mother.

33 *I must perforce*: I was forced to.
compound: come to terms with.
34 *wilful*: i.e. because his eyes want to pour out ('issue') tears. Q and F both read 'mixt-full', which some editors emend to 'mistful'.
35s.d. *Alarm*: call to renew hostilities.
37 *kill his prisoners*: This was contrary to the strict military code of conduct.

15 He cries aloud 'Tarry, my cousin Suffolk.
My soul shall thine keep company to heaven.
Tarry, sweet soul, for mine, then fly abreast,
As in this glorious and well-foughten field
We kept together in our chivalry.'
20 Upon these words I came, and cheer'd him up.
He smil'd me in the face, raught me his hand,
And with a feeble grip says 'Dear my lord,
Commend my service to my sovereign.'
So did he turn, and over Suffolk's neck
25 He threw his wounded arm, and kiss'd his lips,
And so, espous'd to death, with blood he seal'd
A testament of noble-ending love.
The pretty and sweet manner of it forc'd
Those waters from me which I would have stopp'd,
30 But I had not so much of man in me,
And all my mother came into mine eyes
And gave me up to tears.
                                                      King
                                        I blame you not,
For hearing this I must perforce compound
With wilful eyes, or they will issue too.

                    Alarm

35 But hark, what new alarm is this same?
The French have reinforc'd their scatter'd men.
Then every soldier kill his prisoners.
Give the word through.
                                                      [*Exeunt*

Act 4   Scene 7

Llewellyn and Gower discuss the progress of
the battle. They are speaking the king's
praises when Henry comes on to the stage,
angered by the misconduct of the French
and determined to fight to the last. But
Montjoy declares the end of hostilities: the
French are defeated. Montjoy humbly asks
permission to rescue the dead bodies for
burial, and leaves escorted by English
heralds. King Henry, relaxing for a moment,
plays one of his tricks on his followers.

1   *Kill . . . luggage*: The French have killed
    the boys and looted the luggage they
    were guarding.
    expressly: specifically.
2   *law of arms*: code of military conduct.
    arrant: utter.
8   *wherefore*: in consequence; but see Scene
    6, line 37—and Commentary, p. xxvi.
11–50 Llewellyn embarks on a rhetorical
    'comparison' in praise of Henry—
    although it is not easy for him to find
    points of contact.
11 *Monmouth*: A town on the border of
    England and Wales.
14 *Alexander the Great*: King of Macedonia
    (a country, not a town) 356–323 BC; he
    was conqueror of his whole known
    world—and has already in this play
    been compared with Henry V (I, I, 46).
17 *reckonings*: all amount to the same
    thing; in rhetorical exercises a work is
    'varied' by quoting synonyms.

21 *e'en*: indeed.

32 *come after*: follows the same pattern.
    indifferent well: very closely.
    figures: comparisons, parallels.

Scene 7

Enter Llewellyn *and* Gower

Llewellyn

Kill the poys and the luggage! 'Tis expressly against
the law of arms. 'Tis as arrant a piece of knavery
mark you now, as can be offert, in your conscienc
now, is it not?

Gower

5   'Tis certain. There's not a boy left alive, and th
cowardly rascals that ran from the battle ha' don
this slaughter. Besides, they have burned and carrie
away all that was in the king's tent, wherefore th
king most worthily hath caused every soldier to cu
10 his prisoner's throat. Oh, 'tis a gallant king!

Llewellyn

Ay, he was porn at Monmouth. Captain Gower
what call you the town's name where Alexander th
Pig was born?

Gower

Alexander the Great.

Llewellyn

15 Why, I pray you, is not 'pig' great? The pig, or th
great, or the mighty, or the huge, or th
magnanimous, are all one reckonings, save th
phrase is a little variations.

Gower

I think Alexander the Great was born in Macedor
20 His father was called Phillip of Macedon, as I take it

Llewellyn

I think it is e'en Macedon where Alexander is porr
I tell you, captain, if you look in the maps of th
woreld I warrant you sall find, in the comparison
between Macedon and Monmouth, that th
25 situations, look you, is both alike. There is a river i
Macedon, and there is also moreover a river a
Monmouth. It is called Wye at Monmouth, but it i
out of my prains what is the name of the other rive
But 'tis all one, 'tis alike as my fingers is to m
30 fingers, and there is salmons in both. If you mar
Alexander's life well, Harry of Monmouth's life i
come after it indifferent well, for there is figures in a

things. Alexander, God knows, and you know, in his rages and his furies and his wraths and his cholers
35 and his moods and his displeasures and his indignations, and also being a little intoxicates in his prains, did in his ales and his angers, look you, kill his best friend Cleitus.

Gower
Our king is not like him in that. He never killed any
40 of his friends.

Llewellyn
It is not well done, mark you now, to take the tales out of my mouth ere it is made and finished. I speak but in the figures and comparisons of it. As Alexander killed his friend Cleitus, being in his ales
45 and his cups, so also Harry Monmouth, being in his right wits and his good judgements, turned away the fat knight with the great belly doublet. He was full of jests and gypes and knaveries and mocks—I have forgot his name.

Gower
50 Sir John Falstaff.

Llewellyn
That is he. I'll tell you, there is good men porn at Monmouth.

Gower
Here comes his majesty.

Alarm. Enter King Henry, Exeter,
Gloucester, Warwick, *and English* Herald,
and Bourbon *with prisoners. Flourish*

King
I was not angry since I came to France
55 Until this instant. Take a trumpet, herald.
Ride thou unto the horsemen on yon hill.
If they will fight with us, bid them come down,
Or void the field. They do offend our sight.
If they'll do neither, we will come to them,
60 And make them skirr away as swift as stones
Enforced from the old Assyrian slings.
Besides, we'll cut the throats of those we have,
And not a man of them that we shall take
Shall taste our mercy. Go and tell them so.

[*Exit English* Herald

38 *Cleitus*: Alexander's foster-brother, whom he killed in a drunken quarrel.

40 *his friends*: To Gower, Bardolph did not count as one of the king's friends.

47 *great belly doublet*: with his great belly stuffing out his doublet.
48 *gypes*: gibes, taunts.

53s.d. *Alarm . . . Flourish*: The stage-direction starts with a drum-roll of battle and ends with a trumpet-call heralding the royal entrance.

55 *this instant*: Henry has apparently just learned of the attack on the luggage; see Commentary, p.xxvii.
trumpet: trumpeter.
56 *yon hill*: the hill referred to in 4, 2, 30.
58 *void*: clear off.
60 *skirr*: skip.
61 *Assyrian slings*: This seems to be an allusion to weapons described in the Book of Judith (Old Testament Apocrypha) 9:9.
64 *taste*: feel, experience.

Enter Montjoy

Exeter

65 Here comes the herald of the French, my liege.

Gloucester

His eyes are humbler than they used to be.

King

How now, what means this, herald? Know'st thou
      not

68 *fin'd*: staked.

That I have fin'd these bones of mine for ransom?
Com'st thou again for ransom?

Montjoy

No, great king.

70 *charitable licence*: permission granted
   out of Christian charity.

70 I come to thee for charitable licence,
That we may wander o'er this bloody field

72 *book*: put on record.

To book our dead, and then to bury them,
To sort our nobles from our common men,
For many of our princes—woe the while—

75 *mercenary blood*: the blood of soldiers
   fighting only for pay.
76 *vulgar*: common people.

75 Lie drown'd and soak'd in mercenary blood,
So do our vulgar drench their peasant limbs
In blood of princes, while the wounded steeds

78 *fetlock*: ankle.
79 *Yerk*: kick, lash.
   armed heels: iron-shod hooves.

Fret fetlock deep in gore, and with wild rage
Yerk out their armed heels at their dead masters,

80 Killing them twice. Oh, give us leave, great king,
To view the field in safety, and dispose
Of their dead bodies.

King

I tell thee truly, herald,
I know not if the day be ours or no,

84 *peer*: appear.

For yet a-many of your horsemen peer

85 And gallop o'er the field.

Montjoy

The day is yours.

King

Praised be God, and not our strength, for it.
What is this castle called that stands hard by?

87 *hard by*: very near.

Montjoy

They call it Agincourt.

King

Then call we this the field of Agincourt,

90 *Crispin Crispianus*: See 4, 3, 40 *note*.

90 Fought on the day of Crispin Crispianus.

Llewellyn
Your grandfather of famous memory, an't please your majesty, and your great-uncle Edward the Plack Prince of Wales, as I have read in the chronicles, fought a most prave pattle here in France.

King

95 They did, Llewellyn.

Llewellyn
Your majesty says very true. If your majesties is remembered of it, the Welshmen did good service in a garden where leeks did grow, wearing leeks in their Monmouth caps, which your majesty know to

100 this hour is an honourable badge of the service. And I do believe your majesty takes no scorn to wear the leek upon St Tavy's day.

King
I wear it for a memorable honour,
For I am Welsh, you know, good countryman.

Llewellyn

105 All the water in Wye cannot wash your majesty's Welsh plood out of your pody, I can tell you that. God pless it and preserve it, as long as it pleases His Grace—and his majesty too.

King
Thanks, good my countryman.

Llewellyn

110 By Cheshu, I am your majesty's countryman! I care not who know it. I will confess it to all the woreld. I need not to be ashamed of your majesty, praised be God, so long as your majesty is an honest man.

King
God keep me so.

Enter Williams

Our heralds go with him.

115 Bring me just notice of the numbers dead
On both our parts.

[*Exeunt* Montjoy, Gower *and English* Heralds

Call yonder fellow hither.

Exeter
Soldier, you must come to the king.

91 *grandfather*: Edward III—actually the great-grandfather of Henry V.
an't please: if it please, if I may remind.

94 *pattle*: the battle of Crécy.

97–8 *Welshmen . . . grow*: No source other than Llewellyn is known for this account; the wearing of leeks on St David's day (1st March) is thought to commemorate a victory over the Saxons in AD 540.

99 *Monmouth caps*: round, brimless hats with high tapering crowns.

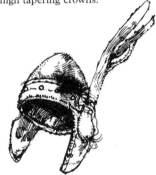

104 *I am Welsh*: Henry V was born in Monmouth.

116s.d. Although the text does not refer to his exit, Gower must go with the heralds: he is not on stage at line 148, when the king sends for him.

King
Soldier, why wear'st thou that glove in thy cap?
Williams
An't please your majesty, 'tis the gage of one that]
120 should fight withal, if he be alive.
King
An Englishman?
Williams
An't please your majesty, a rascal that swaggered
with me last night, who if a live and ever dare to
challenge this glove, I have sworn to take him a box
125 o'th'ear; or if I can see my glove in his cap, which he
swore as he was a soldier he would wear, if a live,]
will strike it out soundly.
King
What think you, Captain Llewellyn, is it fit this
soldier keep his oath?
Llewellyn
130 He is a craven and a villain else, an't please your
majesty, in my conscience.
King
It may be his enemy is a gentleman of great sort,
quite from the answer of his degree.
Llewellyn
Though he be as good a gentleman as the devil is, as
135 Lucifer and Beelzebub himself, it is necessary, look
your grace, that he keep his vow and his oath. If he
be perjured, see you now, his reputation is as arrant
a villain and a Jack Sauce as ever his black shoe
trod upon God's ground and His earth, in my
140 conscience, law.
King
Then keep thy vow, sirrah, when thou meet'st the
fellow.
Williams
So I will, my liege, as I live.
King
Who serv'st thou under?
Williams
145 Under Captain Gower, my liege.
Llewellyn
Gower is a good captain, and is good knowledge and
literatured in the wars.

King
Call him hither to me, soldier.
Williams
I will, my liege.   [*Exit*
King
150 Here, Llewellyn, wear thou this favour for me, and
stick it in thy cap. [*Gives him* Williams's *glove*] When
Alençon and myself were down together I plucked
this glove from his helm. If any man challenge this,
he is a friend to Alençon and an enemy to our
155 person. If thou encounter any such, apprehend him,
an thou dost me love.
Llewellyn
Your grace does me as great honours as can be
desired in the hearts of his subjects. I would fain see
the man that has but two legs that shall find himself
160 aggrieffed at this glove, that is all. But I would fain
see it once, an't please God of His grace, that I might
see.
King
Know'st thou Gower?
Llewellyn
He is my dear friend, an't please you.
King
165 Pray thee go seek him and bring him to my tent.
Llewellyn
I will fetch him.   [*Exit*
King
My lord of Warwick, and my brother Gloucester,
Follow Llewellyn closely at the heels.
The glove which I have given him for a favour
170 May haply purchase him a box o'th'ear.
It is the soldier's. I by bargain should
Wear it myself. Follow, good cousin Warwick.
If that the soldier strike him, as I judge
By his blunt bearing he will keep his word,
175 Some sudden mischief may arise of it,
For I do know Llewellyn valiant,
And, touch'd with choler, hot as gunpowder,
And quickly will return an injury.
Follow, and see there be no harm between them.
180 Go you with me, uncle of Exeter.   [*Exeunt*

148 *Call him hither*: see note to line 116s.d.

150 *favour*: token—the glove given as a pledge in *4, 1, 205*.

152 *Alençon*: Henry was in fact trying to rescue the Duke of York (see *4, 6, 5*).
down together: fighting hand-to-hand ('down' from their horses).
155 *apprehend*: arrest.
156 *an*: if.

158 *would fain*: would very much like to.

165 *go seek him*: at line 148 Williams was sent to bring Gower 'hither'; this new command is issued to ensure that Llewellyn, now showing the glove, meets Williams (who has been authorized to challenge it).

170 *haply*: perhaps.
o'th': on the.
171 *by bargain*: according to our agreement.

177 *touch'd with choler*: fired with anger—set off like a cannon.
178 *return*: pay back.
injury: insult.

Act 4   Scene 8

The king's practical joke on his soldiers gives some light relief after the serious business of the battle. Williams bravely challenges the glove worn by Llewellyn, and the king seems to enjoy his subjects' embarrassment when the truth is revealed. A herald brings a list of the dead and King Henry assesses the losses on both sides.

1 *knight*: Knighting a captain on the battlefield was a usual way of honouring his company.
3 *apace*: very quickly.
4 *toward*: intended for.
  peradventure: very likely, perhaps.

9 *arrant*: utter.
  any's: any is.

11 *You villain*: Gower is offended by the presumption shown by Williams, a common soldier under his direct command, in challenging a superior officer.
12 *be forsworn*: break my oath.
14 *into plows*: easily—even, perhaps, 'in two blows'.

16 *a lie . . . throat*: an outright lie.
  I charge you: These words are spoken to Gower, as Williams's captain.

21 *contagious*: pernicious.

Scene 8

Enter Gower *and* Williams

    Williams
I warrant it is to knight you, captain.

Enter Llewellyn

    Llewellyn
God's will and His pleasure, captain. I beseech yo
now, come apace to the king. There is more goo
toward you, peradventure, than is in yo
5 knowledge to dream of.
    Williams
[*To* Llewellyn] Sir, know you this glove?
    Llewellyn
Know the glove? I know the glove is a glove.
    Williams
I know this, and thus I challenge it.

Strikes him

    Llewellyn
God's blood, an arrant traitor as any's in th
10 universal world, or in France, or in England!
    Gower
[*To* Williams] How now, sir? You villain!
    Williams
Do you think I'll be forsworn?
    Llewellyn
Stand away, Captain Gower. I will give treason h
payment into plows, I warrant you.
    Williams
15 I am no traitor.
    Llewellyn
That's a lie in thy throat. I charge you in his majesty
name apprehend him, he's a friend of the Duke o
Alençon's.

Enter Warwick *and* Gloucester

    Warwick
How now, how now, what's the matter?
    Llewellyn
20 My lord of Warwick, here is, praised be God for i
a most contagious treason come to light, look you, a

21–2 *as . . . day*: A proverbial phrase: the broad daylight shows up the treachery.

you shall desire in a summer's day. Here is his majesty.

Enter King Henry *and* Exeter

King
How now, what's the matter?

Llewellyn
25 My liege, here is a villain and a traitor, that, look your grace, has struck the glove which your majesty is take out of the helmet of Alençon.

Williams
My liege, this was my glove—here is the fellow of it—and he that I gave it to in change promised to
30 wear it in his cap. I promised to strike him if he did. I met this man with my glove in his cap, and I have been as good as my word.

29 *in change*: in exchange.

Llewellyn
Your majesty, hear now, saving your majesty's manhood, what an arrant, rascally, beggarly,
35 lousy knave it is! I hope your majesty is pear me testimony and witness and will avouchment that this is the glove of Alençon that your majesty is give me, in your conscience now.

36 *avouchment*: give testimony.

Gives glove to King

King
Give me thy glove, soldier. Look, here is the fellow of it.
40 'Twas I indeed thou promised to strike,
And thou hast given me most bitter terms.

Llewellyn
An't please your majesty, let his neck answer for it, if there is any martial law in the world.

41 *most bitter terms*: i.e. in striking Llewellyn.

King
How canst thou make me satisfaction?

Williams
45 All offences, my lord, come from the heart. Never came any from mine that might offend your majesty.

44 *satisfaction*: compensation.

King
It was our self thou didst abuse.

Williams
Your majesty came not like yourself. You appeared to me but as a common man—witness the

48 *like yourself*: in your usual appearance.

50 *lowliness*: humble behaviour.

51 *shape*: disguise.

57 *for an honour*: i.e. the honour of having challenged the king himself.

59 *must needs*: will have to be.

60 *mettle*: courage (a pun with 'metal').

61 *twelve pence*: This was a large sum of money—about two days' pay—for a captain to give away.

65 *will none of*: don't want any of.

67 *mend your shoes*: By this stage in the fighting, all the soldiers' clothes were worn out (as King Henry told the French herald at *4, 3, 110–4*).

72 *good sort*: noble birth.

73–101 The list paraphrases that given by Holinshed.

76 *Full*: at least.
common: ordinary.

50 night, your garments, your lowliness. And what your
highness suffered under that shape, I beseech you
take it for your own fault and not mine, for had you
been as I took you for, I made no offence. Therefore I
beseech your highness pardon me. [*Kneels*]

King

55 Here, uncle Exeter, fill this glove with crowns
And give it to this fellow. Keep it, fellow,
And wear it for an honour in thy cap
Till I do challenge it. Give him the crowns.
And captain, you must needs be friends with him.

Llewellyn

60 By this day and this light, the fellow has mettle
enough in his belly. Hold, there is twelve pence for
you, and I pray you serve God and keep you out of
prawls and prabbles and quarrels and dissentions,
and I warrant you it is the better for you.

Williams

65 I will none of your money.

Llewellyn

It is with a good will. I can tell you it will serve you
to mend your shoes. Come, wherefore should you be
so pashful? Your shoes is not so good. 'Tis a good
silling, I warrant you, or I will change it.

Enter Herald

King

70 Now, herald, are the dead number'd?

Herald

Here is the number of the slaughter'd French.

Gives him paper

King

What prisoners of good sort are taken, uncle?

Exeter

Charles, Duke of Orléans, nephew to the king;
John, Duke of Bourbon, and Lord Boucicault.

75 Of other lords and barons, knights and squires,
Full fifteen hundred, besides common men.

King

This note doth tell me of ten thousand French
That in the field lie slain. Of princes in this number

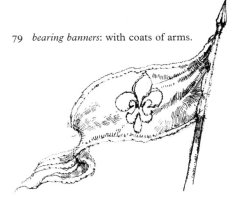

79   *bearing banners*: with coats of arms.

87   *blood and quality*: birth and breeding.

95   *lusty*: powerful.

102   *of name*: of high rank.

103   *five and twenty*: This is the number given by Holinshed—who adds, however, that the French estimated between one and six hundred English dead.

105   *without stratagem*: Shakespeare allows his Henry to ignore the tactics that won the battle of Agincourt; see 'The Sources of *Henry V*', p. 129.

106   *plain shock*: straight attack.
       even play: fair play.

110   *the village*: Maisoncelles, the nearest village to the castle of Agincourt.

111   *be it death*: let sentence of death.

112   *To . . . God*: The Elizabethan saying was 'Give God thanks and make no boast'.

And nobles bearing banners, there lie dead
80   One hundred twenty-six. Added to these,
Of knights, esquires and gallant gentlemen,
Eight thousand and four hundred, of the which
Five hundred were but yesterday dubb'd knights.
So that in these ten thousand they have lost
85   There are but sixteen hundred mercenaries.
The rest are princes, barons, lords, knights, squires,
And gentlemen of blood and quality.
The names of those their nobles that lie dead:
Charles Delabret, High Constable of France;
90   Jacques of Châtillon, Admiral of France;
The Master of the Crossbows, Lord Rambures;
Great Master of France, the brave Sir Guiscard
       Dauphin,
John, Duke of Alençon; Antony, Duke of Brabant,
The brother to the Duke of Burgundy;
95   And Edward, Duke of Bar. Of lusty earls:
Grandpré and Roussi, Fauconbridge and Foix,
Beaumont and Marle, Vaudemont and Lestrelles.
Here was a royal fellowship of death.
Where is the number of our English dead?

Takes another paper

100   Edward, the Duke of York, the Earl of Suffolk,
Sir Richard Keighley, Davy Gam, esquire.
None else of name, and of all other men
But five and twenty. O God, Thy arm was here!
And not to us, but to Thy arm alone
105   Ascribe we all. When, without stratagem,
But in plain shock and even play of battle,
Was ever known so great and little loss
On one part and on th'other? Take it, God,
For it is none but Thine.
       Exeter
                                       'Tis wonderful.
       King
110   Come, go we in procession to the village,
And be it death proclaimed through our host
To boast of this, or take that praise from God,
Which is His only.

Llewellyn

Is it not lawful, an't please your majesty, to tell how
115 many is killed?

King

Yes, captain, but with this acknowledgement,
That God fought for us.

Llewellyn

Yes, in my conscience, He did us great good.

King

Do we all holy rites.
120 Let there be sung *Non nobis* and *Te Deum*,
The dead with charity enclosed in clay,
And then to Calais, and to England then,
Where ne'er from France arrived more happy men.

[*Exeunt*

120 *Non nobis*: Psalm 115 in the Book of
Common Prayer: 'Not unto us, O
Lord, not unto us, but to Thy Name,
give the praise.'
Te Deum: The Canticle 'Te Deum
Laudamus' from the Book of Common
Prayer: 'We praise thee, O God, we
acknowledge thee to be the Lord'.
121 *with charity*: with Christian rites.
enclosed in clay: buried.

Act 5

Act 5   Chorus

The Chorus accounts for the passing of time,
summarizing the events that followed the
battle of Agincourt (1415) until the present
moment, when the audience is escorted to
the signing of the Treaty of Troyes in 1420.

1 *Vouchsafe*: be kind enough.
3 *admit th'excuse*: make excuse for the
    treatment.
4 *due course*: correct sequence.
5 *huge . . . life*: real life size.
7 *Grant*: imagine.
    There seen: having seen him there.
9 *Athwart*: across.
10 *Pales-in*: fences in.
11 *out-voice*: sound louder than.
12 *whiffler*: harbinger, fore-runner—the
    man who was employed to keep the way
    clear for a procession.
14 *solemnly*: in a formal procession.
15 *even now*: already.
16 *Blackheath*: a stretch of open ground,
    south of Greenwich, on the road from
    Dover to London.
17 *to have borne*: to arrange to have carried
    before him (in formal procession).
21 *full . . . ostent*: all the emblems and
    displays of victory.
23 *quick . . . thought*: lively workings of
    your imagination.
25 *his brethren*: the aldermen of the City of
    London.
    in best sort: in civic array.
26 *antique*: ancient.
29 *lower . . . likelihood*: humbler but
    lovingly anticipated possibility.
30 *the general*: the Earl of Essex, whose
    expedition left England on 27 March
    1599 for Ireland, and returned in
    September of that year; see 'Date and
    Text', p. xxxvi.
    empress: Queen Elizabeth I.

Enter Chorus

Chorus
Vouchsafe to those that have not read the story
That I may prompt them, and of such as have,
I humbly pray them to admit th'excuse
Of time, of numbers, and due course of things
5 Which cannot in their huge and proper life
Be here presented. Now we bear the king
Toward Calais. Grant him there. There seen,
Heave him away upon your winged thoughts
Athwart the sea. Behold the English beach
10 Pales-in the flood with men, with wives, and boys,
Whose shouts and claps out-voice the deep-
        mouth'd sea,
Which, like a mighty whiffler 'fore the king,
Seems to prepare his way. So let him land,
And solemnly see him set on to London.
15 So swift a pace hath thought that even now
You may imagine him upon Blackheath,
Where that his lords desire him to have borne
His bruised helmet and his bended sword
Before him through the city. He forbids it,
20 Being free from vainness and self-glorious pride,
Giving full trophy, signal and ostent
Quite from himself to God. But now behold,
In the quick forge and working-house of thought,
How London doth pour out her citizens!
25 The mayor and all his brethren in best sort,
Like to the senators of th'antique Rome,
With the plebeians swarming at their heels,
Go forth and fetch their conquering Caesar in—
As, by a lower but by loving likelihood
30 Were now the general of our gracious empress,

31 *in good time*: fairly soon.
32 *broached*: spitted, impaled.

36–7 *As yet . . . home*: i.e. the grief of the French encourages the English king to remain in England.
38 *the emperor's coming*: The Holy Roman Emperor Sigismund came to England on 1 May 1416.
39 *order peace*: negotiate the terms of peace.
  omit: pass over.
42–3 *myself . . . past*: I myself have performed all the events of the intervening period by reminding you that the time has passed.
44 *brook abridgement*: tolerate the abbreviation.

(As in good time he may) from Ireland coming,
Bringing rebellion broached on his sword,
How many would the peaceful city quit
To welcome him? Much more, and much more cause,
35 Did they this Harry. Now in London place him—
As yet the lamentation of the French
Invites the king of England's stay at home,
The emperor's coming in behalf of France
To order peace between them—and omit
40 All the occurrences, whatever chanc'd,
Till Harry's back return again to France.
There must we bring him, and myself have play'd
The interim, by remembering you 'tis past.
Then brook abridgement, and your eyes advance
45 After your thoughts, straight back again to France.
                                    [*Exit*

Act 5   Scene 1

Although some time has elapsed since the battle of Agincourt (fought on 25 October), we are still on a battle-field in France. Llewellyn has been insulted by Pistol, and he is preparing to take revenge. At the end of the scene Pistol starts off on his return journey to England.

2 *St Davy's day*: 1 March, when the Welsh wear their national emblem.
5 *scald*: scabby.
  pragging: bragging, boasting; Llewellyn's p/b confusion is accentuated by his anger.
10–11 *could . . . contention*: could not start a fight.

Scene 1

Enter Llewellyn *and* Gower

Gower
Nay, that's right. But why wear you your leek today? St Davy's day is past.
Llewellyn
There is occasions and causes why and wherefore in all things. I will tell you ass my friend, Captain
5 Gower. The rascally, scald, beggarly, lousy, pragging knave Pistol, which you and yourself and all the world know to be no petter than a fellow, look you now, of no merits, he is come to me, and prings me pread and salt yesterday, look you, and bid me eat
10 my leek. It was in a place where I could not breed no contention with him, but I will be so bold as to wear it in my cap till I see him once again, and then I will tell him a little piece of my desires.

Enter Pistol

Gower
Why, here he comes, swelling like a turkey-cock.
Llewellyn
15 'Tis no matter for his swellings, nor his turkey-cocks.
God pless you, Anchient Pistol, you scurvy, lousy
knave, God pless you.
Pistol
Ha, art thou bedlam? Dost thou thirst, base Trojan,
to have me fold up Parca's fatal web? Hence! I am
20 qualmish at the smell of leek.
Llewellyn
I peseech you heartily, scurvy, lousy knave, at my
desires and my requests and my petitions, to eat,
look you, this leek. Because, look you, you do not
love it, nor your affections and your appetites and
25 your digestions does not agree with it, I would desire
you to eat it.
Pistol
Not for Cadwallader and all his goats.
Llewellyn
There is one goat for you.

Strikes him with cudgel

Will you be so good, scald knave, as eat it?
Pistol
30 Base Trojan, thou shalt die!
Llewellyn
You say very true, scald knave, when God's will is. I
will desire you to live in the meantime, and eat your
victuals. Come, there is sauce for it. [*Strikes him*]
You called me yesterday 'mountain-squire', but I will
35 make you today a squire of low degree. I pray you,
fall to. If you can mock a leek, you can eat a leek.
Gower
Enough, captain. You have astonished him.
Llewellyn
By Cheshu, I will make him eat some part of
my leek, or I will peat his pate four days. Bite, I pray
40 you. It is good for your green wound, and your
bloody coxcomb.

18   *bedlam*: crazy—an abbreviation of 'Bethlehem', the name of the London hospital for the insane.
     Trojan: hooligan.
19   *fold up . . . web*: cut off your life; the Greek Parcae were the three goddesses of fate who spun, wove, and cut the threads of human life.
20   *qualmish at*: nauseated by.

27   *Cadwallader . . . goats*: Wales and all its creatures. Being a mountainous country, Wales was noted for its goats; Cadwallader was a legendary national hero.

34   *mountain-squire*: landlord of barren property.

36   *fall to*: enjoy your meal, get on with it.

37   *astonished*: stunned, dazed.

39   *pate*: skull.
40   *green*: raw, fresh.
41   *coxcomb*: fool's head.

Pistol

Must I bite?

Llewellyn

Yes, certainly, and out of doubt and out of question too, and ambiguities.

Pistol

45 By this leek, I will most horribly revenge—[*Llewellyn threatens him*] I eat and eat, I swear!

Llewellyn

Eat, I pray you. Will you have some more sauce to your leek? There is not enough leek to swear by.

Pistol

Quiet thy cudgel, thou dost see I eat.

Llewellyn

50 Much good do you, scald knave, heartily. Nay, pray you throw none away. The skin is good for your broken coxcomb. When you take occasions to see leeks hereafter, I pray you mock at 'em, that is all.

Pistol

Good.

Llewellyn

55 Ay, leeks is good. Hold you, there is a groat to heal your pate.

Pistol

Me a groat?

Llewellyn

Yes, verily, and in truth you shall take it, or I have another leek in my pocket which you shall eat.

Pistol

60 I take thy groat in earnest of revenge.

Llewellyn

If I owe you anything, I will pay you in cudgels. You shall be a woodmonger, and buy nothing of me but cudgels. God b'wi'you, and keep you, and heal your pate.   [*Exit*

Pistol

65 All hell shall stir for this!

Gower

Go, go, you are a counterfeit cowardly knave. Will you mock at an ancient tradition began upon an honourable respect, and worn as a memorable trophy of predeceased valour, and dare not avouch in

44 *ambiguities*: uncertainties.

50 *do you*: may it do you.
   scald knave: scab.

55 *groat*: a small coin, worth about fourpence.

60 *in earnest*: as a deposit on.

61 *cudgels*: blows and the weapons with which these are inflicted.
62 *woodmonger*: dealer in wood.
63 *God b'wi' you*: God be with you.
68 *honourable respect*: occasion worthy of honour.

68–9 *memorable . . . valour*: in memory of those who died bravely; see *4, 7, 100*.
69 *avouch*: support.

71 *gleeking and galling*: gibing and scoffing.
73 *garb*: accent.
76 *condition*: behaviour.
77 *hussy*: whore, strumpet.
78 *my Doll . . . Spital*: Doll Tearsheet was
     Falstaff's Doll in *Henry IV Part 2*. Pistol
     seems to think that he took possession
     of her (as well as the Hostess), but he
     knows she has died in the hospital for
     venereal diseases; see *2, 1, 71*.
78–9 *malady of France*: i.e. venereal disease,
     syphilis.
79 *rendezvous*: refuge, last resort.
81 *bawd*: pimp.
81–2 *something . . . cutpurse*: become
     something of a pickpocket.
84–5 *And . . . wars*: The 'Gallia wars' seems
     to allude to the *Gallic Wars* of Julius
     Caesar, so that this final couplet (which
     closes the scene) ends Pistol's career on
     a characteristic attempt at bravado.

70 your deeds any of your words? I have seen you
    gleeking and galling at this gentleman twice or
    thrice. You thought because he could not speak
    English in the native garb he could not therefore
    handle an English cudgel. You find it otherwise, and
75 henceforth let a Welsh correction teach you a good
    English condition. Fare you well.   [*Exit*

Pistol
Doth fortune play the hussy with me now? News
have I that my Doll is dead i'th'Spital of a malady of
France, and there my rendezvous is quite cut off.
80 Old I do wax, and from my weary limbs honour is
    cudgelled. Well, bawd I'll turn, and something lean
    to cutpurse of quick hand. To England will I steal,
    and there I'll steal.
    And patches will I get unto these cudgelled scars,
85 And swear I got them in the Gallia wars.

                                              [*Exit*

Act 5   Scene 2

The year is 1420. In the French king's palace
at Troyes the peace treaty and the marriage
contracts are finally negotiated. Whilst the
lords arrange the political business, Henry
makes his proposal to Katherine. The Duke
of Burgundy introduces a note of smutty
innuendo, but at last the contracts are agreed
by all those concerned.

1 *wherefor . . . met*: which is why we are
   met.
2 *our brother*: brother-king; the greeting is
   courteous.
3 *fair time of day*: good morning.
4 *princely*: royal.
5 *this royalty*: the royal family.
6 *contriv'd*: achieved.
7 *Duke of Burgundy*: The Duke of
   Burgundy was not himself a member of
   the royal family, and was therefore an
   impartial and effective mediator
   between the two kings.

Scene 2

Enter at one door King Henry, Exeter,
Bedford, Westmorland *and other* Lords. *At
another,* Queen Isabel, *the* French King,
the Princess Katherine *and* Alice, *the*
Duke of Burgundy, *and other French*

King
Peace to this meeting, wherefor we are met.
Unto our brother France and to our sister,
Health and fair time of day. Joy and good wishes
To our most fair and princely cousin Katherine.
5 And as a branch and member of this royalty,
By whom this great assembly is contriv'd,
We do salute you, Duke of Burgundy.
And princes French, and peers, health to you all.

French King
Right joyous are we to behold your face,
10 Most worthy brother England, fairly met.
So are you, princes English, every one.

Queen

So happy be the issue, brother England,
Of this good day, and of this gracious meeting,
As we are now glad to behold your eyes,
15 Your eyes which hitherto have borne in them
Against the French that met them in their bent
The fatal balls of murdering basilisks.
The venom of such looks we fairly hope
Have lost their quality, and that this day
20 Shall change all griefs and quarrels into love.

King
To cry amen to that, thus we appear.
Queen
You English princes all, I do salute you.
Burgundy
My duty to you both, on equal love,
Great kings of France and England. That I have
labour'd
25 With all my wits, my pains and strong endeavours,
To bring your most imperial majesties
Unto this bar and royal interview,
Your mightiness on both parts best can witness.
Since then my office hath so far prevail'd
30 That face to face and royal eye to eye
You have congreeted. Let it not disgrace me
If I demand before this royal view
What rub or what impediment there is
Why that the naked, poor and mangled peace,
35 Dear nurse of arts, plenties and joyful births,
Should not in this best garden of the world,

12 *issue*: outcome.
13 *gracious*: noble, honourable; and achieved and blessed by God's grace.
16 *bent*: glance, line of fire.
17 *balls*: (1) eyeballs; (2) cannon balls.
basilisks: (1) mythical beasts with lethal glances; (2) large cannon.
19 *quality*: power.
23 *My duty*: my respect.
on: in.
27 *bar*: court of justice, tribunal.
royal interview: summit conference.
28 *parts*: sides.
31 *congreeted*: greeted each other.
33 *rub*: obstacle.
35 *nurse*: wet-nurse, nourisher.

37 *put up*: raise, show. *visage*: face.	Our fertile France, put up her lovely visage?
	Alas, she hath from France too long been chas'd,
39 *husbandry*: produce, harvest. *on heaps*: in disorder.	And all her husbandry doth lie on heaps,
40 *it*: its.	40 Corrupting in it own fertility.
41 *Her vine . . . heart*: The reference is to Psalm 104:15, 'wine that maketh glad the heart of man'.	Her vine, the merry cheerer of the heart,
	Unpruned, dies. Her hedges, even-pleach'd,
42 *even-pleach'd*: evenly layered.	Like prisoners wildly overgrown with hair
44 *fallow leas*: arable land left untilled.	Put forth disorder'd twigs. Her fallow leas
45 *darnel . . . fumitory*: weeds that grow on uncultivated soil. *rank*: rampant.	45 The darnel, hemlock and rank fumitory
	Doth root upon, while that the coulter rusts
46 *root*: take root. *coulter*: blade in front of the ploughshare.	That should deracinate such savagery.
	The even mead, that erst brought sweetly forth
47 *deracinate*: uproot.	The freckled cowslip, burnet, and green clover,
48 *mead*: meadow. *erst*: formerly.	50 Wanting the scythe, all uncorrected, rank,
49 *burnet*: a herb said to be good for healing wounds.	Conceives by idleness, and nothing teems
	But hateful docks, rough thistles, kecksies, burrs,
50 *Wanting*: for lack of. *rank*: run riot.	Losing both beauty and utility.
51 *Conceives by idleness*: spreads by lying waste. *teems*: breeds.	And as our vineyards, fallows, meads and hedges,
	55 Defective in their natures, grow to wildness,
52 *docks*: dock-leaves. *kecksies*: dry hollow stalks.	Even so our houses, and ourselves, and children
	Have lost, or do not learn for want of time
54 *fallows*: arable land lying fallow.	The sciences that should become our country,
55 *Defective . . . natures*: creatures of the wilderness, wild by nature.	But grow like savages, as soldiers will—
56 *houses*: households, families.	60 That nothing do but meditate on blood—
58 *sciences*: knowledge, learning. *become*: be appropriate for.	To swearing and stern looks, diffus'd attire,
	And everything that seems unnatural.
60 *meditate on blood*: think about nothing but bloodshed.	Which to reduce into our former favour
61 *diffus'd*: disorderly.	You are assembled; and my speech entreats
63 *reduce*: return. *favour*: appearance, approval.	65 That I may know the let why gentle peace
	Should not expel these inconveniences
65 *let*: hindrance.	And bless us with her former qualities.
66 *inconveniences*: injuries.	

68 *you would*: if you desire.
69 *want*: lack.

71 *full accord*: total agreement.
72 *tenors*: general aims.
    particular effects: specific details.
73 *inschedul'd briefly*: summarized.

77 *cursitory*: cursory.
78 *O'er-glanc'd*: looked over.
    Pleaseth: may it please.
79 *presently*: immediately.
80 *better heed*: further consideration.
81 *suddenly*: speedily.
82 *Pass . . . answer*: give you our final
    agreements.

85 *Huntington*: This is the only appearance
    of the character in this play. He was one
    of Henry's kinsmen and fought at
    Harfleur and Agincourt.
86 *free*: complete.
90 *consign*: subscribe.

93 *Happily*: with any luck.
94 *articles*: clauses, conditions.
    too nicely urg'd: too precisely argued
    about.
    stood upon: insisted upon.
96 *capital demand*: first article in the treaty;
    Henry has changed his original
    demands, and is now insisting only that
    his heirs should inherit the crown of
    France.
97 *forerank*: chief.
98 *good leave*: full permission.

King
If, Duke of Burgundy, you would the peace
Whose want gives growth to th'imperfections
70 Which you have cited, you must buy that peace
With full accord to all our just demands,
Whose tenors and particular effects
You have, inschedul'd briefly, in your hands.
        Burgundy
The king hath heard them, to the which as yet
75 There is no answer made.
        King
                                      Well then, the peace,
Which you before so urg'd, lies in his answer.
        French King
I have but with a cursitory eye
O'er-glanc'd the articles. Pleaseth your grace
To appoint some of your council presently
80 To sit with us once more, with better heed
To re-survey them. We will suddenly
Pass our accept and peremptory answer.
        King
Brother, we shall. Go, uncle Exeter,
And brother Bedford, and you brother Gloucester,
85 Westmorland, Huntington, go with the king,
And take with you free power to ratify,
Augment or alter as your wisdoms best
Shall see advantageable for our dignity,
Anything in or out of our demands,
90 And we'll consign thereto. Will you, fair sister,
Go with the princes or stay here with us?
        Queen
Our gracious brother, I will go with them.
Happily a woman's voice may do some good
When articles too nicely urg'd be stood on.
        King
95 Yet leave our cousin Katherine here with us.
She is our capital demand, compris'd
Within the forerank of our articles.
        Queen
She hath good leave.
                                    [*Exeunt all but* King Henry
                                        and Katherine *and* Alice

King
                    Fair Katherine, and most fair,
Will you vouchsafe to teach a soldier terms
100 Such as will enter at a lady's ear
And plead his love-suit to her gentle heart?
Katherine
Your majesty shall mock at me. I cannot speak your
England.
King
O fair Katherine, if you will love me soundly with
105 your French heart I will be glad to hear you confess
it brokenly with your English tongue. Do you like
me, Kate?
Katherine
Pardonnez-moi, I cannot tell vat is 'like me'.
King
An angel is like you, Kate, and you are like an
110 angel.
Katherine
[*To* Alice] *Que dit-il—que je suis semblable à les anges?*
Alice
Oui, vraiment, sauf votre grâce, ainsi dit-il.
King
I said so, dear Katherine, and I must not blush to
affirm it.
Katherine
115 *O bon Dieu, les langues des hommes sont pleines de*
tromperies!
King
What says she, fair one? That the tongues of men are
full of deceits?
Alice
Oui, dat de tongeus of de mans is be full of deceits,
120 dat is de princess.
King
The princess is the better Englishwoman. I'faith,
Kate, my wooing is fit for thy understanding. I am
glad thou canst speak no better English, for if thou
couldst thou wouldst find me such a plain king that
125 thou wouldst think I had sold my farm to buy my
crown. I know no ways to mince it in love, but
directly to say 'I love you'. Then if you urge me
farther than to say 'Do you in faith?', I wear out my

108 *vat*: what.

109 *Que . . . anges*: What is he saying—that I am like the angels?

112 *Oui . . . dit-il*: Yes indeed, begging your grace's pardon, that is what he said.

115–16 *O . . . tromperies*: The king translates the words correctly.

120 *dat . . . princess*: Alice's rendering of the princess's words perhaps suggests something of her own accent.
121 *the better Englishwoman*: i.e. because she seems to prefer plain speaking.

125 *sold my farm*: i.e. was no more than a country farmer.
126 *mince it*: behave like an affected courtier.
128–9 *wear out my suit*: have exhausted my courtship.

129–30 *clap . . . bargain*: shake hands on the deal.
131   *Sauf votre honneur*: saving your grace.

132   *Marry*: by [The Virgin Mary].
        put me to verses: ask me to write poetry.
133   *undid*: would destroy.

135   *measure*: metre.
135   *strength in measure*: sense of rhythm.
136   *measure in strength*: amount of physical strength.
        leapfrog: i.e. by leaping over.
138   *under . . . spoken*: I can say without boasting.
139   *leap into*: achieve (with sexual innuendo).
        buffet: box, fist-fight.
140   *bound my horse*: make my horse leap.
141   *lay on*: hit it out.
        like a jackanapes: as tightly as a monkey.
142–3 *look greenly*: look lovesick.
144   *cunning*: skill, expertise.
        protestation: declarations of love.
145   *urged*: provoked.
145–6 *for urging*: if I am provoked.
146   *temper*: quality.

suit. Give me your answer, i'faith do, and so clap
130 hands and a bargain. How say you, lady?

Katherine

Sauf votre honneur, me understand well.

King

Marry, if you would put me to verses, or to dance for
your sake, Kate, why, you undid me. For the one I
have neither words nor measure, and for the other I
135 have no strength in measure, yet a reasonable
measure in strength. If I could win a lady at leapfrog,
or by vaulting into my saddle with my armour on my
back, under the correction of bragging be it spoken I
should quickly leap into a wife. Or if I might buffet
140 for my love or bound my horse for her favours I
could lay on like a butcher and sit like a jackanapes,
never off. But before God, Kate, I cannot look
greenly, nor gasp out my eloquence, nor I have no
cunning in protestation, only downright oaths,
145 which I never use till urged, nor never break for
urging. If thou canst love a fellow of this temper,

147 *not worth sun-burning*: could not be made worse if it were sunburnt.
148 *glass*: looking-glass.
149 *thine eye . . . cook*: present me more attractively (as a cook garnishes a dish).

153 *uncoined*: not minted—and therefore not in current circulation (i.e. among women).
154 *perforce must*: must necessarily.
do thee right: be faithful to you.
155 *to woo . . . places*: to court other women.
156 *of infinite tongue*: who talk endlessly.
rhyme: sweet-talk.
158 *reason*: argue.
159 *prater*: prattler.
but a ballad: only like a popular song (and therefore unlikely to be remembered for very long).
fall: waste away.
161 *pate*: head of hair.
162 *wax*: grow.
165 *his*: its.

169 *ennemi*: The spelling may indicate Katherine's pronunciation.

177 *thee*: Henry's courtship now uses the 'familiar' second-person singular, pronouns ('thou', 'thee', and 'thy' rather than 'you' and 'your') to address Katherine.
179–83 *Je . . . mienne*: Henry translates his promise of lines 174–5.
181 *St Denis*: patron saint of France.
182 *be my speed*: assist me.

Kate, whose face is not worth sun-burning, that never looks in his glass for love of anything he sees there, let thine eye be thy cook. I speak to thee plain 150 soldier. If thou canst love me for this, take me. If not, to say to thee that I shall die is true, but for thy love, by the Lord, no. Yet I love thee too. And while thou livest, dear Kate, take a fellow of plain and uncoined constancy, for he perforce must do thee right, 155 because he hath not the gift to woo in other places. For these fellows of infinite tongue that can rhyme themselves into ladies' favours, they do always reason themselves out again. What? A speaker is but a prater, a rhyme is but a ballad, a good leg will fall, 160 a straight back will stoop, a black beard will turn white, a curled pate will grow bald, a fair face will wither, a full eye will wax hollow—but a good heart, Kate, is the sun and the moon, or rather the sun and not the moon, for it shines bright and never changes, 165 but keeps his course truly. If thou would have such a one, take me. And take me, take a soldier. Take a soldier, take a king. And what sayest thou then to my love? Speak, my fair, and fairly, I pray thee.

Katherine
Is it possible dat I sould love de *ennemi* of France?

King
170 No, it is not possible you should love the enemy of France, Kate. But in loving me you should love the friend of France, for I love France so well that I will not part with a village of it. I will have it all mine; and, Kate, when France is mine and I am yours, 175 then yours is France, and you are mine.

Katherine
I cannot tell vat is dat.

King
No, Kate? I will tell thee in French, which I am sure will hang upon my tongue like a new-married wife about her husband's neck, hardly to be shook off. *Je* 180 *quand sur le possession de France, et quand vous avez le possession de moi*—let me see, what then? Saint Denis be my speed!—*Donc vôtre est France, et vous êtes mienne.* It is as easy for me, Kate, to conquer the kingdom as to speak so much more French. I shall

185   *move*: persuade.

187–8   *Sauf . . . parle*: With respect, the
        French that you speak is better than the
        English that I speak.

190   *truly falsely*: true in meaning, but false
        (= inaccurate) in grammar.
191   *at one*: the same.

194   *Can . . . tell*: i.e. does anyone else know.

196   *closet*: bedroom.

198   *dispraise*: disparage.

201   *saving faith*: faith that makes me believe.

203   *scambling*: struggling (i.e. in battle).

205   *compound a boy*: generate a son.
206–7   *Constantinople . . . beard*: become a
        crusader and fight against the Turks
        (for control of the Holy Land).
208   *flower de luce*: fleur-de-lis. The French
        heraldic lily became part of the royal
        coat of arms (indicating the English
        claim to the French throne) in the reign
        of Edward III.

210   *'tis . . . know*: after we are married you
        will learn—i.e. to beget a son.
211   *you*: Henry reverts to the formal mode
        of address when he makes a solemn
        proposal.

185   never move thee in French, unless it be to laugh at
        me.

Katherine

*Sauf votre honneur, le français que vous parlez, il est
meilleur que l'anglais lequel je parle.*

King

No, faith is't not, Kate. But thy speaking of my
190   tongue and I thine most truly falsely must needs be
        granted to be much at one. But Kate, dost thou
        understand thus much English? Canst thou love me?

Katherine

I cannot tell.

King

Can any of your neighbours tell, Kate? I'll ask them.
195   Come, I know thou lovest me, and at night when you
        come into your closet you'll question this
        gentlewoman about me, and I know, Kate, you will
        to her dispraise those parts in me that you love with
        your heart. But good Kate, mock me mercifully, the
200   rather, gentle princess, because I love thee cruelly. If
        ever thou beest mine, Kate, as I have a saving faith
        within me tells me thou shalt, I get thee with
        scambling, and thou must therefore needs prove a
        good soldier-breeder. Shall not thou and I, between
205   Saint Denis and Saint George, compound a boy, half
        French half English, that shall go to Constantinople
        and take the Turk by the beard? Shall we not? What
        sayest thou, my fair flower de luce?

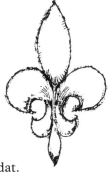

Katherine

I do not know dat.

King

210   No, 'tis hereafter to know, but now to promise. Do
        but now promise, Kate, you will endeavour for your

213 *moiety*: half-share.
214–15 *la plus . . . déesse*: the most beautiful
  Katherine in the world, and my dear,
  divine goddess. The French is not quite
  correct (*mon cher, divin*, should
  correctly be *ma chère, divine*,)—and this
  prompts the king's next comment.
216 *fausse French*: (1) inaccurate; (2)
  deceitful.
217 *sage demoiselle*: wise virgin.
218 *fie upon*: a plague upon.
220 *blood*: spirit.
221 *flatter*: persuade.
222 *untempering*: discouraging.
223 *beshrew*: curse.
223–4 *He . . . me*: It was believed that the
  child's temperament was influenced at
  the moment of conception by the
  father's state of mind.
225 *aspect*: appearance.
228 *layer-up*: preserver.
229 *spoil upon*: ravage to.
230 *wear*: possess and enjoy.

233 *Avouch*: give witness of.

239 *Plantagenet*: The name of the royal
  family between 1154 and 1485.
240 *fellow with*: equal to.
241 *king of . . . fellows*: The king plays with a
  proverbial saying: 'The king of good
  fellows is appointed for the queen of
  beggars'.
242 *broken music*: music in parts, part-song.
244 *break*: break open, tell me.
246 *de roi mon père*: the king my father.
247 *it will . . . it shall*: it will certainly please
  him, and it must please him; Henry is
  well aware that this marriage is the first
  article of the peace treaty.

French part of such a boy, and for my English
moiety take the word of a king and a bachelor. How
answer you, *la plus belle Katherine du monde, mon très*
215 *cher et divin déesse?*
   Katherine
Your majesty 'ave *fausse* French enough to deceive de
most *sage demoiselle* dat is *en France*.
   King
Now fie upon my false French. By mine honour, in
true English, I love thee, Kate. By which honour I
220 dare not swear thou lovest me, yet my blood begins
to flatter me that thou dost, notwithstanding the
poor and untempering effect of my visage. Now
beshrew my father's ambition! He was thinking of
civil wars when he got me. Therefore was I created
225 with a stubborn outside, with an aspect of iron, that
when I come to woo ladies I fright them. But in faith,
Kate, the elder I wax the better I shall appear. My
comfort is that old age, that ill layer-up of beauty,
can do no more spoil upon my face. Thou hast me,
230 if thou hast me, at the worst; and thou shalt wear me,
if thou wear me, better and better. And therefore tell
me, most fair Katherine, will you have me? Put off
your maiden blushes. Avouch the thoughts of your
heart with the looks of an empress. Take me by the
235 hand and say 'Harry of England, I am thine.'—
which word thou shalt no sooner bless mine ear
withal but I will tell thee aloud 'England is thine,
Ireland is thine, France is thine, and Henry
Plantagenet is thine', who, though I speak it before
240 his face, if he be not fellow with the best king thou
shalt find the best king of good fellows. Come, your
answer in broken music, for thy voice is music, and
thy English broken. Therefore, queen of all,
Katherine, break thy mind to me in broken English.
245 Wilt thou have me?
   Katherine
Dat is as it sall please de *roi mon père*.
   King
Nay, it will please him well, Kate; it shall please him,
Kate.

Katherine
Den it sall also content me.
King
250 Upon that I kiss your hand, and I call you my queen.

251–4 *Laissez . . . seigneur*: Let go, my lord,
let go! On my word, I would never want
you to lower your dignity by kissing the
hand of your majesty's unworthy
servant. Excuse me, I beg you, my most
mighty lord.

Katherine
*Laissez, mon seigneur, laissez, laissez! Ma foi, je ne veux
point que vous abaissiez votre grandeur, en baisant la
main d'une de votre seigneurie indigne serviteur.
Excusez-moi, je vous supplie, mon très puissant seigneur.*
King
255 Then I will kiss your lips, Kate.

256-7 *Les dames . . . France*: It is not the custom for women and maidens in France to kiss before they are married.

259 *façon . . . ladies*: fashion for the ladies.

262 *entends . . . moi*: understands better than I do.

265 *Oui, vraiment*: Yes, indeed.

266 *nice*: strict, over-precise.
curtsy: show respect for, yield to.

268 *list*: barriers (the image is from jousting).

269-70 *follows our places*: goes with our status.

270 *stops the mouth*: silences.

270-1 *as . . . yours*: as I will silence your mouth (with a kiss).

281 *would have*: want.

Katherine
Les dames et demoiselles, pour être baisées devant leurs noces, il n'est pas la coutume de France.
    King
Madam, my interpreter, what says she?
    Alice
Dat it is not be de *façon pour les* ladies of France—I
260 cannot tell vat is *baiser en* Anglish.
    King
To kiss.
    Alice
Your majesty *entends* bettre *que moi.*
    King
It is not a fashion for the maids in France to kiss before they are married, would she say?
    Alice
265 *Oui, vraiment.*
    King
O Kate, nice customs curtsy to great kings. Dear Kate, you and I cannot be confined within the weak list of a country's fashion. We are the makers of manners, Kate, and the liberty that follows our
270 places stops the mouth of all find-faults, as I will do yours, for upholding the nice fashion of your country in denying me a kiss. Therefore patiently, and yielding. [*Kisses her*] You have witchcraft in your lips, Kate. There is more eloquence in a sugar touch of
275 them than in the tongues of the French Council, and they should sooner persuade Harry of England than a general petition of monarchs. Here comes your father.

    Enter the French power [French King,
    Queen Isabel, Burgundy], *and the English
    lords* [Exeter, Westmorland]

    Burgundy
God save your majesty. My royal cousin, teach you
280 our princess English?
    King
I would have her learn, my fair cousin, how perfectly I love her, and that is good English.

283 *apt*: a promising pupil.

284 *Our tongue*: the English language; see
    'Background', p. 144.
    condition: behaviour, temperament.
289 *Pardon . . . mirth*: excuse my unseemly
    laughter; Burgundy will twist the sense
    of Henry's words.
290–1 *conjure . . . circle*: i.e. like a magician
    invoking spirits.
291 *his true likeness*: as he really is; Cupid,
    the god of love, was usually depicted as
    a naked and blindfolded boy.

293 *rosed over*: blushing.
294 *deny the appearance*: refuse to admit.
296 *consign*: yield, agree to.
297 *wink*: close their eyes.
303 *wink on her*: give her the wink, indicate.
304 *know my meaning*: i.e. understand about
    sex.
305 *summered*: looked after.
    warm kept: warm-blooded, on heat.
306 *Bartholomew-tide*: the height of summer
    (St Bartholomew's day is 24 August).
307–8 *endure . . . looking on*: allow
    themselves to be handled when before
    they did not wish to be seen.
309 *moral*: comparison.
    ties me over: restricts me to.
310–11 *in the latter end*: at the end of
    summer; Henry also picks up the duke's
    innuendo.
312 *As love . . . loves*: love is blind until it
    really knows what it is loving.
313 *you may*: Henry reminds his listeners
    that this is a serious occasion.

Burgundy
Is she not apt?

King
Our tongue is rough, coz, and my condition is no
285 smooth, so that having neither the voice nor the
heart of flattery about me I cannot so conjure up the
spirit of love in her that he will appear in his true
likeness.

Burgundy
Pardon the frankness of my mirth if I answer you for
290 that. If you would conjure in her you must make a
circle, if conjure up love in her in his true likeness he
must appear naked and blind. Can you blame her
then, being a maid yet rosed over with the virgin
crimson of modesty, if she deny the appearance of a
295 naked blind boy in her naked seeing self? It were,
my lord, a hard condition for a maid to consign to.

King
Yet they do wink and yield, as love is blind and
enforces.

Burgundy
They are then excused, my lord, when they see not
300 what they do.

King
Then, good my lord, teach your cousin to consent
winking.

Burgundy
I will wink on her to consent, my lord, if you will
teach her to know my meaning; for maids well
305 summered and warm kept are like flies at
Bartholomew-tide, blind, though they have their
eyes, and then they will endure handling which
before would not abide looking on.

King
This moral ties me over to time, and a hot summer
310 and so I shall catch the fly, your cousin, in the latter
end, and she must be blind too.

Burgundy
As love is, my lord, before it loves.

King
It is so. And you may, some of you, thank love for my
blindness, who cannot see many a fair French city
315 for one fair French maid that stands in my way.

16 *perspectively*: distanced and distorted, as in a 'perspective glass'.

17 *girdled*: encompassed.

20 *So please you*: if that is your will.

21–2 *so . . . on her*: as long as she brings these cities as a dowry.

22–3 *so . . . will*: thus the maiden that I wanted to have will enable me to satisfy my desire for my heir.

24 The serious business of the scene is now conducted in verse.

27 *in sequel*: following that.

28 *firm proposed natures*: i.e. what has definitely been stipulated. The king is now asking for considerably less than he originally demanded.

29 *subscribed this*: signed his name in agreement.

31–2 *for matter of grant*: in any matter connected with grants of land or titles.

32 *name*: refer to.

33 *addition*: title.

33–4 *Notre . . . France*: Our very dear son Henry, king of England and heir to France.

35–6 *Praeclarissimus . . . Franciae*: The Latin words should have the same meaning as the French, but Shakespeare (like the historians Hall and Holinshed) has copied '*praeclarissimus*' (= most famous) for '*praecarissimus*' (= most dearly beloved).

44 *look pale*: i.e. the white cliffs of Dover and Calais.

French King
Yes, my lord, you see them perspectively, the cities turned into a maid, for they are all girdled with maiden walls that war hath never entered.
King
Shall Kate be my wife?
French King
320 So please you.
King
I am content, so the maiden cities you talk of may wait on her, so the maid that stood in the way for my wish shall show me the way to my will.
French King
We have consented to all terms of reason.
King
325 Is't so, my lords of England?
Westmorland
The king hath granted every article,
His daughter first, and then in sequel all
According to their firm proposed natures.
Exeter
Only he hath not yet subscribed this:
330 where your majesty demands that the King of France, having any occasion to write for matter of grant, shall name your highness in this form and with this addition, in French: *Notre très cher fils Henri, roi d'Angleterre, héritier de France*; and thus in Latin:
335 *Praeclarissimus filius noster Henricus, rex Angliae et heres Franciae.*
French King
Nor this I have not, brother, so denied
But your request shall make me let it pass.
King
I pray you then, in love and dear alliance,
340 Let that one article rank with the rest,
And thereupon give me your daughter.
French King
Take her, fair son, and from her blood raise up
Issue to me, that the contending kingdoms
Of France and England, whose very shores look
    pale
345 With envy of each other's happiness,

346 *dear conjunction*: beloved (*and* dearly-
      bought) union.
347 *neighbourhood*: neighbourliness.
348 *that*: so that.

May cease their hatred. And this dear conjunction
Plant neighbourhood and Christian-like accord
In their sweet bosoms, that never war advance
His bleeding sword 'twixt England and fair France.

Lords
350 Amen.

King
Now welcome, Kate, and bear me witness all
That here I kiss her as my sovereign queen.

352s.d. *Flourish*: a triumphant fanfare.

Flourish

Queen
God, the best maker of all marriages,
Combine your hearts in one, your realms in one.
355 As man and wife, being two, are one in love,

356 *spousal*: marriage.
357 *ill office*: any crooked dealing.
      fell: cruel.

359 *paction*: compact.
360 *incorporate league*: union in one body.

So be there 'twixt your kingdoms such a spousal
That never may ill office or fell jealousy,
Which troubles oft the bed of blessed marriage,
Thrust in between the paction of these kingdoms
360 To make divorce of their incorporate league,
That English may as French, French Englishmen,
Receive each other. God speak this 'amen'.

362 *God . . . 'amen'*: may God say 'amen [=
      so be it]' to this.

All
Amen.

King
Prepare we for our marriage; on which day,
365 My lord of Burgundy, we'll take your oath

366 *surety of our leagues*: security of our
      alliance.
368s.d. *Sennet*: the trumpets signal the
      departure of the king and the royal
      procession.

And all the peers', for surety of our leagues.
Then shall I swear to Kate, and you to me,
And may our oaths well kept and prosperous be.
                                        [*Sennet. Exeun*

Act 5   Scene 3

The Chorus has the last words, speaking a
sonnet that relates *Henry V* to Shakespeare's
earlier history plays.

1 *unable*: unequal, unskilled.
2 *bending*: bending over his writing, or
   taking a bow.
3 *little room*: small space.
4 *by starts*: in fits and starts.
   course: course of events, gallop.
5 *Small time*: for only a short time—
   Henry died in 1422 at the age of 35.
7 *best garden*: i.e. France.

9 *in infant bands*: in swaddling clothes.

11 *state*: estate.
    managing: governing.

13 *oft . . . shown*: i.e. in Shakespeare's
    Henry VI plays.
    their sake: the sake of the other plays.
14 *this*: this play.

Scene 3

> *Enter* Chorus

Chorus
Thus far with rough and all-unable pen
Our bending author hath pursu'd the story,
In little room confining mighty men,
Mangling by starts the full course of their glory.
5 Small time, but in that small, most greatly lived
This star of England. Fortune made his sword
By which the world's best garden he achieved,
And of it left his son imperial lord.
Henry the Sixth, in infant bands crown'd king
10 Of France and England, did this king succeed,
Whose state so many had the managing
That they lost France and made his England bleed,
Which oft our stage hath shown—and for their
    sake,
In your fair minds let this acceptance take.
                                              [*Exit*

The Sources of *Henry V*

The three plays presenting the career of the hero of Agincourt in Shakespeare's second tetralogy may all have been inspired initially by an anonymous play, *The Famous Victories of Henry the Fifth*. The only surviving text of this play (1598) is a debased and abbreviated version of a lost original, and it is this which Shakespeare is most likely to have known. He had recourse, also, to various semi-official histories, and especially to Holinshed's *Chronicles of England* (1587) and Hall's *Union of the Two Noble Families* (1548). A few passages from Holinshed are reprinted below to give a rough idea of Shakespeare's working, but the serious student of Shakespeare's sources should consult Kenneth Muir's book, *The Sources of Shakespeare's Plays* (London, 1977), and see the complete texts published in *The Narrative and Dramatic Sources of Shakespeare*, vol. iv, by Geoffrey Bullough (London, 1973).

Act 1, Scene 1, lines 1–19

[Early in his reign Henry summoned the high court of parliament which passed many laws, but some petitions were deferred] . . . Amongst which, one was that a bill exhibited in the parliament holden at Westminster in the eleventh year of King Henry the Fourth (which, by reason the king was then troubled with civil discord, came to none effect) might now with good deliberation be pondered and brought to some good conclusion. The effect of which supplication was: that the temporal lands devoutly given, and disordinately spent by religious and other spiritual persons, should be seized into the king's hands, sith the same might suffice to maintain, to the honour of the king and defence of the realm, fifteen earls, fifteen hundred knights, six thousand and two hundred esquires, and a hundred almshouses, for relief only of the poor, impotent, and needy persons, and the king to have clearly to his coffers twenty thousand pounds, with many other provisions and values of religious houses . . .

Act 1, Scene 2, lines 35ff.

. . . Herein did he much inveigh against the surmised and false
feigned law Salic, which the Frenchmen allege ever against the
kings of England in bar of their just title to the crown of France.
The very words of that supposed law are these, *In terram Salicam
mulieres ne succedant*; that is to say, into the Salic land let not
women succeed. Which the French glossers expound to be the
realm of France, and that this law was made by King Pharamound;
whereas yet their own authors affirm that the land Salic is in
Germany, between the rivers of Elbe and Sala; and that when
Charles the Great had overcome the Saxons, he placed there
certain Frenchmen, which having in disdain the dishonest manners
of the German women, made a law that the females should not
succeed to any inheritance within that land, which at this day is
called Meissen. So that, if this be true, this law was not made for
the realm of France, nor the Frenchmen possessed the land Salic
till four hundred and one-and-twenty years after the death of
Pharamound, the supposed maker of this Salic law; for this
Pharamound deceased in the year 426, and Charles the Great
subdued the Saxons, and placed the Frenchmen in those parts
beyond the river of Sala, in the year 805 . . .

. . . The archbishop further alleged out of the Book of Numbers
this saying: 'When a man dieth without a son, let the inheritance
descend to his daughter' . . .

Act 3, Scene 7, lines 38ff.

. . . A soldier took a pix out of a church, for which he was
apprehended, and the king not once removed till the box was
restored and the offender strangled . . .

Act 3, Scene 7, lines 154ff.

. . . King Henry advisedly answered: Mine intent is to do as it
pleaseth God, I will not seek your master at this time; but if he or
his seek me, I will meet with them, God willing. If any of your
nation attempt once to stop me in my journey now to Calais, at
their jeopardy be it; and yet wish I not any of you so unadvised as
to be the occasion that I dye your tawny ground with your red
blood . . .

Act 4, Scene 3, lines 16–67

. . . It is said, that as he heard one of the host utter his wish to another thus: I would to God there were with us now, so many good soldiers as are at this hour within England! The king answered: I would not wish a man more here than I have, we are indeed in comparison to the enemies but a few, but if God of his clemency do favour us and our just cause (as I trust he will) we shall speed well enough. But let no man ascribe victory to his own strength and might, but only to God's assistance, to whom I have no doubt we shall worthily have cause to give thanks therefore. And if so be that for our offences' sake we shall be delivered into the hands of our enemies, the less number we be, the less damage shall the realm of England sustain . . .

Act 4, Scene 8, line 105

. . . He sent privily two hundred archers into a low meadow, which was near to the vanguard of his enemies, but separated with a great ditch, commanding them there to keep themselves close till they had a token to them given, to let drive at their adversaries . . . he caused stakes bound with iron sharp at both ends, of the length of five or six foot to be pitched before the archers, and of each side the footmen like a hedge, to the intent that if the barded horses ran rashly upon them, they might shortly be gored and destroyed . . . This device of fortifying an army was at this time first invented . . .

Act 5, Chorus, lines 17–22

. . . The king, like a grave and sober personage, and as one remembering from whom all victories are sent, seemed little to regard such value [of] pomp and shows as were in triumphant sort devised for his welcoming home from so prosperous a journey, insomuch that he would not suffer his helmet to be carried with him, whereby might have appeared to the people the blows and dints that were to be seen in the same . . .

What the Critics have said

Samuel Johnson
[*Act V*, Scene iv]
'The truth is, that the poet's matter failed him in the fifth act, and
he was glad to fill it up with whatever he could get; and not even
Shakespeare can write well without a proper subject. It is a vain
endeavour for the most skilful hand to cultivate barrenness.'
                    The Works of Shakespeare, ed. Samuel Johnson (1765)

William Hazlitt
'Henry V it is true, was a hero, a king of England, and the
conqueror of the king of France. Yet we feel little love or
admiration for him. He was a hero, that is, he was ready to sacrifice
his own life for the pleasure of destroying thousands of other lives:
he was a king of England, but not a constitutional one, and we only
like kings according to the law; lastly, he was a conqueror of the
French king, and for this we dislike him less than if he had
conquered the French people. How then do we like him? We like
him in the play. There is he a very amiable monster, a very splendid
pageant. As we like to gaze at a panther or a young lion in their
cages in the Tower, and catch a pleasing horror from their
glistening eyes, their velvet paws, and dreadless roar, so we take a
very romantic, heroic, patriotic, and poetical delight in the boasts
and feats of our younger Harry, as they appear on the stage and are
confined to lines of ten syllables; where no blood follows the stroke
that wounds our ears, where no harvest bends beneath horses'
hoofs, no city flames, no little child is butchered, no dead men's
bodies found piled on heaps and festering the next morning—in
the orchestra! . . . '
                    from *Characters of Shakespeare's Plays* (1817)

A.W. Schlegel
'King Henry the Fifth is manifestly Shakespeare's favourite hero in
English history: he paints him as endowed with every chivalrous
and kingly virtue; open, sincere, affable, yet, as a sort of
reminiscence of his youth, still disposed to innocent raillery, in the

intervals between his perilous but glorious achievements. However, to represent on the stage his whole history subsequent to his accession to the throne, was attended with great difficulty. The conquests in France were the only distinguished event of his reign; and war is an epic rather than a dramatic object.'

from *Lectures on Dramatic Art and Literature* (1809–11)

R.G. Moulton

'In *Henry V* Shakespeare has embodied his conception of supreme heroism; and in order that the conception may be individualized, and not remain a mere poetic ideal, his choice of subject has given it the practical tinge, which of all aspects of heroism is the one most congenial to the English mind. Or rather, the hero of the poem is the English nation itself, as typified in the popular king who has caught the spirit of every class amongst his people, and concentrates them all in himself.'

from 'On Character Development in Shakespeare as illustrated by *Macbeth* and *Henry V*', in *Transactions of the New Shakespeare Society* (1880–86)

W. B. Yeats

'Shakespeare watched Henry V not indeed as he watched the greater souls in the visionary procession, but cheerfully, as one watches some handsome spirited horse, and he spoke his tale, as he spoke all tales, with tragic irony.'

from *Ideas of Good and Evil* (1903)

George Bernard Shaw

'One can hardly forgive Shakespeare quite for the worldly phase in which he tried to thrust such a Jingo hero as his Harry V down our throats. The combination of conventional propriety and brute masterfulness in his public capacity with a low-lived blackguardism in his private tastes is not a pleasant one. No doubt he is true to nature as a picture of what is by no means uncommon in English society, an able young Philistine inheriting high position and authority, which he holds on to and goes through with by keeping a tight grip on his conventional and legal advantages, but who would have been quite in his place if he had been born a gamekeeper or a farmer . . . His popularity, therefore, is like that of a prizefighter: nobody feels for him as for Romeo or Hamlet.'

from *Dramatic Opinions and Essays* (1907)

J. I. M. Stewart

'Falstaff's corner of *Henry V* is extremely wonderful; the rest is a slack-water play, stirred here and there by simple patriotic feeling. For comedy now Shakespeare had so little list that he fell back upon comic Scots, Irish, and Welshmen—the recourse, I think I may say, of a professional entertainer hard pressed indeed. Moreover, that the poet of *Romeo and Juliet* should have executed the wooing of Katherine—that *ne plus ultra* of all obtuseness—must fill us with dismay until we persuade ourselves (with a school of critics romantic, no doubt) that there here glints at us from behind the mask the master's most inscrutable smile.'

from *Character and Motive in Shakespeare* (1949)

Classwork and Examinations

The works of Shakespeare are studied all over the world, and this classroom edition is being used in many different countries. Teaching methods vary from school to school, and there are many different ways of examining a student's work. Some teachers and examiners expect detailed knowledge of Shakespeare's text, others ask for imaginative involvement with his characters and their situations; and some teachers want their students to share in the theatrical experience of directing and performing a play. Most people use a variety of methods. This section of the book offers a few suggestions for approaches to *Henry V* which could be used in schools and colleges to help with students' understanding and *enjoyment* of the play.

> A Discussion
> B Character Study
> C Activities
> D Context Questions
> E Comprehension Questions
> F Essays
> G Projects

A   Discussion

Talking about the play—about the issues it raises and the characters who are involved—is one of the most rewarding and pleasurable aspects of the study of Shakespeare. It makes sense to discuss each scene as it is read, sharing impressions—and perhaps correcting misapprehensions. Large classes can be divided into smaller 'sub-committees' of four or five students (with a group-leader) to investigate specific points and then report their findings back to the main body. It can be useful to compare aspects of this play with other fictions—plays, novels, films—or with modern life.

Suggestions

A1 What is *your* nationality? Do you have a sense of being English—or Scots, Welsh, Irish, Jewish, Muslim, African . . . ? Or are you a European? How do you determine this? Does the history of your country/nation/race mean much to you?

A2 Should rulers (either kings, presidents, or governments) have the right to confiscate private property for public use?

A3 Would you fight for your king/queen and country—or would you resist the Chorus's call to arms (Chorus *3*, 22–4)?

A4 Does 'obedience to the king' (or to any individual in authority—commanding officer, employer, teacher) override personal morality?

A5 Before the battle of Agincourt, King Henry promises his followers that they will be taking part in a historic event worthy of remembrance:

> He that shall see this day and live old age
> Will yearly on the vigil feast his neighbours,
> And say 'Tomorrow is Saint Crispian.'
> Then will he strip his sleeve and show his scars,
> And say 'These wounds I had on Crispin's day.'

(4, 3, 44–8)

How would you choose to commemorate/celebrate such an occasion?

B Character Study

Shakespeare is famous for his creation of characters who seem like real people. We can judge their actions and we can try to understand their thoughts and feelings—just as we criticize and try to understand the people we know. As the play progresses, we learn to like or dislike, love or hate, them—just as though they lived in *our* world.

Characters can be studied *from the outside*, by observing what they do, and listening sensitively to what they say. This is the scholar's method; the scholar—or any reader—has access to the whole play, and can see the function of every character within the whole scheme of that play.

Another approach works *from the inside*, taking a single character and looking at the action and the other characters from his/her point of view. This is an actor's technique in creating a character—who can have only a partial view of what is going on; and it asks for a student's inventive imagination. The two methods—both useful in different ways—are really complementary to each other.

Suggestions

a) from 'outside' the character

B1 'The king has two faces': contrast the character that Henry presents in public with what you can see of his private self.

B2 Is the Archbishop of Canterbury more a man of the world than a man of God?

B3 Do King Henry's practical jokes indicate a sense of humour, or are they cruelly manipulative?

B4 Describe the characters and dramatic functions of

a) Exeter
b) The Dauphin
c) Burgundy

B5 'Apart from the king himself, Llewellyn is the only character worth the name in *Henry V*—and his personality seems excessive for his part in the action.' How far would you agree with this statement?

b) from 'inside' the character

B6 Record King Henry's thoughts in a 'stream-of-consciousness' narrative as he listens to the archbishop's exposition of the 'law Salic that they have in France'.

B7 As one of the French ambassadors, describe your feelings before, during, and after the audience with the English king.

B8 'Confessions of a Conspirator': write—or ghost-write—the musings of one of the three traitors (Cambridge, Scroop, and Gray) before the execution day.

B9 Deliver the *Act 3* soliloquy of the Boy, formerly Falstaff's page, in a modern idiom.

B10 'The Seige and Surrender of Harfleur': the Governor writes an official communiqué, or a personal letter, to explain (or excuse) his action.

B11 Emulate Bourbon's rhapsodies on his horse: expatiate on the wonders of your own favourite—bike/car/footballer/pop star/pet animal.

B12 In the character of Pistol (and remembering Gower's observations in *Act 3*, Scene 7)

> a) write a letter to the Hostess describing your conquest of the Frenchman
> b) devise a ballad recounting your exploits in the 'Gallia wars'.

B13 Tell the story of the night before Agincourt from the viewpoint of one of the soldiers, Bates, Court or Williams.

B14 Send despatches from the Agincourt front to the French king, giving the account of Bourbon, Constable, or Grandpré describing

> a) the English army before the battle
> b) the state of the French morale
> c) the defeat of the French forces.

B15 'A winning match!' As the Princess Katherine, confide your thoughts and emotions to your diary before and after your encounter with the English king.

B16 'She told me everything': a series of letters/articles for the press from Alice, describing the progress of the courtship you have witnessed and the part you played in it.

B17 The French royal family speak their minds at last! The story of the engagement which has been fought, won (or lost), and arranged between Henry V and the French princess told in the character of

> a) The French king
> b) The French queen
> c) The Dauphin

C   Activities

These can involve two or more students, preferably working *away from* the desk or study-table and using gesture and position ('body-language') as well as speech. They can help students to develop a sense of drama and the dramatic aspects of Shakespeare's play—which was written to be *performed*, not studied in a classroom.

C1 Traditionally the Chorus's speeches have always been delivered by a single actor; in the workshop divide them between several speakers or groups of speakers. Which method do you prefer?

C2 Hold a 'round-table' discussion after the declaration of war on France, making sure that all interests are represented (the churchman, the politician, the agnostic philosopher, the 'statutory' woman, the member of an ethnic minority).

C3 In small groups, devise models—like the archbishop's beehive—for the harmonious state; present these for criticism to the entire class.

C4 War has been declared, and men are enlisting for service: interview as many as you can for radio/TV news, questioning them about their motives, hopes, and fears.

C5 The usual war correspondents are gathered at Harfleur, preparing copy for their different media. Write their reports, bearing in mind the intended audience (radio/TV) or readership (newspapers). Compare the different 'angles'.

C6 Find out all you can about Prince Hal and Falstaff, then devise a scene in which the Hostess, Pistol, Nym, Bardolph, and the Boy (Falstaff's page) reminisce about 'the good old days'.

C7 Improvise a scene between four officers about the proper conduct of a modern-day battle, using stereotypes such as Gower, Llewellyn, Jamy, and Macmorris. These could be representatives of different ethnic groups, or even of different services (army, navy, air-force . . .).

C8 The Battle of Agincourt—a television documentary looking back on the first (or any subsequent) anniversary. How the land lay: the deployment of troops on either side. 'I was there': interviews with survivors. 'The right and wrong': debate by politicians. 'Oh God, Thy hand was here': discussion by churchmen.

C9 Organize media coverage at Troyes—what are the hopes and fears of the two parties? Interview Burgundy before and after the summit conference and peace talks.

D   Context Questions

In written examinations, these questions present you with short passages from the play, and ask you to explain them. They are intended to test your knowledge of the play and your understanding of its words. Usually you have to make a choice of passages: there may be five on the paper, and you are asked to choose three. Be very sure that you know exactly how many passages you must choose. Study the ones offered to you, and select those you feel most certain of. Make your answers accurate and concise—don't waste time writing more than the examiner is asking for.

D1 Fortune is —'s foe, and frowns on him. For he hath stolen a pax, and hanged must a be.

    (i) Who is the person speaking, and to whom ('—') does he refer?
    (ii) To whom is he speaking, and what does he want?
    (iii) What do we know of '—'; what happens to him?

D2 The offer likes not, and the nimble gunner
With linstock now the devilish cannon touches.
               Alarm, and chambers go off.

    (i) Who delivers these lines, and to whom are they addressed?
    (ii) What was the 'offer', and to whom was it made?
    (iii) What follows the *Alarm*?

D3 Alas, she hath from France too long been chas'd,
And all her husbandry doth lie on heaps,
Corrupting in it own fertility.

    (i) Who is 'she' and why has she been chased from France?
    (ii) Who has been chasing her?
    (iii) Who is the speaker of these lines, and what is the occasion?

E   Comprehension Questions

These also present passages from the play and ask questions about them, and again you often have a choice of passages. But the extracts are much longer than those presented as context questions. A detailed knowledge of the language of the play is asked for here, and you must be able to express unusual or archaic phrases in your own words; you may also be asked to comment critically on the effectiveness of Shakespeare's language.

E1   Suppose that you have seen,
  The well-appointed king at Hampton Pier
  Embark his royalty, and his brave fleet
  With silken streamers the young Phoebus feigning.
  Play with your fancies, and in them behold   5
  Upon the hempen tackle ship-boys climbing.
  Hear the shrill whistle, which doth order give
  To sounds confus'd. Behold the threaden sails,
  Borne with the invisible and creeping wind,
  Draw the huge bottoms through the furrow'd sea,   10
  Breasting the lofty surge. O do but think
  You stand upon the rivage, and behold
  A city on th'inconstant billows dancing,
  For so appears this fleet majestical,
  Holding due course to Harfleur . . .   15

  (i)   Give the meanings of 'threaden' (line 8); 'Breasting' (line 11); 'rivage' (line 12).
  (ii) Express in your own words the sense of lines 3–4 'his brave fleet . . . feigning'; lines 7–8 'the shrill whistle . . . sounds confused'; line 13 'A city . . . dancing'.
  (iii) What do these lines show of the attitude and function of the speaker (the Chorus)?
  (iv) How appropriate is the reference to 'young Phoebus'?

E2 I did never know so full a voice issue from so empty a heart. But the saying is true, the empty vessel makes the greatest sound. Bardolph and Nym had ten times more valour than this roaring devil i'th'old play, that everyone may pare his nails with a wooden dagger, and they are both hanged, and so would this   5
be if he durst steal anything adventurously. I must stay with the lackeys with the luggage of our camp. The French might have a good prey of us if he knew of it, for there is none to guard it but boys.

(i) Express in your own words the meaning of 'the empty
. . . sound' (lines 2–3); 'lackeys' (line 7); 'good prey of
us' (line 8).

(ii) Who are the characters described in this speech, and what
is their importance to *Henry V*?

(iii) Explain the reference to 'this roaring devil i'th'old play'
(line 4).

(iv) How does this speech prepare us for subsequent events in
the play?

E3   . . . On, on, you noble English,
Whose blood is fet from fathers of war-proof,
Fathers that like so many Alexanders
Have in these parts from morn till even fought,
And sheath'd their swords for lack of argument.   5
Dishonour not your mothers. Now attest
That those whom you call'd fathers did beget you.
Be copy now to men of grosser blood,
And teach them how to war. And you, good yeomen,
Whose limbs were made in England, show us here   10
The mettle of your pasture. Let us swear
That you are worth your breeding, which I doubt not,
For there is none of you so mean and base
That hath not noble lustre in your eyes.

(i) Give the meanings of 'fet' (line 2); 'war-proof' (line 2);
'yeomen' (line 9).

(ii) Express in your own words the sense of lines 4–5, 'from
morn . . . argument'; lines 6–7, 'Dishonour . . . beget you';
lines 8–9, 'Be copy . . . war'.

(iii) Comment on the 'class-distinction' shown in these lines.

(iv) What persona is Henry trying to present in this speech?
How convincing is he?

F   Essays

These will usually give you a specific topic to discuss, or perhaps a
question that must be answered, in writing, *with a reasoned
argument*. They *never* want you to tell the story of the play—so
don't! Your examiner—or teacher—has read the play, and does not
need to be reminded of it. Relevant quotations will always help you
to make your points more strongly.

F1 'There is only a single character in *Henry V*': how far is this true?

F2 'As well as writing history, Shakespeare also criticizes its events and heroes.' Discuss.

F3 'For King Henry, doing the will of God is only an excuse for doing what is politically expedient.' Do you agree?

F4 *Henry V* is a very long play, and often needs to be cut for stage (or film) presentation; what scenes or episodes would you be willing to discard?

F5 Give your reasons for disputing or sharing these comments made by previous critics (see p.126).

- a) 'The truth is, that the poet's matter failed him in the fifth act' (Dr Johnson).
- b) Shakespeare 'spoke his tale, as he spoke all his tales, with tragic irony' (W. B. Yeats).
- c) 'His [Henry's] popularity . . . is like that of a prizefighter: nobody feels for him as for Romeo or Hamlet' (G. B. Shaw).
- d) 'the hero of the poem is the English nation itself' (R. G. Moulton).

F6 Arbitrate between Hazlitt—'We feel little love or admiration for [Henry V]'—and Schlegel—'King Henry the Fifth is manifestly Shakespeare's favourite hero'.

G Projects

In some schools, students are asked to do more 'free-ranging' work, which takes them outside the text—but which should always be relevant to the play. Such Projects may demand skills other than reading and writing: design and artwork, for instance, may be involved. Sometimes a 'portfolio' of work is assembled over a considerable period of time; and this can be presented to the examiner as part of the student's work for assessment. The availability of resources will, obviously, do much to determine the nature of the projects; but this is something that only the local teachers will understand. However, there is always help to be found in libraries, museums, and art galleries.

G1 The historical Agincourt.

G2 Shakespeare's sources for *Henry V*.

G3 Great performances by great actors.

G4 Weaponry at the time of *Henry V*.

G5 'The wooden O': Shakespeare's theatre.

G6 Research the origins and symbolism of
'. . . the balm, the sceptre and the ball,
The sword, the mace, the crown imperial . . .' — 4, 1, 233–4.

Background

England c. 1599

When Shakespeare was writing *Henry V*, most people believed that the sun went round the earth. They were taught that this was a divinely ordered scheme of things, and that—in England—God had instituted a Church and ordained a Monarchy for the right government of the land and the populace.

'The past is a foreign country; they do things differently there.'

L. P. Hartley

Government

For most of Shakespeare's life, the reigning monarch of England was Queen Elizabeth I. With her counsellors and ministers, she governed the nation (population about five million) from London, although not more than half a million people inhabited the capital city. In the rest of the country, law and order were maintained by the land-owners and enforced by their deputies. The average man had no vote—and his wife had no rights at all.

Religion

At this time, England was a Christian country. All children were baptized, soon after they were born, into the Church of England; they were taught the essentials of the Christian faith, and instructed in their duty to God and to humankind. Marriages were performed, and funerals conducted, only by the licensed clergy and in accordance with the Church's rites and ceremonies. Attendance at divine service was compulsory; absences (without good— medical—reason) could be punished by fines. By such means, the authorities were able to keep some check on the populace— recording births, marriages, and deaths; being alert to any religious nonconformity, which could be politically dangerous; and ensuring a minimum of orthodox instruction through the official 'Homilies' which were regularly preached from the pulpits of all parish churches throughout the realm. Following Henry VIII's break away from the Church of Rome, all people in England were able to hear the church services *in their own language*. The Book of Common Prayer was used in every church, and an English translation of the Bible was read aloud in public. Shakespeare would be most familiar with the Bishops' Bible, which he would hear in church, and with the Geneva version of the New Testament which, being a small volume, he probably possessed. The Christian religion had never been so well taught before!

Education

School education reinforced the Church's teaching. From the age of four, boys might attend the 'petty school' (French *'petite école'*) to learn the rudiments of reading and writing along with a few prayers; some schools also included work with numbers. At the age of seven, the boy was ready for the grammar school (if his father was willing and able to pay the fees).

A thorough grounding in Latin grammar was followed by translation work and the study of Roman authors, paying attention as much to style as to matter. The arts of fine writing were thus inculcated from early youth. A very few students proceeded to university; these were either clever scholarship boys, or else the sons of noblemen. Girls stayed at home, and acquired domestic and social skills—cooking, sewing, perhaps even music. The lucky ones might learn to read and write.

Language

At the start of the sixteenth century the English had a very poor opinion of their own language: there was little serious writing in English, and hardly any literature. Latin was the language of international scholarship, and Englishmen admired the eloquence of the Romans. They made many translations, and in this way they extended the resources of their own language, increasing its vocabulary and stretching its grammatical structures. French, Italian, and Spanish works were also translated, and for the first time there were English versions of the Bible. By the end of the century, English was a language to be proud of: it was rich in synonyms, capable of infinite variety and subtlety, and ready for all kinds of word-play—especially the *puns*, for which Shakespeare's English is renowned.

Drama

The great art-form of the Elizabethan and Jacobean age was its drama. The Elizabethans inherited a tradition of play-acting from the Middle Ages, and they reinforced this by reading and translating the Roman playwrights. At the beginning of the sixteenth century plays were performed by groups of actors, all-male companies (boys acted the female roles) who travelled from town to town, setting up their stages in open places (such as inn-yards) or, with the permission of the owner, in the hall of some noble house. The touring companies continued, in the provinces, into the seventeenth century; but in London, in 1576, a new building was erected for the performance of plays. This was the Theatre, the first purpose-built playhouse in England. Other playhouses followed, including Shakespeare's own theatre, The Globe, which was completed in 1599. The English drama reached new heights of eloquence.

There were those who disapproved, of course. The theatres, which brought large crowds together, could encourage the spread of disease—and dangerous ideas. During the summer, when the plague was at its worst, the playhouses were closed. A constant censorship was imposed, more or less severe at different times. The Puritan faction tried to close down the theatres, but—partly because there was royal favour for the drama, and partly because the buildings were outside the city limits—they did not succeed until 1642.

Theatre

From contemporary comments and sketches—most particularly a drawing by a Dutch visitor, Johannes de Witt—it is possible to form some idea of the typical Elizabethan playhouse for which most of Shakespeare's plays were written. Hexagonal in shape, it had three roofed galleries encircling an open courtyard. The plain, high stage projected into the yard, where it was surrounded by the audience of standing 'groundlings'. At the back were two doors for the actors' entrances and exits; and above these doors was a balcony—useful for a musicians' gallery or for the acting of scenes 'above'. Over the stage was a thatched roof, supported on two pillars, forming a canopy—which seems to have been painted with the sun, moon, and stars for the 'heavens'.

Underneath was space (concealed by curtaining) which could be used by characters ascending and descending through a trapdoor in the stage. Costumes and properties were kept backstage, in the 'tiring house'. The actors dressed lavishly, often wearing the secondhand clothes bestowed by rich patrons. Stage properties were important for defining a location, but the dramatist's own words were needed to explain the time of day, since all performances took place in the early afternoon.

Suggested Further Reading

Bate, J., 'Hal and the Regent', *Shakespeare Survey 38* (1985), 69–76.

Brown, J.R., *Shakespeare's Plays in Performance*, (London, 1966; Penguin Shakespeare Library, Harmondsworth, 1969).

Edwards, P., *Threshold of a Nation*, (Cambridge, 1979).

Gurr, A., '*Henry V* and the Bees' Commonwealth', *Shakespeare Survey 30* (1977), 61–72.

Holderness, G. (ed.), *Shakespeare's History Plays: 'Richard II' to 'Henry V'*, New Casebooks, (Macmillan, 1992).

Jones, G.P., '*Henry V*: The Chorus and the Audience', *Shakespeare Survey 31* (1978), 93–104.

Quinn, Michael (ed.), *Shakespeare: 'Henry V'*, Casebook Series, (Macmillan, 1969).

Reese, M.M., *The Cease of Majesty*, (London, 1961).

Ribner, Irving, *The English History Play in the Age of Shakespeare*, (Princeton, NJ, 1957; rev. edn., 1965).

Tillyard, E.M.W., *Shakespeare's History Plays*, (London, 1944).

Traversi, Derek A., *Shakespeare: From 'Richard II' to 'Henry V'*, (Stanford, Calif., 1957).

Background Reading

Blake, N.F., *Shakespeare's Language: an Introduction*, (Methuen, 1983).

Muir, K., and Schoenbaum, S., *A New Companion to Shakespeare Studies*, (Cambridge, 1971).

Schoenbaum, S., *William Shakespeare: A Documentary Life*, (Oxford, 1975).

Thomson, Peter, *Shakespeare's Theatre*, (Routledge and Kegan Paul, 1983).

William Shakespeare, 1564–1616

Elizabeth I was Queen of England when Shakespeare was born in 1564. He was the son of a tradesman who made and sold gloves in the small town of Stratford-upon-Avon, and he was educated at the grammar school in that town. Shakespeare did not go to university when he left school, but worked, perhaps, in his father's business. When he was eighteen he married Anne Hathaway, who became the mother of his daughter, Susanna, in 1583, and of twins in 1585.

There is nothing exciting, or even unusual, in this story; and from 1585 until 1592 there are no documents that can tell us anything at all about Shakespeare. But we have learned that in 1592 he was known in London, and that he had become both an actor and a playwright.

We do not know when Shakespeare wrote his first play, and indeed we are not sure of the order in which he wrote his works. If you look on page 150 at the list of his writings and their approximate dates, you will see how he started by writing plays on subjects taken from the history of England. No doubt this was partly because he was always an intensely patriotic man—but he was also a very shrewd business-man. He could see that the theatre audiences enjoyed being shown their own history, and it was certain that he would make a profit from this kind of drama.

The plays in the next group are mainly comedies, with romantic love-stories of young people who fall in love with one another, and at the end of the play marry and live happily ever after.

At the end of the sixteenth century the happiness disappears, and Shakespeare's plays become melancholy, bitter, and tragic. This change may have been caused by some sadness in the writer's life (one of his twins died in 1596). Shakespeare, however, was not the only writer whose works at this time were very serious. The whole of England was facing a crisis. Queen Elizabeth I was growing old. She was greatly loved, and the people were sad to think she must soon die; they were also afraid, for the Queen had never married, and so there was no child to succeed her.

When James I came to the throne in 1603, Shakespeare continued to write serious drama—the great tragedies and the plays based on Roman history (such as *Julius Caesar*) for which he is most famous. Finally, before he retired from the theatre, he wrote another set of comedies. These all have the same theme: they tell of happiness which is lost, and then found again.

Shakespeare returned from London to Stratford, his home town. He was rich and successful, and he owned one of the biggest houses in the town. He died in 1616.

Shakespeare also wrote two long poems, and a collection of sonnets. The sonnets describe two love-affairs, but we do not know who the lovers were. Although there are many public documents concerned with his career as a writer and a business-man, Shakespeare has hidden his personal life from us. A nineteenth-century poet, Matthew Arnold, addressed Shakespeare in a poem, and wrote 'We ask and ask—Thou smilest, and art still'.

There is not even a trustworthy portrait of the world's greatest dramatist.

Approximate order of composition of Shakespeare's works

Period	Comedies	History plays	Tragedies	Poems
I	Comedy of Errors	Henry VI, part 1	Titus Andronicus	
	Taming of the Shrew	Henry VI, part 2		
1594	Two Gentlemen of Verona	Henry VI, part 3		Venus and Adonis
		Richard III		Rape of Lucrece
	Love's Labour's Lost	King John		
II	Midsummer Night's Dream	Richard II	Romeo and Juliet	Sonnets
	Merchant of Venice	Henry IV, part 1		
1599	Merry Wives of Windsor	Henry IV, part 2		
	Much Ado About Nothing			
	As You Like It	Henry V		
III	Twelfth Night		Julius Caesar	
	Troilus and Cressida		Hamlet	
1608	Measure for Measure		Othello	
	All's Well That Ends Well		Timon of Athens	
			King Lear	
			Macbeth	
			Antony and Cleopatra	
			Coriolanus	
IV	Pericles			
1613	Cymbeline			
	The Winter's Tale	Henry VIII		
	The Tempest			